GW00585319

Risdon Beazley

Marine Salvor

Roy Martin
&
Lyle Craigie-Halkett

*This book is dedicated to
the many thousands of people
who worked for Risdon Beazley*

Published by the Authors

First published December 2006

Reprinted, with additions & corrections, March 2007

Reprinted, with postscript, August 2007

Reprinted, incorporating postscript and additions January 2008

©Roy Martin & Lyle Craigie-Halkett 2006.

All rights reserved. No part of this publication may be reproduced, stored in a retrieval system, or transmitted in any form or by any means, electronic, mechanical, photocopying, recording or otherwise, without the prior written permission of the copyright owners.

Printed by Ashford Press, Southampton

ISBN 978-0-9557441-0-5

Published by:
Roy Martin & Lyle Craigie-Halkett
Brook House, Roman Road,
Chilworth, Southampton SO16 7HE
United Kingdom

sales@risdonbeazley.co.uk

Contents

Illustrations

Introduction & Acknowledgements

Risdon Beazley went to great lengths to avoid publicity; but we feel that his story is worth recording as part of Britain's maritime history and to recognise both his achievements and those of the thousands who worked for his company throughout it's 55 year history.

Roy Martin wrote chapters one to six, Lyle Craigie-Halkett wrote chapters seven to nine; chapter ten was a joint effort. When the company closed down, the records were taken to Rotterdam, we are now in touch with those who look after the files and are hoping to get at least some of them back to Southampton. Other records were kept at Mrs Beazley's house at Littlebourne; the house was cleared in 2005 and these were shredded.

We would appreciate any further information, or corrections, that will aid us in making any future edition of this book more complete. Most of the photographs we have used come from the personal collections of individuals or from company brochures and records; many were provided by the family of the company's last Works Manager, the late Eric Ralls. It has not been possible to check the origin of all of these pictures. We apologise if we have, unintentionally, infringed any copyright.

The first edition of this book, if you can call a publication of 44 pages a book, was written because no one had recorded the history of Risdon Beazley Ltd much beyond their own experiences in cargo recovery. Neither of us aspire to be writers. We approached several organisations to keep a copy on file and Mr Jim Brown of the Bitterne Local History Society at Southampton offered to edit that first book and BLHS then published it. So this present edition would not have been written without Jim's initial help. We publicised the book on Mrs Siri (Holm) Lawson's website www.Warsailors.com and sold most of our small stock through this channel. Through the same route we received most interesting information from a number of people. Many thanks to Siri and Jim.

The original information that we had to go on was sketchy; this particularly applied to the record of Beazley's war service, where we only found a few files at the National Archives. We are now fortunate to have new information from a number of sources. Especially the experiences of four men who were on Risdon Beazley managed ships during the war – they are Tom Bray, the late Syd Day (via Mrs Sally Self, his daughter, who has also been our proof reader), Tony Hodge and Cyril Smith (with the help of Mrs Susan Roberts, his daughter); Bruce Benson typed up Tommy Thomson's diaries and scanned his photographs. They have all been of great help, in fact without them this book may never have been written.

Others who have helped include: Linda Abend (Bermuda Maritime Museum), David Asprey, Dennis Biggs (through his grandson Gage Holding), Captain & Mrs Don Brackenbury (Mrs Brackenbury, who as Miss Hunt, was Risdon Beazley's private secretary), Allan Crothall, Charles Cooper, Michael Davis (Bermuda). Keith Gordon (New Zealand), David Hancox (Australia), Fergus Hinds, Don Jones, Mac MacKay (Canada), Alan Martin (Australia), Philip Simons, David Sowden. Finally thanks to Sylvia Craigie-Halkett and June Martin, they have had to live with the various drafts of this book for several years and have been most helpful with their input.

Lyle Craigie-Halkett & Roy Martin
Southampton 2006

Third Reprint

We have included the postscript material in this reprint. At Southampton Archives we have also seen some of the Arthur Daniel Cox diaries that he kept throughout the war. Mr Cox 'worked as a joiner for Beazley's, a local ship repairer'

We are now in touch with Robert Bennett, who's father Tom was the accountant for the company and after that for the family. The material we already have has enabled us to expand the fleet list. Mr Bennett also has 'substantial material' on:

- Admiralty relations (1946-1952)
- SORIMA
- Ulrich Harms
- Office staff, plus masters and consultants
- Directors and payments
- Yard and buildings, when bought and sold etc
- Ship sales 1946-70
- Equipment purchases
- Wreck accounts and cargo receipts (*see also the cargo ledger at Smit's office*)
- Agent and other relations

Abbreviations

ANCXF	Allied Naval Commander, Expeditionary Force
ASDIC	Anti Submarine Detection Investigation Committee (Sonar)
ASV	Admiralty Salvage Vessel
bhp	Brake Horse Power
BISN	British India Steam Navigation Co.
CinCXF	Commander in Chief, Expeditionary Force
CSV	Coastal Salvage Vessel
DEMS	Defensively Equipped Merchant Ships
DEMS gunners	Army or Navy gunners on above (usually shortened to DEMS)
DSC	Distinguished Service Cross
DSO	Distinguished Service Order
DUKW	'Duck' an amphibious vehicle US
DHB	Dover Harbour Board
HMS	His Majesty's Ship. Now Her Majesty's Ship
IHP	Indicated Horse Power
L&GSA	Liverpool and Glasgow Salvage Association
LCT	Landing Craft Tank
LMC	Lloyd's Machinery Classification
LOF	Lloyd's Open Form
LSF	Lloyd's Salvage Form
MOWT	Ministry of War Transport
OTS	Overseas Towage & Salvage
P&O	Peninsular & Oriental
RAB	Risdon Archibald Beazley
RAF	Royal Air Force
RN	Royal Navy
RNR	Royal Naval Reserve (a reserve of professional seamen)
RNVR	Royal Naval Volunteer Service (mainly non seafarers)
RB	Risdon Beazley Ltd
RBM	Risdon Beazley Marine Ltd
RBMT	Risdon Beazley Marine Trading Co
RBUH	Risdon Beazley Ulrich Harms Ltd
SISEA	Smit International South East Asia (Pte.) Ltd.
SV	Salvage Vessel

Chapter One - The Early Years 1926 to 1940

> "RAB was a superb entrepreneur who inspired great loyalty and hard work from his staff. He provided in return a very interesting working life for us all with a very high element of satisfaction, which lasts even to the present. The story ... is certainly a part of the maritime history of Southampton – but, knowing him as we both did, had he still been alive we feel sure he would not have approved of this or any publication of what he considered his private achievements. He was a very private man and to us a friend we sadly miss. Anyway, neither the firm nor he exists anymore and there is no reason at all why the story should not be told."
>
> *Part of a letter from the late Captain D E Brackenbury & Mrs B Brackenbury, Nov.02*

Risdon Beazley (RAB) was born in 1903, he was the eldest child of Henry Joseph and May Annie Beazley (nee Whale). When his birth was registered at South Stoneham, Southampton; his father's trade was given as 'bicycle maker'; he was christened Risden (sic)[1] Archibald Beazley on 13 March 1904. His brother Jasper Gilbert was born just over a year later and his sister Olive May was christened in February 1907. Throughout this time the family lived in Shirley, Southampton.

When Henry bought a 33 foot motor boat, called **Coo-ee**, he registered the vessel in his own name, giving his address as The Towers, Onslow Road *(now Swift Road)*, Woolston, Hants. The boat had been built in Amsterdam in 1901 and first registered under the British Registry in 1902; presumably H J Beazley bought it later as the original Port of Registry was Great Yarmouth.

By 1913 Henry was a yacht builder at Ferry yard, 10 Elm Road *(now Hazel Road)*, Itchen[2]. A year later Henry had formed a partnership with R Kemp, where they traded as Beazley & Kemp, yacht builders. This partnership continued throughout the First World War; war work was regarded as a 'reserved occupation' and the workers wore a badge to indicate that they were exempt from call up. By 1920 R Kemp had taken over the yard and were trading as Engineers and Shipbuilders. They are still in business today as Kemp's Shipyard, yacht builders, brokers and marina owners, also as Kempsafe, makers of ships galley ranges. At about this time Henry J Beazley seems to have acquired Clausentum Yard at Bitterne Manor and was listed in Kelly's as – Beazley H. J., shipbuilding and engineering, ship repairing, docking &c Clausentum Yard, Northam Bridge Rd., Bitterne.

In 1920 the Beazley family lived at Heathfield House in Westend Road, Bitterne, Southampton. In a book titled Memories of Bitterne[3] by Irene Pilson, that is in Southampton Library (*Special Collections, Local Studies*), there is a story with the title The House Warming at Heathfield House, which is about the Beazley family. The article talks of Mrs Beazley, and her daughters – so we are obviously missing some! In the late 1930's H.J.B. and his wife owned what is now Botleigh Grange Hotel. In her will dated 1959, Annie May had become May Annie and was living at Chandlers Ford; she owned more than twenty houses at Millbrook (Southampton).[4]

RAB formed the Risdon Beazley Marine Trading Company Ltd in 1926, when he was 22 years old. In the same 1927 edition of Kelly's they were listed as Marine Engineers, Hawkeswood Road, Bitterne Park. In a subsequent edition the company were described as yacht builders and by 1933 were subscribers to Lloyd's Register of

---

[1] He seems to have adopted the name Risdon before the war.
[2] Woolston and Itchen did not become part of Southampton until 1920
[3] This book was published by the Bitterne Local History Society, it is now out of print.
[4] Rodney Whale, Andover, July 2007 and Christening Records

Yachts where they were also listed as yacht builders. By 1939 the company had become Risdon Beazley Ltd, other ships are shown as managed by R A Beazley. At the same time the House Flag, dark green with a white diamond, was changed from a pennant to a flag On post 1952 ships this was also on the buff funnel.

Throughout the 55-year life of the company and its successors the base remained at Clausentum Yard on the site of the Roman port settlement in what is now Bitterne Manor, Southampton. Before the war they worked from No. 36 and 38 Hawkeswood Road and during the war they acquired much of the property in that road, plus Lloyd's Albert Yard (at Keswick Road Woolston?). They retained numbers 32 to 38 and all of the buildings on the West Side of the road after the war. When Jasper Beazley set up office with his brother in 38 Hawkeswood Road, he was described as a motor trader; later he moved to Bullar Road, where he traded as Criterion Garages. Olive married a William Henderson Gray, O. M. Henderson Gray was on the board of Risdon Beazley Ltd, in 1951. Her second marriage was to Esmond Ayton Beevor who warranted an entry in Burke's Peerage[1]; Olive's father is there described as living in Bitterne, Southampton, Hampshire, England. Olive died 31 Aug. 2001.

Gossip on the **Droxford,** which was correct about the boys and their father, had it that there were two more brothers, Kim and Henry. A Kim Beazley did take over Blakes Ltd of Gosport; he may have been a cousin. Henry George owned and operated the Southampton 'sludge boat' **Bargate** and two small tugs, **Seldom In** and **Bonaparte.** He worked from Bonaparte Yard, Quayside Road, Bitterne Manor. The **Bargate** was included in a fleet list provided by Risdon Beazley Ltd, in 1940[2].

RAB and his wife, Dorothy, had three daughters so the name died out on that side. It was said that one daughter became a barrister, another married a Major Gotto and lives in Cork, Eire. Some years after his first wife died RAB married Mavis a daughter of the Andrews family, who operated Overseas Towage and Salvage, London. This Mrs Beazley was apparently told by her parents "you had better go down and look after Risdon"[3] (now that he is a widower). This lady had the misfortune of seeing both her father's company and her husband's company acquired and then closed down by L.Smit & Co of Rotterdam.

By the mid thirties RAB was living in 44 Westwood Road Southampton, he also registered his ships there. **Recovery of Leith** was registered in 1936, **Aid** was acquired by a Vyvyan Drury in 1937 and put under RB management. By the next year the tug was also registered at Westwood Road as owned by RAB.

Risdon Beazley moved to the village of Twyford, about seven miles north of Southampton[4], in 1940, presumably to protect his family from the bombing. There he bought a property called Littlebourne. The house had once been called The Bourne but when a previous owner moved into a bungalow in the grounds he took the name with him and renamed the original property Littlebourne.

Though not particularly imposing RAB set about upgrading the house with teak floors and panelling from an Atlantic liner (**Aquitania**?) that was being broken up ; the balance of the panelling was used in a subsequent refurbishment of 36 Hawkeswood Road. He also acquired sporting rights over land near the Mountbatten estate at Romsey. One of his salvage officers – Bill Robinson – was appointed to run the estate.

---

[1] *Burke's Peerage, Baronetage & Knightage 107th edition, 3 volumes (Wilmington Delaware, USA ...) ??*
[2] See the chapter on the war
[3] Source Mrs Mavis Beazley, 2002
[4] The village is named after it's two fords (river crossings) and should not be confused with Twyford Berks.

The house, the shooting and fishing and a Rolls Royce completed RAB's transition to a country gentleman; though even in this he was private as always.

He became an underwriting name at Lloyd's but apparently resigned when he made a loss, saying 'I didn't join Lloyd's to make a loss'. He enjoyed an extremely low premium on his Hull & Machinery insurance ~ ½%, this was probably because he never made a claim, for him marine insurance was 'total loss only'. He worked with the same professionals, certainly throughout the post war years. His metal brokers were Henry Gardner in London and Tennants in New York; his lawyers were Ingledew, Brown, Bennison and Garrett and his insurance brokers were Bain Dawes.

By the mid thirties RBMT Ltd was doing demolition work on piers and small-scale wreck removal. In 1936 RAB convinced Peter Kleyn van Willigen, who later became Chairman of Smit Internationale, that his company was a suitable partner for the salvage of the square-rigger **Herzogen Cecile.** Back in Rotterdam KvW's family was less than happy that he had been hoodwinked[1]. When the wreck broke up outside of Salcombe, mainly because the harbour authority would not allow the vessel to enter port after she had been re-floated, a team from Risdon Beazley cut it down and took the steel scrap into the Dart.

In 1937 the **Kantoeng,** then the largest tin dredge in the world, capsized under tow of Smit tugs whilst bound for Bintang and the wreck threatened to block the port of Fowey. Risdon Beazley Ltd removed the hull, using their ship **Recovery of Leith,** and scrapped it on Par Sands; the buckets and chains remain at the wreck site.

Wreckage from English Trader   Photograph RAB's office.

In previous editions this picture was captioned '**Wreckage at Kingswear, from Hertzogen Cecille?**' A railway buff, had identified the site as Kingswear[2], but we did not know of a job that the firm had done near Kingswear (Dartmouth Devon U K).

With kind help from Mr Dave Griffiths, son of the former Dartmouth Harbour Master, this wreckage was identified as coming from the **English Trader.** He has sent us copies of photographs from a book about this casualty, with hand written notes his father made. (Dave Griffiths has also sent a picture of one of RBs salvage craft dismantling slipways and piles after the war.)

---

[1] Source Mr P. Kleyn van Willigen, 1982

[2] Dennis Roberts, a friend

Captain Griffiths wrote:

"The English Trader was entering Dartmouth for bunkers pilot George Ridalls on board, the Master came from Brixham . At 4 AM on the 23ʳᵈ Jan 1937. I was wakened by a ship blowing, soon I knew that a ship was ashore just outside the Castle. Contact was made with Dartmouth Coastguard and Brixham Lifeboat weather at the time light to moderate SW swell. I made contact with Mr Risdon Beazley of Southampton who arrived at Dartmouth at 8 AM. He soon had a crowd of coal lumpers¹ on board. Vessel was loaded with maize, (many?) tons were discharged overboard, and when weather was calm, Dutch coasters loaded alongside this made little difference as the vessel was fast for'd, with rocks well inside No1 hold."

Left - coal lumpers   Below English Trader minus bow

By the 22ⁿᵈ February the bow had been 'amputated' and the casualty was towed into the Dart and beached at Kingswear. Captain Griiffiths continues: *"This day was the most worrying for me, to give the salvage officer ²the OK to burn the foredeck just for'd of No2 hold, I had demanded extra heavy pumps to be added to the very many others, all pumps were working while the ship was towed close to the Kingswear shore the extra pumps were really needed."³*

The Lloyd's Casualty Reports make interesting reading, though without Captain Griffiths' reports we would not have known that RAB himself was on site from 8AM on the first day: *" ...Jan. 23 ... British steamer English Trader at 4.30 a.m.* "am ashore west side of Dartmouth": *Dutch tug Witte Zee at 5 3 a.m. GMT "proceeding to assistance of steamer English Trader": Rotterdam Jan. 23 "Witte Zee proceeding from Falmouth on Lloyd's Form; tug Zwarte Zee proceeding from Douarnenez....."* Other vessels involved include the **Tor Bay lifeboat**, the tugs **Verne** and **Venture**, the destroyer **HMS Keppel, HMS Witch**, destroyer **HMS No 89** and Admiralty tug **Retort**. Captain Doust *'attending'*, presumably as the Salvage Association's *'Special Officer'*

¹Coal lumpers were dock labourers

²Presumably this was Bill Robinson, one of RB's two salvage officers, though there is no way of proving that; but Bill is shown proudly standing on the pile of ship scrap at Kingswear several months later.

³A Court of Inquiry considered that the cause of stranding was "Steering jammed hard aport, master and pilot exonerated"

On the 24th in a heavy, and worsening, southerly gale the tugs lost control and " *Vessel swept broadside to wind and sea bumping heavily on starboard bilge. In view of situation and seas breaking on board master decided to abandon vessel. Landed Dartmouth with crew and labour in Brixham lifeboat ... Zwarte Zee proceeding to shelter"* Also on the 24th *"during a lull in the storm boarded vessel at noon. Navigation bridge smashed by seas and No. 2 hold now flooded to tide level"* On the 25th the engine room and stokehold were flooded, but after this the salvors regained the initiative, laying out ground tackle and raising steam. On the evening of the 25th Risdon Beazley's salvage vessel **Recovery of Leith** arrived after what must have been a hair raising trip and she laid out further ground tackle and placed pumps on board.

By the 17th February, despite constructing a wooden bulkhead in No2, the salvors had accepted that, in Doust's words, *"View starting of fore-well deck plating no reasonable hope of bows being lifted when the remainder of vessel refloated"* On Feb. 22 the **English Trader** was refloated by the Smit tugs **Ostzee** and **Ebro**: *"minus foreship"* - the **Witte Zee** and the **Zwarte Zee** had returned to their stations.

It was not until April 2 that the casualty was ready fro tow and the tugs **Crested Cock** and **Atlantic Cock** arrived to tow her to Southampton. On April 4 these two tugs, plus the **Recovery of Leith**, left with their tow. But on the following day the casualty was leaking badly and she was towed into Portland, leaving again on the morning of the 23rd. Berthing at Southampton late on the same day.

English Trader was drydocked on the 27th and on May 5 the **Recovery of Leith** returned to Dartmouth *"'to remove the bows of steamer English Trader"* On May 29th the vessel left Southampton in tow of three United Towing tugs, bound for the Tyne where permanent repairs were to be made. The vessel was rebuilt from the boiler room forward in 100 days.

The **English Trader** rescued survivors from the Ben line ship **Benvenue**, which had been torpedoed on the 15th May 1941. But in October 1941 **English Trader** herself was wrecked, most of the crew were rescued by two lifeboats; the **Cromer boat** was skippered by the famous coxswain Henry Blogg.

Clausentum Yard   ca 1970 (with approximate limits outlined)   Photo Roy Romsey

English Trader

Top - aground, middle- outbound, bottom – passing own bow!
Salvage ship - Recovery of Leith, Bibby's trooper - Lancashire

Chapter Two - Admiralty Salvor 1940 to 1943

At the outbreak of the First World War the Admiralty had neither salvage vessels nor a department to run them. Commercial salvage was fragmented, the largest salvage organisations were those operated by the big ports such as London and Liverpool; the smaller ports relied on local commercial salvors. A number of ship owners also operated salvage craft and there were specialist organisations, many could trace their history back to the 19th century. Seeing the need, the Admiralty acquired such vessels as were available and converted a number of small warships for the work. Civilian managers, such as the Liverpool and Glasgow Salvage Association, (L&GSA) provided the management and expertise. Most of the vessels were old at the beginning of the war and at the end they were disposed of. The longest lived of the salvage vessels was L&GSA's **Ranger** that had been built in 1880 as a steam gunboat and which continued in service until the 1950s. Only a few dumb (non propelled) lifting craft were left and these went in the 1930s. Most of the expertise was also lost, though, fortunately, some skilled people went back to the commercial companies.

As a new conflict became more likely the Nation again found itself without a unified salvage organisation. As Britain was short of just about everything, the absence of a salvage capability probably did not seem of great importance. That was until it was realised how easily aircraft bombing, mining or torpedoing ships in the approaches could block the ports. The Admiralty set up a committee to report on how a salvage organisation could be built up. The committee suggested that the quickest way was to requisition all suitable ships and to hand them over to civilian managers, who were often the owners of the ships that had been requisitioned. This is what happened when war began.

Presumably because of their stalwart work in WW1, Liverpool and Glasgow were to look after the West Coast from Cape Wrath to Lands End. Metal Industries, who had taken over the famous Scapa firm of Cox & Danks, were to look after the East Coast from Cape Wrath to Harwich – including the Northern Isles. The Port of London Authority (PLA) were to handle Harwich to North Foreland. From here to Lands End was left to Commander (later Captain) Doust to 'coordinate'. The East Coast section was later sub divided to include Leith Towage and Salvage and T Rounds, Scarborough

Doust and his team then looked to the South Coast. They approached Dover Harbour Board (DHB), who had for many years operated their own sea going tugs; DHB agreed to take from North Foreland to Beachy Head. Now the problem was, what to do about the rest of the English Channel. Doust obviously knew of RB's from the **English Trader**, if not before. By the summer of 1940, there was no cover for the South Coast and many of the requisitioned ships were still without managers.

The Doust's team seemed somewhat surprised by what they found at Southampton: here was an operator with a fleet of ships, albeit some of them were rather small, and an impressive store of salvage equipment – mostly ex-Admiralty stock from the earlier war. RAB, never the man to overlook an opportunity, had over the preceding three years, bought up just about every ship that had, or could have, a salvage capability. He was young and he had assembled a keen young team around him. Their base fronted onto the River Itchen and extended from there to the trunk road that joined Portsmouth and Southampton. Bitterne had a railway station on the line from Southampton Central and Docks to Portsmouth. There was also a local airport (the home of the Spitfire fighter plane). During the visit it was agreed that Mr S W

Giddings, the Company Secretary, would provide a list of the ships that RB operated and the equipment would be catalogued on behalf of the Admiralty.

Then the conversation turned to the surplus ships; we only have Doust's account of this part of the conversation – though that agrees with the tale that was handed down in later years. It was said to have gone "well Mr Beazley we have more ships on our hands than we would like", RAB " how many do you have ", "well with your vessels we will have over 30", RAB "we'll take them" Doust adds that Beazley also said, "as far as I am concerned the sky is the limit": the phrase does not sound like one of RAB's, but the willingness to accept a challenge does.

When Gidding's letter arrived in London it listed a total of nineteen ships, including even the Southampton 'sludge' vessel **Bargate**: times were difficult but the Admiralty decided that they were not so desperate that they needed a sludge boat. The Ministry of War Transport also questioned whether RB's coaster **Palmston** would not be more useful as a cargo carrier. As it was, only the **Bargate**, the **Poole Dredger No 2** and the **Topmast No 3** and **Aid** are not listed in the 1945 fleet. The additional ships that came under RB's management were as varied as the fleet that RB had contributed; they included the **Lady Southborough, Forde** and the **Gallions Reach** who had all been at Dunkirk. The other salvage vessels included: **Akershus (1944), Dapper, Doria, Dormouse, Empire Demon (1943), Foremost 18, Freija, Longtow, Maggie Lough, Nessus, Ramier, Richard ll, Roselyne, Thoma ll, Trottebec, Venture lll, Watercock** and **Wayfarer.** There seem to have been other vessels, such as the drifter **Vine,** which were presumably transferred to others before 1945.

Beazley's area of responsibility was to be from Beachy Head to Lands End. The boundaries seem to have been somewhat fluid as three of the RB managed vessels were based at Harwich and journeyed even further afield (at least one went as far as Scapa Flow). The three – **Freija** (Captain Austin and later Goddard), **Foremost 18** and **Forde** (Captain Trodden[1]) worked that section of the East Coast.[2] [3]

When it came to the question of remuneration Metal Industries had dug their heels in, but eventually had to accept a lump sum of £7,000. This was "Still a great deal less than Risdon Beazley had negotiated for roughly the same service"[4]. As we have seen Risdon Beazley had provided more ships and had taken others under their management, the £20,000 they were awarded reflected this.

The occupation of France meant the closure of the port of Southampton to deep-sea ships; it also marked the beginning of the Blitz, which was probably at its worst in November 1940, when much of the town was destroyed. The Inner Dock, where many of the RB ships were moored, was badly damaged, but none of the vessels were lost. Everywhere in Southampton the citizens had burrowed into the ground to make air raid shelters. RB dug two at Clausentum and the following finds are recorded :

A large ditch-like feature was found probably in the eastern section. It cut the natural gravel, and was at least 6m wide, with gently sloping sides. ...A cooking pit was recorded, together with a second hearth. Three stones on the edge of the second hearth, and a thin layer of burnt soil may mark a third hearth. ...The most interesting find was the lower part of a limestone altar, dedicated apparently to Mercury. Only Mercury's feet clad in winged boots survived. They were carved in hard white limestone, probably from the Oxford area.

---

[1] Or Trüden according to one of Sally Self's references

[2] *Forde & Foremost 18* were to be involved in Operation Neptune – D-Day.

[3] 'The Battle for the East Coast' by J P Foynes – self published.

[4] Admiralty Salvage in Peace & War 1906 – 2006 Tony Booth. Apparently RB provided three salvage officers, Bill Robinson, Perc Carrington &? (Rodney Paul or John Polland?)

At the end of November 1940, the RB tug **Aid** and the ex French tug **Abeille XIV** (R A Beazley, manager) were towing the barge **BHC No. 10** from Southampton to Falmouth: they were attacked by the German destroyers, **Richard Beitzen**, **Hans Lody** and **Karl Galster**. **Aid** sank with the loss of five crew and the barge sank with a loss of three; **Abeille XIV** survived, but two of her, British, crew were killed. The destroyers went on to sink the **Pilot Boat No. 4**. In another engagement with the trio, later that day, the RN destroyer **HMS Javelin** had her bows blown off by a torpedo, 48 of her crew were killed. On the 23rd April the salvage vessel **Miss Elaine** was bombed, but survived.

Though ships coming in from the Atlantic could no longer use Southampton because of the occupation of France, coasters still used the port. The most regular visitors were another group of unsung heroes, the colliers, who were later called the 'coal scuttle brigade'. They had to brave attacks by E-boats, surface craft, aircraft and shore batteries on their voyage from the North East Coast: others from the South Wales ports were attacked by surface craft and submarines. A supply of coal was essential for the running of Southampton and every other town; coal fired the power station and the gasworks, as well as the grates and cooking stoves in the homes. When these smaller vessels were wrecked, the salvage crews had three tasks – to keep the port functioning, salve the vessel and the cargo.

The Admiralty staff who listed the equipment that was available at Clausentum Yard also noted the boat building and repair capability there. The principal facility was the large boat shed that had been built in the 1930s; two slipways ran into this shed, which was served by the fitters shop and the shipwrights shop. Several smaller covered slips could be used for boats of up to 65 feet long.

By the autumn of 1941, RB were building the first of the 22 Fairmile motor vessels for Coastal Forces. The first group of nine B type vessels were delivered between February 1941 and May 1942, these were all fitted out as Motor Launches. Beazley's average building time for boats of this class was 21 weeks, against a national average of 24.8 weeks. Whilst the raids on the town of Southampton had eased, the banks of the Itchen and the nearby airport, the home of the Spitfire, were still frequently bombed. A raid on the 8th March 1941 damaged Northam Bridge, just down stream from the Yard, but despite this ML 208 was completed on the 12th of the month. One C type – MGB 327 was completed on the 22 August 1941 – a building time of 27 weeks, 2 weeks less than the UK average.

As soon as the first production run was completed, work started on the D type. In all, 12 of these were delivered in an average building time of 33 weeks, a full 10 weeks better than the UK average: all but one of these vessels were completed as Motor Torpedo Boats[1]. RB also built ten smaller Harbour Service Launches and at least one 36 foot motor launch, which still survives. as **Cerf lll**

There are some records of the **Forde** and the **Longtow's**[2] work, mainly in the narrative of Sydney Day. **Forde**, a sloop in the First World War, was converted to a cross Channel car ferry on the Dover to Calais route in 1928. She was among the vessels requisitioned early in the Second World War and was pressed into use as a salvage vessel, or as Syd Day more correctly calls her – a pump carrier.

Syd's father found the pub that Captain Trodden of the **Forde** and a few of his crew drank in and Syd went there with his discharge book, was accepted and did a 'pier

---

[1] John Lambert "Allied Coastal Forces of World War II

[2] Thanks mainly to Mrs Sally Self, Sally has transcribed tapes that her father made about his time as a crew member of several of the salvage ships managed by RB. She intends to publish the book as "Those Were the Days," it should be a good read.

head jump'. Having been brought up in small Coastguard gigs and cutters, he seems to have been looking for a change from being a steward on a Union Castle mail boat. He found that he was still a steward and on something far less grand than a Castle boat, but here he had a chance to get on deck from time to time.

At the same time that Syd was making his move into salvage another young Southampton lad, Tom Bray, who was to become one of RB' stalwarts, was also joining the Union Castle Line[1].   Tom had done his six months training at the Prince of Wales Sea School, which he finished on the 21st March 1940.   He joined the **Athlone Castle** as a bridge boy on the same day. After two trips to the Cape sixteen year old Tom was given leave as his parents had been bombed out, while he was helping the family he worked on the local Red Funnel tugs.

After a year he joined RB and was sent to the **Lady Southborough** (Captain MacClean) as an Ordinary Seaman.   The **Lady Southborough** sailed from Southampton in November 1941 to work at the entrance to the River Fal.   From Falmouth they sailed for South Wales; they had a rough trip, losing a lifeboat in heavy weather.   Those crew who were not seasick were ill from eating mussels that they had harvested and pickled while working near the mussel beds in the Fal.

With Syd on board **Forde's** first job was the salvage of the **Domala** of BISN[2;] The vessel had been bombed and there were many casualties.   After some pumping, the tugs towed the vessel to the Western Solent where she was beached off Oxey Lake, near Syd's home, and, after further patching and pumping, was moved to Netley.

Syd writes of the shortage of food on the salvage ships, which were only equipped with small refrigerators: they often had to rely on dried fruit and beans taken from the casualties.   **Forde** then went to Harwich, where she was to be based, and then to the Tyne and the Firth of Forth, later they then moved up to Scapa expecting to have to deal with casualties from the Narvik landings.   By April 1940 they were no longer required at Scapa and returned to Harwich: importantly for the crew, they were now victualled by the Navy, receiving considerably more than civilian rations.

In May they were moved to Dover and, along with the fleet, went from there to Dunkirk to assist in the evacuation of troops.   On return to Dover they assisted the ferry **Mona's Isle** and then the paddle steamer **Royal Daffodil**.   The only damage they sustained was caused by three French destroyers who passed them at full speed, despite requests to slow down. They returned to Harwich and on to London were they and their 'chummy ship,' **Recovery of Leith**, stayed through the worst of the Blitz. Syd gives a graphic description of this time:

"After this we went back to Harwich for a time before being called up to the Port of London. With the beginning of the Blitz there were many casualties that needed lifting to keep the river clear. We spent several weeks up there through the worst of it, next door to our chummy ship the Recovery of Leith."   This was a time that Syd always spoke of with considerable awe and depth of feeling.

---

[1] Tom has also kindly written out his experiences in RB, both during and after the war.

[2] **Clyde-Built Database:** Under the command of Capt Fitt, DOMALA suffered a severe bombing attack on Saturday March 2nd 1940. She was carrying a total of 295 people, 46 British and 249 Indians from London via Antwerp to Calcutta. At Antwerp she had boarded 143 British Indian subjects repatriated by Germany. A Heinkel bomber dropped four bombs onto the ship causing terrible casualties amongst the passengers and crew. Capt Fitt was killed with 18 other British people and 81 Indians, of whom 36 were crew. Before flying off the bomber sprayed the liners decks with machine gun fire. The JONG WILLEM from the Netherlands picked up 48 survivors in a boat, and even as she performed this task, she too was bombed and fired upon by machine gun, fortunately without damage or casualties. DOMALA was in a very bad state, the government purchased her and had her converted to a cargo vessel: on a voyage from the Mersey she was torpedoed by U582. Tragically all of her 59 crew perished.

"It had a terrible beauty. The fires and the searchlights together created a scene that was intensely colourful. The Thames became so polluted, with the chemicals from the paint and chemical factories that it was black for days on end. It tasted on your lips and right down into your stomach. Where the mud and water was thrown up on to us, it burnt the paintwork on the funnels, so Christ help anyone who fell in. During the nights we stayed on the Forde and spent time feeding people who came along, getting some drink in from a local friendly pub, whose owners were in the shelters, and playing daft games like 'priest of the parish, a fearsome game, where you ran between two lines, where every one was armed with a knotted handkerchief."

It was while in this berth at Brunswick (Wharf) that attempts were made to sabotage the **Forde**. They were having a boiler clean at R H Green and Silley Weir's, the builders of the Blackwall frigates. "Someone pinched our bikes that we used to go to the country dances: then far more seriously someone made a die and blanked off a steam pipe in the engine, luckily for the firemen it blew out through the gauge. There was no chance of finding out who did it. I reckoned that they (the dockyard workers) were generally a miserable lot. They knocked off if there was an air raid: mind you they had had it for 60 or so consecutive nights. It wasn't all 'London can take it.' In the Dockyard, it got so bad, Admiral Keyes, who was in charge, had to publicly apologise to the men (dock workers) for making remarks about ships being always late coming out of refits there. The Forde always was weeks late finishing a refit in London. The blokes ... used to put in for overtime they weren't doing. To us silly sailors it seemed wicked, all we wanted was to get back to sea to do the job.

There were others out in the thick of it, pinching from bonded warehouses. Tidder would take the usual, booze and fags, but he also had a taste for the exotic, and at various times had antelope horns and grandfather clocks. It was he (Tidder) who when we were based in Harwich used to do moonlight jaunts to the fruit fields to pick the strawberries. He would use purloined sugar from some casualty, would brew up strawberry jam to sell around the local houses. He even pinched paint from the ships and took himself off to paint the houses in Harwich. A most enterprising man, for most of the stuff was bound for the bottom of the sea or to be burnt up!

At Brunswick Wharf they were lying in the old rigging out dock for the Blackwall Frigates. 'The trouble was it used to dry out at low tide, so there was no water for the pumps; so if we got a fire bomb on board you couldn't do what you usually did, which was to blow them over the side with the pressure from the pumps. Otherwise you had to kick 'em over and swear at them. The stuff used to come down in shovelfuls; the boat was plastered with mud. I stood under the bridge and watched bombs go right under the ship, but they didn't explode, which was lucky as in that shallow water, she would have just gone to bits." It would be shortly after this that Risdon Beazley took over the management of the **Forde** and the other vessels, though Syd has them as managing the **Forde** when he joined her.

By October 1942 things were somewhat quieter in the Nore area and **Forde** was no longer needed. She was sent to Southampton and then on to Milford Haven where she was handed over to a Liverpool & Glasgow Salvage Association. In all the **Forde** assisted thirty casualties whilst based at Harwich.

After some leave most of the crowd from the **Forde** joined the **Longtow**, still under the command of Captain Trodden; by now Syd was on deck – where he had always wanted to be. Trodden seems to have been well liked and his crew stayed with him, the **Longtow** became a happy ship. She had been built as a fish carrier in the days when there had been a fleet of such ships to get the catch quickly to market. With improvements in rail transport she was no longer needed for this work and was modified to work as a salvage vessel. The crews of the salvage ships were civilians on six monthly running agreements.

Though there were many of "the old crowd" left on the ships they were by now getting "some funny men along, some you would have to work out of the ship, as we were a really happy crew." When the Steward left, Syd was taken off the deck to go back to his old job; but he soon persuaded a pal from the Union Castle to take over the cooking and got back to the job he liked best. The Castle boat man seems to have been less than impressed with his first sight of the old fish carrier, but he stuck with it and was 'a good cook.'

SS Longtow   *photograph from Website*

One of **Longtow's** first jobs was in the Bristol Channel were she worked with the Lifting Craft **LC1** & **LC3**, later Syd was to become Bosun of the **LC3.** After some time there, Captain Trodden was transferred. The new master was 'mad' and by the sound of it useless; he damaged the ship so badly that he was eventually relieved. A Captain Barker took over and things returned to normal. After more time at Swansea, working with the **Lady Southborough,** they returned to Southampton and then back to Harwich, where their area was from Cromer to Dover.

Tom Bray was on the **Lady Southborough** and he remembers this period as being a time when they all worked 24 hour days and had frequent air raid alerts. The two ships and their lifting craft worked from the Mumbles to Swansea, Port Talbot, Barry, Cardiff and Avonmouth. An interesting diversion was when they were sent to North Devon to experiment with, what they learnt later was, the PLUTO. The pipeline had been laid from Swansea, across the Bristol Channel, to the coast off Ilfracombe. Another length had been laid from Ilfracombe and the **Lady Southborough's** job was to recover both ends so that the Royal Engineers could splice them together. After the splice was made the line was lowered to the seabed and tested successfully. Several years later Tom and his shipmates realised the importance of their task[1].

Back at Harwich Syd found that there were "bursts of frantic activity, followed by days of more mundane work". The most notable salvage operation of 1943 was probably the **Josefina Norden**, a Finnish tanker. This vessel had been blown up by a mine on 6 April, the stern half had sunk while under tow and the salvage crews were told to save the fore-body with its cargo of oil. A Navy Salvage Officer and

---

[1] Pipe Line Under The Ocean. PLUTO was the line that carried the fuel across the English Channel for D-Day

another officer, together with Syd and a second seaman, Wills, from the **Longtow** boarded the casualty to connect the tow. The tow wire parted, the tug broke down and the tanker drifted on to the Shivering Sands.

Again without food, Syd set about finding lunch for them all; the only food he could find was that stowed under the Chief Steward's settee. Finally the tug **Woodcock** came to rescue them from a "decidedly unpleasant situation", they had to leap from the tanker onto the tug's heaving deck, one of the Naval Officers having ensured that he was first off! Syd and his pal received a commendation from the Flag Officer Harwich via the Chief Admiralty Salvage Officer for "helping so gallantly in a difficult and dangerous operation"; the leaping Naval Officer received a DSO.

Tom was also transferred to Harwich, by this time he was a diver's linesman doing occasional dives because they were permanently short-handed. One of the more hair raising occasions was when he was diving on the wreck of the Norwegian collier **Skagerak,** not the cargo ship of the same name. Working from a small landing craft they had found a piece of what they thought was the structure projecting above the mud line. The other diver was on deck making up a charge that he wanted Tom to place on the object to save work. After fixing a strop to this 'vent' Tom came back to the surface to help the others wind the object in on a small hand winch and when this did not work the skipper went full astern on both engines and dragged the object clear. They returned to the mother ship at a meal time and proudly told the master about the shiny object that they had slung under their craft. The meal was abandoned and the object was taken well out to sea where it was detonated, even then it shattered many local windows.

By 1943 new salvage vessels were being delivered., those for the British were divided into three classes.

The British built King Salvor class, 200 feet in length, 1,500 IHP steamers, were designed for salvage work in distant waters, they were equipped with workshops, diving gear, welding and cutting tools. They were not, however, designed as lifting craft and this shortcoming meant that they seem not to have been popular with the salvage officers[1]. Six were put under RB management, one under L&GSA (who also were to operate the tug/salvage vessel **Salveda**) and five were RN operated.

The American equivalents of the King Salvor class were the USN BARS salvage ships. These wooden vessels were 183 feet in length and were propelled by Diesel Electric engines of 1.200 BHP. A number of these were built for operation by US forces and only four were put under RB management. Most of the crews were from the Montreal and New York seamen's pool. The **American Salvor** arrived in the UK in November 1943 with convoy SC146. Captain G L Wallwork assumed command on the 1st December and R W Lennard, the Mate, took over command of the **Help** for the landings; he was awarded an OBE for his services in France. The **Lincoln Salvor** arrived in January 1944 with convoy SC 152. Six of her crew had deserted in the US, they seem to have been 'big ship men' who must have been horrified at the thought of crossing the Western Ocean in so small a vessel. Captain Griffith took command and later the Mate, Mr Walker, was promoted Master. The last two, the **Boston Salvor,** Captain Eidick, a Latvian**,** and the **Southampton Salvor** did not arrive until the end of March 1944 with convoy SC155, which included 25 LSTs (Landing Ship – Tank). All were part of the salvage fleet for the D-Day landings as were several of their US flagged sisters.

---

[1] Though in the right hands they did good work

The remaining self-propelled class of salvage vessel was the Coastal Class. These were an Admiralty design, but detailed work was handed to Smith's Dock. Smith's was an old established yard who were quite innovative. In the mid thirties they had designed an improved type of whale catcher, this formed the basis of the workhorse of the North Atlantic escort fleet, the 'Flower'-class corvette, 277 of these were built in the UK and Canada. Smith's did a similarly good job on the Coastals, in all nine were built, RB managed seven of these. These handy ships were 179 feet in overall length, 150' BP and of 600 IHP. They could lift 100 tons over the bow or up to 250 ton underslung as a 'belly lift', they could also be used in pairs.

Additionally dumb (non propelled) lifting craft were built, these were the LCs mentioned above, these also operated in pairs and were capable of lifting about four times as much as the Coastal Class. 'Camels'[1] provided further lifting capacity.

This influx of vessels needed crewing, the new deliveries alone required a total of almost 500 men, additionally extra yard and office staff were needed. Merchant seamen of all ranks were sent to the company, many of these men had been torpedoed and, on reporting to the Merchant Navy Pool, were re-assigned to RB. The sight that greeted them when they reported for their new duty at Clausentum Yard must have surprised them. Once past the guard, they found a series of workshop buildings on the left that stretched all the way to the river. On the banks of the river the Fairmiles and smaller boats were being built and the river itself was full of smaller craft and rows (or herds?) of Camels. The offices were situated in houses on the opposite side of the road as were temporary buildings.

Once assigned to a ship they would have been surprised to find that this was only part of the operation. Many of the ships were based in the older part of Southampton Docks, but some were working as far apart as Falmouth and Felixstowe. Others would be sent to newly built vessels all over the UK and about a quarter of them found themselves taking over US built ships that had been delivered by run crews. Most enjoyed the work, but others found it too demanding and returned Deep-Sea at the first opportunity.

Dispenser, the first of the Coastal Class vessels, was completed on 8 October 1943. Captain F R Hunter, who transferred from the **Prince Salvor**[2], opened articles for the ship at Middlesborough: she was thus a merchant ship. Hunter remained in command until 15 June 1946 when he was superseded in Malta. By early November she had completed trials and stored for sea, she is wrongly shown in the Admiralty 'Pink List' as being RN manned, allocated to Gibraltar but currently in the Clyde.

Tom Bray joined the vessel[3] as Diver Ernie Goodman's AB/Linesman. The low powered **Dispenser** had a difficult passage to the West Coast, spending two days in the Pentland Firth, "looking at the same lighthouse" because of bad weather and strong tides. After a day anchored off Gourock they sailed for Milford Haven to join an outward convoy KX11.

After a day in Gibraltar they set out for Malta in convoy KMS31. On the next day they were twice attacked by aircraft with 'missiles'. Tom describes the effect of the attack: "after a day in Gib we joined a convoy for Malta, we were attacked a couple of times (in the night?) the first time a large tanker (he later told me that he wasn't sure

---

[1] These were steel cylinders, not unlike large mooring buoys, that could be attached to a sunken ship, then the water would be blown out and the camel would become buoyant: they were usually rigged in pairs.

[2] Tom Bray remembers that Frank Hunter had just completed survivors leave, having been torpedoed whilst serving in a Blue Funnel ship and he was suffering from dermatitis, brought on by being in the sea covered with fuel oil.

[3] Having spent five months working on the wreck of HMS Foylebank in Portland Harbour.

that the ship was a tanker) in the next line abreast got hit.   I was on the wheel at the time and the blast was horrific.   Both wheelhouse doors were open and the blast from the explosion ripped through like a hurricane."

Coastal Class Vessel on trials (Lifeline?)[1]   RB picture

The convoy was KMS 31, with an escort of eight, it was attacked by aircraft launching bombs and aerial torpedoes. In all four ships were sunk in this attack – **Indian Prince (Br), Birchbank (Br), Nivose (Fr)** and **Carlier (Bel); Nivose** was a tanker and **Carlier** was carrying ammunition, which exploded.

Tom continues "On our arrival in Malta a British Navy destroyer met us and remarked over his loud hailer (that we), a rusty looking ship with two equally rusty anchors hung over the stern, 'resembled St Peter looking for Anchorage'".   They were based at Malta and went with the invasion fleets to Sicily and Sardinia and then on to Naples where they were employed clearing berths so that supplies could be off loaded. Captain Doust, who was Deputy Principal Salvage Officer in newly occupied Naples, records that she arrived on 20th November, in convoy VN9 from Augusta (Sicily).

Two of the Beazley managed King Salvor vessels were in convoy KMS 29, they were the **Ocean Salvor** and the **Prince Salvor**, the first destined for Colombo and the second for Alexandria.   The **Sea Salvor**, which was described as a repair ship, was sent to Naples with KMS 69.   There were other movements of the Beazley vessels, **Salventure** was in Alexandria, but was later at Malta.   **Salviking** went to Colombo and was torpedoed in the Indian Ocean whilst on salvage duty, this incident is covered later.

Though five BAR class boom defence vessels had carried out good work in clearing Naples port, the arrival of the **Dispenser** was welcomed by all concerned.   The

[1] The Admiralty war built vessels were mostly managed by commercial firms. They are correctly referred to as Admiralty Salvage Vessels (ASVs) and normally wore the Red Ensign of the Merchant Navy. When an Admiralty Salvage Officer was board they wore the Blue Ensign of the Reserve. Some books and websites (and official convoy records) quote the ship's names with the prefix HMS (His Majesty's Ship) but this is incorrect.   The crews were merchant seamen, they signed Ship's Articles (mostly Eng. 1), which are now in the National Archives.   The salvage ships are listed on the Pink Lists, generally under the name of their base port, say Clyde, Malta, Gibraltar.

Dispenser was given two days to break out her gear and then set to work.   In total British and American salvage crews cleared 160 wrecks from the port.   The retreating Germans had not only scuttled ships throughout the port, they had added lighters, locomotives, cranes and trucks to the mess, so that when the Allies arrived the port had only one working berth.   The harbour was covered with fuel oil and the installations providing power and water had been wrecked.   *Dispenser's* work included clearing Berth 10 of the wreck of a 150 ton crane (22/27 November); then clearing the whole of Berth 71.   After this she spent much of December lifting and clearing the wreck of a destroyer, *Dispenser* lifted the bow whilst the rest of the lift was provided by camels.   From Boxing Day 1943 until the end of that month she was engaged in moving the two sections of a damaged dock caisson.

On New Years Day she went to the Corsican port of Bastia where, together with the **Barholm**, she cleared that port of wreckage, raising seven wrecks in eight days.   On this occasion she had Lt Cdr Dolmage, two Italian divers and a team of riggers on board.[1]   The two salvage ships were escorted to Corsica and through the minefields by **HMS Loyal.**   Their task was to clear the dock so that a cargo of runway mats could be landed.   One operation, that Tom remembers very clearly, was the removal of a landing craft loaded with high octane fuel.   The Bar boat took the bow section while the *Dispenser*, with her higher lifting capacity, lifted the stern[2].

Once the weight was taken the two salvage ships were held together with mooring wires so that they could manoeuvre as one.   The wreck was taken out to the breakwater near the entrance and they began lowering the wreck to the seabed.   Throughout drums of fuel were popping up and the surface of the sea became covered with high octane fuel.   Once the bow touched bottom the Bar boat let go her gear.   *Dispenser's* end was still clear of the bottom and it was getting dark.   At this point the cook on the Bar boat was seen dumping hot ashes from the galley fire and, whoosh, the sea caught fire with the *Dispenser* held by the strops in the middle of the flames, which were being continually supplied with fuel from the wreck.

Captain Hunter put the engines astern to wash the fire forward and called the launch, which had the cutting gear on board, alongside so that Tom could cut the lifting strops; he managed to cut the port wire, this would have shot off the deck with a crack and the *Dispenser* took an alarming starboard list.   With his burning goggles on Tom was almost blinded, but it appeared to him that the bridge of the ship was on fire.   Taking his goggles off he attacked the starboard wire: this was under enormous strain and hot metal was being flicked up at his face and body.   He was encouraged by the shouts of cut that f***ing wire.   After what seemed an age the wire parted and the engines on the ship and the launch were put full astern and, because of their different speeds the burning gear was whipped out of Tom's hands.   The Bar boat had departed rather promptly and there is no record of what Hunter said to the Captain of that ship afterwards.

Their fear then was that German reconnaissance aircraft would see the flames and join in the fun.   Because of bad weather Allied troops were not able to begin the Anzio landings until the 23rd January 1944.   Those on the *Dispenser* heard a while afterwards that the cargo ship which brought the air strip mats in was sunk, though most of her cargo had been discharged and divers recovered the remainder.

---

[1] The Primary Source for information on salvage work in and around Naples is ADM1/17017 and 17183, but David Sowden's book 'Admiralty Coastal Salvage Vessels' has been particularly helpful – see Appendix 8. Tom Bray does not remember the Italian team being on board his ship.
[2] The divers placed 6" & 9" circumference (48mm & 72mm diameter) diving strops under the wreck, or through the propeller apertures and hawse pipes. The eyes of the strops are then shackled to the fully extended six fold purchases and the wreck is lifted off the bottom in this way.   Sometimes the performance has to be repeated several times.

The two vessels returned to Naples on 25th January where *Dispenser* started work on another destroyer that was blocking berth 33. Again *Dispenser* was supplemented with camels and compressed air and there was an incident when a compartment of a camel exploded, blowing the kapok off the bridge front. By this time young Tom was a regular diver, though he still had to complete his diving course. *Dispenser* lifted the destroyer's bow section clear of the channel. During the third week in February she went to Torre del Greco where, working with the captured sheerlegs *Titano*, she cleared a number of wrecks, including a 600-ton sailing vessel and a block laying barge. Gales at the end of February caused work to be suspended and added new work when *HMS Boxer* dragged her anchors and grounded, then the tug *LT 221* also grounded whilst assisting the RN ship. *Dispenser* and two BAR boats refloated the *Boxer* on 3rd March and *Barholm* re-floated the tug.

The Boom Defence Vessels employed in the British Sector were *Barholm, Barmond, Bardale, Barhill*, and *Barflake (all H.M.S.)*. Other British vessels recorded as arriving in the port were *Empire Dace, Candida, Valor, King Salvor, Salveda, Merno, Salvestor* and *Salventure* (another RB managed vessel). Recommendations were: *Salvestor* "to place in a seaworthy condition" and *Salventure* was sent to Malta because of "poor performance". The sub standard performance of the *King Salvor* Class of vessel was more likely to have been the result of unsuitability for the task of wreck removal than poor crew performance. It was remarked that these vessels should only be used for distant water salvage and it is noticeable they were not included in the subsequent Normandy operations.

The British, under Captain Doust, dealt with 115 wrecks in the western part of the port; whilst the Americans under Commodore Sullivan USN removed 55 wrecks from the eastern part; this was despite salvage and clearance equipment being in short supply. Because of this colossal effort the throughput of the port was exceeding peacetime levels by April 1944.

In 1943 Cyril Smith[1] was serving as a Radio Officer with Marconi International Marine when he was informed that he would be transferred to Risdon Beazley Limited of Southampton at the request of the Royal Naval Authority. The Naval Officer in charge sorted out the transfer and Cyril was sent to Colombo to join the *Salviking*[2] as First Radio Officer/ Purser. His No. 2 also came from the UK, he had a war time certificate to act as a Junior Telegraphist, a job he combined with that of Storekeeper. *Salviking's* task was to remove the wreck of the Destroyer *HMS Tenedos*, which the Japanese had sunk in a raid in 1942.

At approximately 1600 on the 12th February 1944 the *Salviking* was ordered to sea as the trooper *Khedive Ismail* (Managed by British India S N Co for the M.O.W.T.) had been torpedoed by the Japanese submarine I – 27. The troop ship was being escorted by the HM Destroyers *Paladin* and *Petard,* which succeeded in sinking the submarine: However *Paladin* suffered damage from the submarine's hydra plane that had opened up a hole 20' long and 2' wide in her hull. Her crew had moved everything possible to the starboard side to bring the damage above the water and she was beached on a island in Addu Atoll in the Maldives.

Salviking set sail that evening after embarking six Royal Navy divers under the command of a Warrant Officer, who were to assist *Salviking's* two divers if required.

---

[1] This report is from Cyril Smith's records.
[2] Like the other Admiralty salvage vessels that RB managed *Salviking* is often described as *HMS Salviking,* but crew members from these ships are adamant that the vessels flew the Red Ensign of the Merchant Service and their crews were civilians. This is confirmed by the fact that they signed Articles and had Discharge Books..

The sea was flat, the moon made everything as bright as if it was daylight and every movement produced brilliant phosphorescence.

Cyril continues " It was the first time my No. 2 and I had both been called upon as Radio Officers to keep radio watch. At the change of the watch at midnight going into 14th February 1944 the Second Mate on watch shouted through the wireless cabin port hole that we were being attacked. He had quite clearly seen a torpedo going under the ship in the phosphorescence. He gave me a position but at the same time the submarine was adjusting the depth of the second torpedo which hit the Salviking in the stern partly destroying some of the accommodation aft. As the Salviking was only 1500 tons, voices could be heard from one end of the ship to the other. It became clear that everyone was heading towards the life boat which was launched together with a diesel engine boat. The Captain did not go onto the bridge but went straight onto the deck to ensure everyone who could get off the ship was going into one or the other of the boats. Meanwhile I was sending a message which in those days was "SSS" and indicated we were being attacked by a submarine. A dog and a monkey were also attached to the crew and both were taken into the lifeboat! My No.2 had the job of taking an emergency transmitter in the first boat to get away. He had completed part of his job by putting the emergency transmitter into the boat but then came back to the wireless cabin to see how long I was going to be. The Chief Officer, acting on his own initiative and I was told against orders, went to search below deck for any survivors and was instrumental in rescuing the Third Engineer.

To cut a long story short, the submarine surfaced which caused considerable concern as we had no way of knowing whether she was German or Japanese. The Germans had a reputation of treating survivors much better than the Japanese at that time. After the event, on reflection, she appeared to look at us to check if we were alright and then disappeared. Many years later we learned that she was in fact the German submarine *U-168* which the Royal Navy sank the following October with the loss of all hands.

For me, the night was full of anxiety since the only measure of the success of the distress signal would be the appearance of a rescue vessel. Sea conditions continued to be in our favour and the next morning an Indian Navy converted trawler appeared on the horizon which took us on board and took the diesel engine motor boat in tow. We headed for Addu Atoll some 60 miles away".

The trip home was also full of adventure. They were sent via Bombay, where they were to join a returning passenger vessel. To pass the time Cyril and his No.2 went to the cinema, during the performance there was an enormous explosion and debris rained down on the building. As soon as it was safe to come out they emerged to a scene of devastation, they both volunteered to help but were told that there was nothing that they could do. The SS *Fort Stikine*, with a cargo that included a large amount of explosives, had caught fire and suffered two massive explosions. Twelve other ships were wrecked, either by the explosion of the ensuing tidal wave, thousands died. After some leave Cyril joined the RB managed **Salventure**, again as 1st Radio Officer & Purser. He remained on that ship, based in Malta, until September 1946, when he retired from the sea.

Chapter Three - Admiralty Salvor 1943 to 1946

Planning for what became known as the D-Day Landings, Operation Overlord, started a couple of years before the event; the maritime part of the landings was termed Operation Neptune.   Once it was realised that the King Salvor class vessels were not suitable for beach and port clearance attention turned to the alternatives: in addition to the requisitioned craft, these were the dumb lifting craft, the US built vessels and the Coastal Class vessels (CSVs).   Four US built BARS vessels were available to the British and, in addition to the *Dispenser,* four Coastals would be delivered in time.   These, plus three pairs of Lifting Craft and numbers of Camels, would be the backbone of the operation.   There were insufficient CSVs to operate in the most efficient way – in pairs, so each was paired with one of the requisitioned lifting craft.

All of the salvage vessels were civilian manned sailing under the Red Ensign and, irrespective of their manager they were controlled by Risdon Beazley for this operation.   Salvage equipment and smaller craft were stored at Clausentum, as were the Camels.   Though the company was known to some as 'the circus' obviously high ranking people had gained faith in them, they reported directly to the CinCXF, later ANCXF.   Rear Admiral A R Dewar, the UK Director of Salvage, appointed Cdre Thomas McKenzie RNVR (Sp), of Metal Industries[1], to be in charge of the British salvage effort in Northern Europe and Cdre Sullivan USN returned from the Mediterranean to oversee the US Navy's part in the operation.

In preparation for D-Day the 'salvage store carriers' were to assemble in the 'Isle of Wight Area' on Y-21,[2] making them the first of the salvage fleet to be in position.   The vessels were *Palmston, Forde, Carmenita, Dorita, Polita* and *Alita* (at just over 100 GRT the last four were little more than coastal barges;) all were to come from Southampton except the *Forde* which arrived from Swansea.   These vessels, and the salvage ships that arrived later, anchored in an arc between south west and west of Hillhead Beacon at the southern end of Southampton Water.   As they could not encroach on the North Channel, they were limited to between two and three point five meters of water at Chart Datum.   The after draft of a Coastal Class vessel is around three point five meters and during the last week in May there was only 0.3 meters of water at Low Water!

The salvage ships *Uplifter, Lifeline, Sea Salvor, Foremost 17, Foremost 18, Lincoln Salvor, American Salvor, Bertha, Help, Lady Southborough, Salvage Chieftain* and *Abigail* arrived at Y-14.   The Wreck Removal Vessels H.M.S. *Jezo* , H.M.S *Jacinta* and H.M.S *Lune* and the Ocean Going tugs *Zwarte Zee* and *Thames* (both L Smit and Co.[3]) and the Assurance class tug HMS *Jaunty* also joined them..

There is no record of where the Lifting Craft were moored; anchoring points are shown inside the salvage anchorage in two meters, some could have been at Clausentum with the Camels.   To the east was an anchorage for no less than 69 tugs, many of these were required to tow refloated units of the Mulberry Harbour.

---

[1] There were two McKenzies in Admiralty Salvage, they were the brothers.   Thomas became Commodore RNVR and was made a Member of the Order of Bath (CB) in addition to being a CBE.   He was Principal Salvage Officer (North West Europe)   His elder brother James Fenwick was on the staff of the Flag Officer Normandy Landings and then became his brother's deputy, he retired as a Captain RNVR.   Had I read Brack's notes properly I would have picked this up.   Brack was in the USA from 1943 to1944, supervising the construction of the four 'Salvor class' ships, he then he became RB's marine superintendent in the Mediterranean.

[2] Y was the 1st June 1944

[3] Five Smit tugs were already outside Holland in May 1940, *Thames, Roode Zee, Seine, Hudson* and *Donau..*   The first four were on Admiralty service: the *Roode Zee* was lost with all hands when she was torpedoed in April 1944.   .The book **Smit 150** says that 12 Smit tugs escaped from Holland.   Others that escaped were *Zwarte Zee , Witte Zee, Schelde, Ebro* and *Lauwerzee;* the first three of these were in Admiralty Service and the last was lost in 1940.   The tugs based in the UK were managed by J D McLaren of London, Smit's pre-war UK salvage agents.   David Asprey, his source **Colledge - Ships of the Royal Navy**

There have been a number of accounts, including at least one from the USA, on the lines of 'but for so-and-so these things would never have worked'; but the tale in Admiralty Salvage in Peace & War seems to have the ring of truth:

Salvage Officer William 'Bill' Robinson[1] was sent to Littlehampton, Sussex, to refloat a stranded craft.   What he found, when he arrived on site, was 200 feet a box like concrete caisson.   Robinson had never seen such a craft and called John Polland at the Admiralty for advice.   Polland was quickly on site and was as mystified as his colleague.   He requested plans from the War Office and found that this was a 'Pheonix Unit'. But the unit that he looked at differed from the drawing he had been sent, penstocks were missing, bulkheads were not watertight and the outlet holes at 6" diameter, would not take the flanges of a 6" pump piping as they were supposed to. They were tasked with refloating the unit and towing it to nearby Selsey Bay.   They decided to visit Selsey, as they got close Polland said they could see, "dozens of these monstrosities", the bay "was cluttered up with concrete and steel equipment"

The chapter goes into some detail about the raising of the Mulberry Harbour units. There are some discrepancies: it says that Polland was only loaned three vessels, the one from RB being 'an old Dutch dredger'. We know from Syd Day's account that there at least the **Longtow** and **Roselyne** were on site.   Tony Booth also says that the salvage officers were those "deemed too old for active service" - Bill Robinson was a fairly young man then.   Of course the main problem was that the bulk of the salvage vessels were allocated to the invasion fleet and were not permitted to leave their anchorages.

The section of the Solent anchorage is shown below:

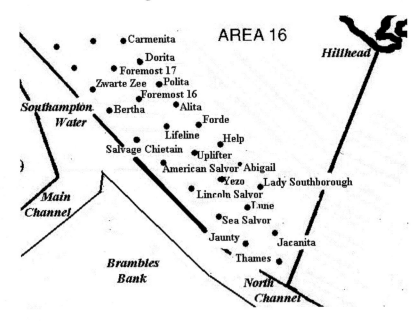

Salvage ships at the Solent anchorage, June 1ˢᵗ - John Winser, D-Day ships[2]

Other assembly points were Plymouth: **Salvictor, Southampton Salvor** and **Le Leutter** together with the WDVs, H.M.S. **Marie** H.M.S. **Admiral Sir John Lawford**[3] and H.M.S. **Tehana;** and the Nore, where the **Succour, Salveda** and **Gallions Reach** assembled.   The US salvage vessels were at Portland and Plymouth.

---

[1] RB's salvage officer though Tony Booth does not say so
[2] **Salvage Chietain**, should be **Salvage Chieftain.**
[3] Requisitioned Fleetwood trawler

On the 4th June 1944 the **Boston Salvor** was sent to the Owers Bank to assist **HMS Northcote**. **Boston Salvor** waited by the Nab Tower in gale conditions until a tug arrived, then the two of them proceeded to the casualty, where the salvage ship put a team of five seamen on board under the charge of her salvage officer, a Mr Brown. Two of the team, G F French and J Taylor, were lost when the casualty foundered; the rest of the team were snatched from the water and hospitalised in Portsmouth. **Boston Salvor** was an unlucky ship, she was destroyed by a V2 rocket in March 1945 whilst in a dry-dock in Antwerp.

The D-Day plan was to allocate a pair of salvage vessels to each of the two British beaches and another pair to the Canadian beach; these were to arrive at D+1. One RN Wreck Dispersal Vessel was allocated to each beach. A further two pairs were allocated to the Mulberry Harbours. Five vessels were kept in reserve to begin the clearance of the captured ports. The US Navy vessels included **U.S.S Brant, U.S.S Diver** and **U.S.S Swivel** – sisters of the US built vessels serving under the British flag. Various defects with some of the vessels caused substitutions to be made and many salvage vessels, including some of those eventually destined for Normandy, were first assigned to Mulberry pumping duties in the UK.

Longtow and her chummy ship **Roselyne** were sent to Selsey, where about 60 sections were parked, each had to be pumped out and re-floated with the crews racing one another to ensure that they did not end up with the unit listing towards them, which would mean more work for that ship's crew. With all the haste and the rivalry there were a few crushed arms and legs. Once the units were re-floated the pumps were stripped off and the units handed over to the 'pongees' (probably pongoes – a seaman's word for soldiers, or more correctly a primitive African ape!), then the tugs would tow them away.

The lack of food was an ever present problem, if none could be had from the depot ships the crews were forced to go ashore and beg for what they could – and there was precious little food left ashore. The situation was not helped when a Naval Officer ordered the catering crew on the **Longtow** to feed his team of ratings; they refused and he attempted to have them sacked.

George Major, who became Second Engineer on the **Droxford**, was launchman on a Coastal class waiting to go to the 'far shore': he was sent ashore to Hillhead with the ration books to queue up and get what he could. George was not too familiar with the waters at the Haven, he took a short cut and went ashore on a falling tide. It was only then, when the sky became full of aircraft and gliders, that he realised that the great day had come[1]. Syd too talks of the tremendous excitement and the masses of ships, aircraft and gliders. Had he been on shore, he would have found these and the seemingly endless convoys of troops and guns equally exciting, as we boys did.

Early in 1944 Tony Hodge[2] joined the A.S.V. **Gallions Reach** at Immingham. Like several of the requisitioned units this ship had been built for the PLA as a self-propelled mud hopper and had been equipped with the pumps, wires and even Polar Blasting Gelignite that made her suitable for salvage work.
In May they signed Articles to sail for the 'Mass Invasion of Europe', their Identity Cards were stamp 'V', for volunteer, and they became entitled to a free issue of 200 cigarettes or 4 oz. of tobacco a week. Crews were to work on board or ashore as required, this may well be when they came under the T124X arrangement. They left the Humber on the 19th May and anchored off the Medway to await their convoy. They sailed with convoy ETC 5 on the 9th June.

---

[1] George could always be relied to respond to the enquiry "what did you do on D-Day" with "I sat on a mud bank"
[2] Tony Hodge kindly provided information from a draft of his Memoirs, which he has since self published, very interesting.

When considering Risdon Beazley's contribution to the invasion effort, it is worth noting that at least nine of the Beazley built Fairmiles also played their part at Normandy.

A plan change came about when the Americans realised that they too needed lifting craft, so **Help** and **Abigail** were sent to assist. Commander Byron S. Huie Jr. USNR, who was in charge of US salvage operations off the Normandy beaches in June and July, 1944 writes of this part of the operation:

"Our force was further augmented by the assignment to it of some other craft which comprised the combat salvage and fire fighting unit operating off the UTAH Beach under Admiral Moon.

American Salvor at Dover 1946[1]   *Photograph 'Ken' Kenny, Tony Hodge*

The storm had not caused such great damage there. Several large coasters were aground and these were easily refloated by our salvage unit up there so that soon afterwards the USS *Bannock* and the *ATR 3* were assigned to our unit off OMAHA Beach. Also, three British Wreck Disposal Craft, which were laying off the beach area waiting for Cherbourg to fall to commence port clearance operations, were sent in to assist us. These were *HMS Marie, HMS Tehana* and the *HMS Sir John Lawford*. These ships carried divers and explosives for demolition purposes. They were soon busily engaged in blowing down sunken wrecks off the shore.

About the middle of July, two other British craft from another of Commodore Sullivan's units were sent to assist us. These were the *Help* and the *Abigail*, two large lifting craft known by the British as BAR boats (*sic*). They proved to be of great value in lifting sunken wrecks so as to remove them as obstructions close off shore. By the 20th of July, beach clearance operations were completed. The only thing remaining were a few of the LCIs sunk on D and D plus 1 day by enemy action, and a few of the large metal bombardons which the storm had driven high and dry on the shore and which were to be removed in sections later by the Seabees."

---

[1] 'S' on funnel indicates that this ship was part of the salvage fleet for the Normandy Landings in 1944

"Our divers rigged for raising thirty-six underwater obstructions sunk off the beach. These obstructions were Sherman tanks, half tracks, DUKWs, jeeps, and equipment such as that which had been lost overboard either during the first two days of the attack or during the storm. They were raised principally by means of a 30-ton floating crane loaned to us by the Army and by using the two British ships *Help* and *Abigail* previously mentioned. The figures for craft taken from the beaches do not include approximately the fifth, which were able to retract under their own power after salvage methods had been employed to remove others blocking their exit. A total of thirty-two craft of all types were sunk by the unit as menaces to navigation. Up until the time Cherbourg fell, Commodore Sullivan was aboard the flagship of Admiral Kirk, the *Augusta*...."

When Cherbourg fell, however, the Commodore was one of the first to enter. Following the completion of our work on the beaches on 20 July, the many ships assigned there were dispatched to other areas. The *Help* and the *Abigail* went in to Cherbourg to help the harbor clearance parties operating there under the Commodore. The *Swivel*, which I had not previously mentioned, and which served as the task unit commander's headquarters ship, also went into Cherbourg. The *Diver* and the *Brant* likewise entered Cherbourg to begin harbor clearance operations".

According to ADM1/17274 the salvage vessels were allocated as follows:

Juno and Sword beaches - *Foremost 17, Lifeline, Lady Southborough, Southampton Salvor, American Salvor, Sea Giant* and *Antic*[1]. They worked on until the end of October. In all 704 casualties of all types were assisted at the beach-heads. (this figure may include the wrecks at Cherbourg and/or Le Havre)

Arromanches - *Lady Southborough* September/October. Eight salvages including the stern half of the cargo ship *Harpagus* 7,271 grt; which was refloated, towed to Southampton and from there to Wallsend where a new 190' forebody was joined.

Bassin A Flot - *LC14* later *Lifeline* – Eight wrecks removed by *LC14*, one by *Lifeline*

Port Maree – *LC14, LC20, Lifeline & Foremost 18* – Four wrecks removed.

Cherbourg – *Help, Abigail, LC 15,17,21,22*, plus **USS Swivel, USS Diver** and **USS Brant** and twelve lifting Camels entered the port in early July. The Germans had held out here until 27 June. Though the port was in the American sector it had been agreed that the clearance should be an Anglo-American project. Immediately after the capitulation Commodores McKenzie and Sullivan flew into Cherbourg and found the port devastated. Many of the quays had been demolished and sixty-seven ships had been scuttled within the port; cranes, railway wagons and other debris had been added to complicate the task. They knew from previous clearance work that there was a risk that the wreckage had been booby trapped.

Before the salvage crews could start their work the port had to be cleared of mines. This was achieved by a combination of conventional and 'human' minesweepers. These were teams of fit young men who, working at low water, avoided the trip wires and cleared the basins. It is hard to think of a job that required more raw courage than this. By early September the port was handling about 12,000 tons of cargo per day, about half of the normal capacity. Not long afterwards, Cherbourg was exceeding its peacetime capacity, like Naples before it.

Port en Bessin – Nine casualties assisted.

---

[1] An Antic is shown as having been sunk earlier in the war.

Le Havre – *Help, Abigail, LC 17, LC21.* Mine sweeping started immediately after the Germans had surrendered and was completed in an amazing three days. McKenzie records 60 casualties assisted, the balance are probably included in the figure for the Seine Approaches.

Rouen & Seine Approaches – *Salvictor, Salvage Chieftain.* - 162 casualties assisted.

Ouistreham (Caen) – ***Succour*** – Eight wrecks removed & one casualty assisted.

Dieppe – 12 casualties assisted, mostly by local salvage vessels.

Boulogne - *Lifeline, Foremost 18, LC14, LC2. WDV Martenet & WDV Maria*
23 wrecks removed and six allied casualties assisted.

Bassin Loubet – *Lifeline, Foremost 18, LC14, LC20. WDV Martenet & WDV Maria*
Ten wrecks removed, plus nine mine carcasses & 3 trolleys.

Calais – *Gallions Reach, Rampant, LC15, LC22.* 29 casualties assisted. Wreck removals included a number of fishing vessels and floating cranes.

Zeebrugge – *Lincoln Salvor, Dexterous, LC19, Abigail.*

Ostend – *Uplifter, Lincoln Salvor, Salvage Chieftain.* 37 casualties assisted. About half were wreck removals, the balance being allied vessels.

Terneuzen – *Swin, Lady Southborough & Gallions Reach* (from March 1945.)
Nine casualties assisted, wreck removal included two tugs, a bridge and a lock gate.

Schelde – *American Salvor, Lincoln Salvor, Dexterous, Bertha, Euston Cross, Freedom & Antic* Nov/Dec 1944. Over 50 allied casualties assisted.

Flushing – *Kingarth, Uplifter, Salvage Chieftain.* - 60 casualties assisted

Antwerp – *Salveda* – most of the work carried out by local contractors, several unfinished vessels scuttled at Cockerill shipyard, Hoboken.[1]

London Gazette entries:

British Empire Medal, Hugh Ross ALLAN, Diver, Salvage Vessel " Uplifter."[2] *Allan was serving in operations off Normandy during the invasion of Europe. He was one of the first divers to make a descent at Port-en-Bessin when operations were in active progress and when the extent of mining was unknown. His skilful work in mined areas and in strong tides greatly contributed to the successful salvage of H.M. ships and merchant vessels.*

Awarded the British Empire Medal: Harry William BENTLEY, Boatswain, s.v. " Kingarth."[3] . *The Salvage Vessel " **Kingarth**" was engaged on the important and arduous work of clearing the harbour at Flushing, which included the lifting of the lock gates. Boatswain Bentley was outstanding in his enthusiasm, great ability and complete disregard of his own safety. He supervised and undertook the slinging of the lock gates which weighed 150 tons. This proved to be a very difficult and hazardous operation. On one occasion, when working under adverse conditions of sea and wind and in a current of some seven knots, a sling broke and Boatswain Bentley immediately jumped on to the gate, which was being lifted, to fix a new one. The gate was then in a most precarious position and was likely to capsize at any moment, in which event Boatswain Bentley would have had but little chance of survival.*

---

[1] ADM1/17274 does not seem to be complete as in Tony Hodge has the ***Gallions Reach*** working at Arromanche, Calais, Ostend, Terneuzen , Antwerp and Flushing.
[2] Uplifter was managed by Metal Industries Ltd.
[3] Kingarth was managed by Risdon Beazley

The following entries appeared in the Supplement to the London Gazette dated 10 August 1945:

To be Additional Members of the Civil Division of the Most Excellent Order of the British Empire:

Captain Rieth Stonehouse LENNARD, Master, s.v. " **Help**" (Risdon A. Beazley),
Captain James WHITE, Master, s.v." **Abigail**" (Leith Salvage and Towing Co. Ltd.).

Awarded the British Empire Medal, John Gordon SMITH, Senior Diver, s.v."**Help**" (Risdon Beazley).

The Salvage Vessels " **Help** " and "**Abigail** " were continuously employed after D Day in salvage operations and port clearance in France and N.W. Europe. This work, which was often carried out in conditions of extreme discomfort and danger, was of incalculable value, in terms of shipping and cargo saved, to the Allied cause.
Captain Lennard of the s.v. " **Help** " demonstrated unusual skill throughout the operations. He showed outstanding seamanship when a strong gale and heavy tide caused the anchors to drag and the vessel was lifted by the high seas and pounded on top of the quay breaking the stem frame. He succeeded in getting her clear until tugs arrived and anchors were relaid.
Captain White of the s.v. " **Abigail** "handled his ship with outstanding skill and seamanship throughout and he was responsible for the expeditious raising of many sunken ships and obstructions.

Senior Diver Smith displayed a high sense of duty throughout under most difficult conditions. He was the only diver working on two occasions in January when the temperature of the water was below freezing point. In Cherbourg, where mines were plentiful and were exploding, he remained under water until he had a complete picture of the obstruction to be cleared. He also placed sweep wires under a barge loaded with mines and thus enabled it to be successfully removed.

There were Commendations for:

James Sangster Melville CRAIG, Carpenter & Diver, s.v. " **Abigail** " (Leith Salvage & Towing).

William Charles Sidney IRONS, Second Mate and Boatswain, s.v. " **Help**" (Risdon A .Beazley).

James McKENZIE, Boatswain, s.v. " **Abigail** " (Leith Salvage and Towing Co. Ltd.).

William Gardner MCPHERSON, Esq., Chief Engineer Officer, s.v. " **Abigail** " (Leith Salvage & Towing Co.)

Acting Temporary Lt. Cdr D J R Davies, RNR was recommended for a decoration for 'salvage operations on the Normandy beaches and port clearance in the US Sector'

Member of the Order of the British Empire: Percy Harold CARRINGTON, Salvage Officer, Risdon A Beazley.

The KING has been graciously pleased to give orders for the following appointment to the Most Honourable Order of Bath:

To be an Additional Member of the Military Division of the Third Class... of the said Most Honourable Order: **Commodore Second Class Thomas McKenzie C.B.E. R.N.V.R.,** for distinguished service in organising salvage operations in the liberated ports in the British Assault Area in France.

Other decorations listed in Seedies: "For back up to Normandy & salvage operations":

Foremost 18 - Dalton WG, Captain; Kirby W, Boatswain; Munson D, A.B. – Mentioned in despatches

American Salvor – Haliday J J, Diver – Mentioned in Despatches

Lincoln Salvor – Whiting WC, Chief Engineer – Mentioned in despatches

Lifeline – Storr Geoffrey, Captain – Distinguished Service Cross
Before they left the Humber they had a visit from Army Intelligence on security and they especially warned them not to keep diaries, as Tony says, it became apparent after the war that their own senior officers disobeyed these instructions.

Tony's recollections of **Gallions Reach** at Arromanches need to be included in full:
"The convoy regrouped off Portsmouth on the night of the 10th June and we sailed for Normandy, a bright moonlight night, the sort that during the blitz was referred to as a Bomber's Moon and it turned out that the E-boats from Le Havre liked it too.   We felt rather naked when the firing started as one of the escort had a breakdown and had to return to Portsmouth and one of the others was hit although it still continued firing. The Convoy was in two lines and a small tanker on our port side was torpedoed, exploded, and showered us with oil.   At least two people survived as we saw red life-jacket lights in the water and though we couldn't do anything I think an escort picked them up astern.   Meanwhile we were happier when we had another ship abeam between the action and us.

We got to our designated anchorage in what was being turned into Mulberry Harbour and already a line of old ships had been sunk and the huge concrete caissons were being sunk to extend the breakwater.   This being my birthday I had a tot of rum, the first time I remember tasting it.   At that time the Royal Navy ratings got a tot of rum every day but we had just one gallon jar on board for a sweetener after cold or hazardous work but we soon found out that we could replenish our stock very easily!

My feelings that day were of being very proud to be part of such an endeavour.   I believe that there were something like five thousand ships spread out along the beach head from battleships to small tankers and workhorses like us and in between them host of landing craft, launches and DUKWs scurrying around.   Landing ships and Landing craft were running up on the beach discharging men, guns, tanks, ambulances, and lorries with everything bound inland.

A battleship, the "Rodney" I think, was offshore shelling targets ashore with the shells passing over our heads so there was quite a bit of noise but there was very little enemy air activity during the day.   To avoid being opened fire on by trigger-happy gunners all allied Aircraft had, at the very last moment, been painted with very distinctive black and white stripes.   Friendly Fire was very well known then too!
The nights were very noisy as German aircraft tried to fly over the beachhead to drop mines and presumably to gather intelligence.   All gunnery officers had been allocated a section of the sky into which to fire, i.e. creating a box barrage.   With all H.M. Ships including special AA Cruisers firing and as all units comprising the breakwater had Bofors Guns it really was a Brock's Benefit, and with smaller 20mm tracer shells cross-crossing the sky it was really beautiful.   Our Radio Officer, Dave Wicks, a wartime recruit who had been studying at the Royal Academy of Art, was apt to be so entranced that on at least one occasion he stood out on the deck wearing only his underpants and a steel helmet working on a scratchboard with the odd shell splinters clanging on the deck and spitting into the water alongside the ship.   I wonder if he ever showed his sketches – some years after the war I did go to the Royal Academy show and saw one of his line drawings but it was not of the beachhead.

There was one German plane that used to come over during the day on reconnaissance and we rather admired his cheek as he flew very low, too low for the gun battery on the cliff to depress their guns and the ships could not fire at it without hitting other ships or troops ashore.   One day, at low tide, gunners had 20mm guns mounted on lorries down on the beach and as we watched they caught him as he made his run.   There was a brief cheer and then someone said "Poor sod" our tribute to him and we all went back to work rather quietly.

About this time there was a sudden flurry of air activity concentrated over the beachhead, fighters overhead instead of flying to the front inland and Naval ships up to something and we found out soon afterwards that King George V1 had paid a visit. It was said that Churchill had told the King that he would go over on D Day but the King said 'If you go – I go' which put a stop to that.

Apart from the noise from the AA guns at night there were constant patrols through the anchorage dropping small charges against midget subs and frogmen.   I never heard of these intruders having any success inside the anchorage though they did sink at least one destroyer – the "Quorn" – outside the anchorage.   The effects of these small depth charges when one was laying in one's bunk was like someone hitting the bulkhead next to you with a very large hammer so I preferred to sleep on deck as the weather was quite warm.

The weather however changed again and we had an on-shore gale blowing.   We had at one stage both anchors down and we were steaming up to them – every sailor's nightmare to be caught on a lee shore.   The off loading of stores into DUKWs stopped and very little could be landed on to the beach or via the temporary metal causeways which were being constructed.   We had the worst case of seasickness that I had ever seen at the time.   The lad would not go down below so we sat him in a lifebuoy and lashed him to a funnel stay otherwise he would have gone overboard via the scuppers and wash port and it was patently obvious that he didn't care anyway.

As soon as the weather moderated slightly, we set out to help ships in trouble and I remember particularly going to the Tank Landing craft adrift in the Channel that was very low in the water and listing badly.   It had a couple of canvas topped 3 tons lorries on board and the soldiers were huddled on top of them and looked very pleased to see us.   It's nice to know that you're wanted!

The success of the whole Invasion was in jeopardy as very little supplies could be landed. One ammunition ship had been blown ashore and was sitting upright on the sand and our Captain, Lawrence, was ordered to steam alongside her at high water and beach ourselves.   He was not a happy Cappy as he said, he was told to do something that he'd spent all his life trying to avoid! Having bilge keels we managed to tie up alongside her and dry out and the Royal Engineers used our derricks and winches to off load the ammunition over on to lorries on the beach at low tide and into DUKWs when the water rose.   This went on through the night under floodlights, which were only turned out when enemy planes were overhead.   In spite of having been under water the shells went straight up to the front line, which certainly wouldn't have pleased any Armament Supply Officer under normal circumstances!

Before we left Arromanche Capt. Lawrence was awarded the D.S.C[1]. and I think it was probably this episode that gained him it.   He, of course, described it as a 'Roti' gong, (i.e. came up with the rations)

Shortly after this was the big raid of 450 Lancasters on Caen where the British, facing the main concentration of German Armour, were being held up.   With the naked eye we could see the planes suddenly rise as they released their bombs.   There was something very unreal about drinking mugs of tea on deck and watching all this

---

[1] I have not yet been able to find reference to this award and believe that it is one of a number that I have missed.

happen and I was reminded of this feeling when I turned on the T/V on Sept 11th and watched the events unfold at the Twin Towers of New York. The thought that you ought to be horrified at knowing that people are being killed and yet feeling very detached. There was some AA fire and we saw one Lancaster limping home and losing height and counted the crew bailing out. When six had left the aircraft one of our lads said that there was one chap still left and the pilot bravely waited until the plane had cleared the anchorage and then he too jumped and was soon picked up."

He continues:

"I got ashore occasionally, once on the back of a motorcycle driven by a mad Canadian R.N.R. Officer attached to us as Salvage Officer. I wasn't happy in the lanes torn up by tank tracks and shell holes and even less happy when I saw a Military Police notice saying that we were in sight of enemy observation posts. I don't know where we went or why – all I remember is hanging on for dear life and clutching a couple of round boxes of Camembert Cheese. I'm not awfully keen on Camembert but having been too young for such tastes before the war I still look on them as the first fruits of victory.

Another time ashore I met a matelot who told me that he was in H.M.S. "Albatross" which I think was a converted Seaplane Carrier and he told me that his captain was trying to get them all killed, refusing to up anchor when being shelled by shore batteries and 88s in Sword Area, the eastern extremity of the Beach Head. This Captain had rebuked an officer who ducked down behind a canvas (sic) dodger when a shell came over saying that he should behave like a gentleman. When he conducted a funeral service of some of his men that had been killed he said that he envied the men killed in action and trusted that the rest of the ship's company felt the same! I thought that this was just a matelot's whinge or at least an exaggeration, but in 1994 I saw a detailed account basically confirming this and even named the Captain, Capt.Mcgrath R.N. I only hope that the relatives of men killed on board her never read this account.

During the storm the harbour that the Americans had built at Port-en-Bessin, which was in an exposed position, was wrecked as in their quest for speed in construction they had not put the specified number of anchors out. The units they salvaged were added to the British harbour and some of their vessels used the anchorage. About a month after our arrival at Arromanche and having sustained no damage except a few shell splinters in our funnel we were minding our own business in Mulberry Harbour when an American Tank Landing Ship with the tide under her stern careered through the anchorage and hitting us a glancing blow carried most of our bow ramp away and we were sent ignominiously home to Southampton for repairs."[1]

For the salvage vessels that remained on the UK side times were equally busy, **Longtow** was then based in Dover and covering casualties caused by the long distance shelling from the French side and vessels that grounded on the Goodwin Sands. Syd recalls that, if you did not get them off within 48 hours, they started to break up. At least the salvage ships found food and supplies on the damaged Liberty ships. Their counterparts on the French side were amazed to find that there was much more food in France than they were used to seeing; perhaps this was why many of the French were none too keen to be 'liberated.'

All crews remember the rough times clearing up on the casualties with the stink of cordite still around as they shovelled debris over the side; debris that included body

---

[1] There is a good photograph of a Coastal salvage ship alongside a canal barge, this is reproduced in "D-Day Ships"by John Winser; it is credited to the Imperial War Museum, but they cannot seem to find the negative.

parts. There was not even time to deal with the corpses properly. Some of the crew could not cope, but most were so weary that they 'accepted it'. Syd says how sorry he felt for the dead 'Yanks, floating around in their fancy uniforms', as he says, 'to come all that bloody way and to end up like that.'

After repairing in Southampton, the **Gallions Reach** arrived at Calais in September 1944. Tony Hodge writes: "The Canadians, having taken the town, pushed on and were still fighting at Dunkirk. There was an Army "Town Major" and a handful of soldiers and after the 'Sweepers' had done their job we were the first ship to enter the harbour. We did not go alongside as the Germans had caught a couple of ships in Boulogne by putting ordinary sea mines behind the steel shuttering that formed the quay wall so that as the vessels went alongside the mines went off. Instead we moored in the middle of the harbour rather like a spider at the centre of a web with mooring lines out from each bow and quarter. Soon we could land by dinghy at a safe place marked by the REs with mine tapes that also marked a swept path to the town.

With our divers the job was to clear the harbour of obstructions so that ferries could start running on the short route from Dover. Being just nineteen I couldn't wait to go ashore and we were supposed to take a DEMS rating with sidearm with us though I don't think we were in any danger from residual Germans. Weeks later more troops arrived and there was a drive and they rounded up nearly three hundred German deserters most of whom I was told had been hidden by French girl friends or wives. The biggest danger was from people claiming to be of the F.F.I. (Free Forces of the Interior) mostly young men who hung around with all sorts of weapons and German stick bombs, of which there were plenty laying round and with which they were liable to let fly just for the hell of it.

The docks and centre of the town were flattened as the town had been fought through in 1940, (one of the Rifle Brigades holding out very courageously,) and had been bombed and again fought through after the Invasion...there were places where people had been buried under the rubble and I still dislike the smell of Freesias, which always brings back memories.

The REs soon made it safe for us to go alongside what had been the Gare Maritime. At this time our Captain, Capt Harvey, had to be taken ashore with a nervous breakdown. If it was the constant worry about the ship setting off a mine, then I must have had blind confidence in him or been completely stupid as I never remember being frightened during this period of the war."

After time at Calais, the **Gallions Reach** moved to Ostend and then across to Terneuzen, [1] among the wreck removal work that the vessels undertook, was the removal of the wreckage of 12 MTBs that had been destroyed by fire at Ostend. Whilst at Terneuzen, **Gallions Reach** sustained damage when two RN minesweepers passed the ship at full speed and ranged her against the dyke wall. Having been damaged by an American LST at the Mulberry Harbour the crew felt, just as the crew of the **Forde** must have felt after Dunkirk "With friends like that, who needs enemies".

"At Antwerp little had changed but we met some of the crew of the "Boston Salvor" who were being repatriated. While their ship was in dry dock, with nothing constructive to do, some of the crew had adopted the cafés of Schipperstraat as their haunts and others had taken to attending meetings of a religious sect. A bit exaggerated but we used to say that when you went aboard the ship, half the crew

---

[1] Fairmiles lost at Ostend 462/465/255/461/466/438/459/444/776/791/798/789. see ADM 116/5493 and 6077

would say 'Brother, are you saved?' and the others would say, slurring their words, 'Have a drink old boy'.

Luckily for both saints and sinners they were saved when a V2 landed on their ship while they were ashore at their various pursuits. The "Boston Salvor" had a very large towing Capstan aft and the rocket had landed on that, the blast went sideways and killed fourteen workers on the dockside but the three shipkeepers who were forrard emerged shocked but uninjured. The drunks got back first and fed them hearty tots of rum & it was alleged that the next morning they asked "V2, what V2?" Tony continues:

"Christmas time 1944 and through to the New Year was a very worrying time as, just when it was thought that victory was in sight, the Germans made a very strong counter attack that had been very carefully planned. It was spear headed by crack troops, some of whom spoke English, riding in captured transports and wearing U.S. uniforms, penetrated the American positions and every tank that they could muster followed these up. The whole push, which was known as the Battle of the Bulge, one objective being to re-take the port of Antwerp, was initially very successful and they had got within thirty miles of Brussels when they were pushed back, General Montgomery being sent to organise the counter attack"

After repairs had been completed **Gallions Reach** went to work at Flushing in January 1945, Tony says:

"The island of Walcheron had been liberated on the 2nd November 1944 after a costly assault by Marine Commandoes made very difficult by the Germans who had opened the sluice gates of the dykes and flooded large areas of the island. When we arrived the harbour of Flushing was cluttered up with all sorts of wrecks, some sunk by allied bombing and some scuttled by the retreating Germans to stop it being used for landing supplies. The clearance had not been given priority, as Antwerp, nearer the battle lines and with rail and road communications, was now open to shipping.

One wreck that gave us a certain amount of amusement was a tug, which had sunk upright, and was submerged except for the bridge and the funnel. Early on April the 1st we took the dinghy out to her and hung a bucket of oily waste inside the funnel. We lit this and it looked, in the slight wind, as though she was steaming along half under water and we sat back and enjoyed watching the puzzlement of passers by though it was a bit of an anti-climax to trying to explain the concept of "April Fool" to a Dutchman.

Another ship, a large liner, was still on the stocks having been laid down in pre-war days. The tide was such that the opportunity to launch her occurred only about twice a year and just before this time the RAF dropped a small bomb on her and I believe this happen again until the Germans gave up the idea of using her. They had built a wall under her bilge keels and used her as an Air Raid Shelter. One night a soldier with a very fine voice stood under her enjoying the resonance and sang "Jerusalem" and I've never heard it sung more beautifully or more movingly since. The ship was completed and launched in July 1946 and when I saw the "Willem Ruys" at sea, shipmates looked a bit sideways at me when I said that I remembered her as an Air Raid Shelter.

There was plenty of arms and ammunition lying around and in our spare time we rigged up a rifle range. One of the ABs said he'd been a gunnery instructor in the Royal Navy and though we rather doubted it he'd obviously been on a range before and so we accepted it and he took charge to make sure that there were no accidents.

There had been so many needless deaths through the careless or uninhibited use of guns – I was told later and I've no authority for it but I must have believed the person that told me – that twenty-seven deaths occurred on V.E.day from bullets and shells fired this way."

Dispenser arrived at Marseilles on 13 February 1945, she was the first ship to enter the port after she cleared a block ship sunk in the locks. Once they had cleared the entrance they sailed for Le Ciotat, where there was a small shipyard and an inoperable dry dock.   A trawler had been scuttled at the entrance and three smaller vessels (tugs) had been sunk to block the fitting out berth. The first task was to lift the tank landing craft that was at the entrance; a South African salvage vessel the *Gantous* (incorrect spelling?) assisted but left after a week.   From there they went east to Antibes where they lifted a yacht, as they afterwards received 'a small reward' they realised that this was an independent job.   *Dispenser* is recorded in the Pink List leaving for Malta on 2 March.

The following announcement appears in a Supplement to the London Gazette dated 24th April 1945:

To be an Additional Officer of the Civil Division of the Most Excellent Order of the British Empire:

Captain Frank Ronald Hunter, Master, Admiralty Salvage Vessel " *Dispenser.*"

To be an Additional Member of the Civil Division of the Most Excellent Order of the British Empire:

Ernest Frederick Goodman, Esq. Chief Diver, Admiralty Salvage Vessel " *Dispenser.*"
When the invasion of the South of France took place the opening of the port of Marseilles necessitated the clearance of blockships and the removal of numerous wrecks and obstructions before the port could be thoroughly effective. These waters were known to be mined, and the salvage vessel " Dispenser " played a prominent part in the dangerous and difficult work of clearance.

The Master displayed outstanding courage, coolness and skilful seamanship whilst manoeuvring his ship in these dangerous waters. His expert knowledge and ability in rigging and lifting work was undoubtedly a major factor in the rapid clearance of a number of essential alongside berths. His cheerfulness and tireless energy kept his ship's company working with excellent results on an almost non-stop programme of raising and removing of wrecks.

Chief Diver Goodman showed exceptional courage in sustained diving operations in heavily mined areas. On one occasion he was rendered unconscious by the explosion of a nearby mine but he insisted on continuing his diving the next day. He showed remarkably endurance and outstanding ability in the diving operations.

It is difficult to think that all this was achieved in 17 days, but however long it took there can be no doubt that *Dispenser*, her master, officers and crew performed very well in the Mediterranean[1].

Back at Malta Tom passed his diving test, not surprising as by now he seems to have had a great deal of experience, and he was sent to Alexandria on an Italian Cruiser to join the *Prince Salvor* (Captain Vise). After three weeks the *Prince Salvor* sailed for the UK and he was transferred to the *Salventure* on the 3rd August 1945; here he joined two of his former shipmates Bert Jurd and Harry Furnel.   Cyril Smith was Chief Radio Officer / Purser on this ship and they have remained friends ever since.

---

[1] In March 1944 Dispenser is shown in convoy NV29 Augusta-Naples

They started work on a trawler that had been sunk alongside a berth; fleet salvage divers had cut the wreck down to the mud line and only her stern post protruded. They burned a hole in the stern piece to allow a large shackle to pass through and rigged a strop up to the ship and attached this to a tackle, actually the topping lift of the ship.   After having to go back to put a charges on the keel, to complete the work that should have been done by the previous team, they lifted that half of the wreck; the other half soon followed.   So the King Salvor class vessels were of use - in the right hands.

Tony says "V.E. (Victory in Europe Day) came on the 8th of May and it seemed a bit of an anti-climax.   The Japs were still in it, we were still stranded in a bombed and flooded town and all we could find to make merry with was Crème de Banane!

We returned to London on the first of June and I paid off on the 28th of July1945. The Gallions Reach was no beauty but we'd been through some interesting times together."   Syd was the last man to leave his **Longtow** after VE Day.   Then he was called to the Yard as he was wanted as bosun on the **LC3**, this was a less than happy time as the barge was short of gear, much of it having been sold on the black market in Antwerp and the only lighting was by Tilley lamps.   Syd went from Bosun to Mate and then became Skipper when the Master went sick.   Most of their work was in and around Southampton Docks.   Then, with everything running down he was moved to the **American Salvor** as Bosun. He was later offered the Mate's job but turned it down, the job wasn't what it used to be.   He decided it was time to 'swallow the anchor' and get married, which he did.

Tony worked for a time in the Risdon Beazley office and was accommodated on a former private yacht the **Zaza,** which was long past her glory days.   He was so relieved to be sent to the **American Salvor**, that he walked, lugging his kit bag, from the Old Docks to the far end of the New Docks to join the **Twickenham Ferry** for his trip to France.   Once he had made it to Rouen and joined his ship they were involved in the task of patching and re-floating the former whale factory ship **Ole Wegger**, which the Germans had scuttled so as to block the Seine.   Little help was forthcoming from the French, so it was decided that the wreck was to be towed to Falmouth by Admiralty tugs with the **American Salvor** as escort.

They were then told that they could come home to Southampton for Christmas.   They were so keen that they sailed into a gale, with reports of all sorts of things adrift in the Channel and with few navigational aids restored.   They arrived safely at Southampton and were amused to be berthed opposite to one of the **Queens**.

After Christmas at home they were sent to Dover were they carried on the work that the **Longtow** had been involved in.   Tony then transferred to the **Southampton Salvor** and was detailed to do the stores off-survey, prior to the vessel being handed back to the Americans.   After this the crews were drifting away, he followed and joined the Royal Fleet Auxiliary.   He later became a Senior Purser in Union Castle.

Thus the biggest salvage effort in history came to a close.   Obviously there was much removal work to complete, but, without the efforts of Cyril, Syd, Tom and Tony and the many hundreds like them, the ports would have been unusable and the liberation would have ground to a halt.   Obviously if Risdon Beazley Ltd had not existed others would have risen to the occasion.   But this does not alter the fact that these men and their company did take on the task and did everything that was asked of them.

Not too long after the war some, mostly those who had not played a part, tended to play down the achievements of what they decided to call 'the circus' and RAB's dislike of any sort of publicity aided these people in their efforts. But those who know what that organisation achieved, and went on to achieve in the years that followed, do remember.

Captain Doust wrote many years later that RBs salved "over 3,500 ships and 3.5 million tons of cargo[1] – a contribution of vital importance to the war effort beyond the reach of any other of the managers.   He got no official recognition for it," he went on to say that, by 1944, RB had grown into "the biggest salvage organisation in the world – managing 77 vessels, tugs and lifting craft."

But the men never fell into the trap of taking themselves too seriously; Tony ends his story with:

"During my time with the Salvage vessels someone had pinned up in the mess a quotation from Churchill that referred to "The heroic and marvellous feats of the Salvage Services" but we rather preferred the cartoon that one of the lads had drawn. This showed a cargo ship beset with all sorts of trouble, planes strafing it, subs torpedoing it, and mines floating all around and from its bridge to the Salvage ship steaming toward it, the signal "Go away – don't you see we've got enough trouble already!"

Freija   ***Photo David Sowden***

Foremost 18. Photograph - World Ship Society

---

[1] This is an exaggeration, the best estimate that we can make was that the firm completed around 2,000 jobs in it's time.

Chapter Four   Down Under - Cumberland & Niagara

Foremost 17 in Mort's Yard, Sydney.   Photograph – Keith Gordon & Tommy Thomson

*'Cumberland'. Steamship, steel, 9471 tons. Built 1915. 474 x 60 x 36.6 feet. Owned by the Federal Steam Navigation Company, under the command of Captain McGibbon. Struck one of the fourteen mines laid in June by the German raider **Wolf**, and was beached near Gabo Island in a sinking condition, 15 July 1917. A salvage crew worked for some weeks patching and re-floating the vessel, but after rounding Green Cape on the tow to Sydney, heavy seas forced her abandonment and she foundered. An attempt was made to tow the patched-up **Cumberland** to Sydney but she foundered whilst underway. SS **Merimbula** was involved in the rescue of crew. It was not until 1952 that salvage crews finally recovered her cargo of valuable metal, estimated at the time to be worth £300,000.*

By September 1951 **Foremost 17** had completed her season's work in the Thames Estuary, this work site was appropriate as the vessel had been built for the Port of London Authority to carry dredging spoil to sea for dumping. The vessel returned to Southampton where a rumour started that she was to be sent to work overseas.   As so often happens the 'galley wireless' proved to be correct when Mr Paul, the Salvage Officer, told the crew that the ship was to go to Australia and he would like to keep the same crew with him.   The company were said to be interested in several wrecks in that part of the world and it was expected that the work could take up to five years to complete, but annual leave would be given.   Everyone volunteered for this adventure[1].

As was usual with RB the ship was given a full overhaul, dry-docked and painted before the crew loaded her with all the necessary equipment.   Then a steel cover was welded over the hatch and every door, porthole, ventilator or opening also had a steel cover welded in place.   The Dutch tug **Pool Zee** (L. Smit & Co) was engaged to tow the vessel to Eden in Australia, near where the wreck of the **Cumberland**, lay.   A run crew of three boarded the salvage ship with their stores and oil lamps etc and the **Foremost 17's** crew helped with rigging the towlines and cast off their ships moorings before they went home on leave.

---

[1] I have relied mostly on the record of the late Mr Tommy Thomson as transcribed and provided by Mr Bruce Benson; as, unfortunately, the files that refer to the salvage of the gold from the Niagara, which were at TNA, have been 'lost while on loan to a government department'.

Back from leave, armed with their new passports and vaccination certificates, they signed ship's articles on 28th November1951. They left in two batches the engineers, fireman and catering staff left on the Qantas flight on the 1st December and the deck department flew out on the following day, arriving in Sydney early in the morning on the 6th December. The crew occupied all of the seats on the starboard side of both aircraft. Tommy describes the route and the stopovers in detail. RB must have been among the first to fly a ship's crew across the world and to offer them an annual flight home for leave!

"This operation up to now had been carried on under a cloak of secrecy, and we were told that any one caught giving information to newspaper reporters would be instantly dismissed and sent home. But the papers were not long in getting wind of something going on, and there were photographs of the crew disembarking from the plane in next day's newspapers. The refusal to talk only made them more curious. They were at Darwin to meet us."

The crews were divided among small hotels in Pambula and Eden, 12 miles further south and about halfway between Sydney and Melbourne. When the **Pool Zee** arrived in Eden two days before Christmas, after an 84 day tow, they all moved to Eden Hotel until they had their ship opened up and ready to live in. They also built a compound for their heavy stores and with the intention of the ship's crew landing the recovered cargo and storing it there. In the event the engineers got steam up very quickly and all were able to enjoy their Christmas dinner on their ship.

Within a few days the ASDIC dome was fitted and the ship sailed for the site. They found the **Cumberland** immediately and after laying their moorings, put the grab and the chamber down on the wreck, having bars of copper in the salvage ship's hold that night. Within a week they were back in Eden with a full load, which they discharged and stored in their compound. They also removed and boxed up the ASDIC equipment, sending that and their two ASDIC operators back to the UK.

But none had reckoned with the Australian Customs, who impounded the recovered cargo; or the wharfies who were notoriously awkward. For the next landing the awkward squad were brought down from the nearest port, Fathra; this proved to be too expensive and the ship was sent to Sydney to land all subsequent cargoes. This too proved to be expensive, especially as the ship's stock of explosives had to be transhipped to a "Powder Hoy"[1] before entering the port and reloaded after departure. To avoid this expense a plywood barge was acquired and moored near Boyd Town, but this broke adrift and was wrecked on the nearby beach; so the crew had to spend a day 'beach-combing, recovering all the bits of gelignite that they could find'. After that it was back to using the "Powder Hoy".

One wonders who had 'helped' by telling the customs and the wharfies what was going on. As it was the **Foremost 17** only worked this one wreck in Australia, leaving the **City of Rayville** and the **Port Kembla** (New Zealand) for others – to the best of my knowledge these two are still untouched. In all they recovered 1,858 tons of copper and lead from the wreck and had the pleasure of meeting many interesting people including some who had come from the Shetlands.

On the 11th July 1952, once the winter weather had set in, and before the **Cumberland** job had been completed they took their ship to Melbourne for refit and were rewarded with the promised trip to the UK for some well-earned leave. This time they flew with home with BOAC. They returned to Southampton and re-signed articles on the 19th September and again flew out with Qantas. They spent a week in

---

[1] A barge or hulk that was moored well clear of the port.

Melbourne whilst the ship repairers completed their work. On this occasion their agent was Captain (later Sir) John Williams of United Salvors.   He had made his name during the war by recovering all but 35 bars of gold cargo from the **RMS Niagara** off New Zealand.

During the latter part of 1952 a colleague of Captain Williams, his Chief Diver Johnno Johnstone had travelled to the UK to contact RAB about the salvage of the remaining 35 bars of gold in the **Niagara.** According to Tommy, Johnno was to get £250 for each bar that was recovered, whilst the Bank of New South Wales would get £500, leaving more than £4,000 for RB. With the **Foremost 17** within a week's steaming of the casualty this job appealed to RAB.

Once they had completed work on the **Cumberland** the **Foremost 17** was slipped at Morts Dock in Balmain, Sydney for a scrape and paint and to carry out a few repairs. After this the crew stowed for sea and waited for a favourable weather forecast for the 1,279 mile trip across the stormy Tasman Sea to New Zealand.   When the favourable forecast came the little ship sailed to the "Powder Hoy" to reload her explosives and dropped the pilot outside Sydney Heads at 1230 on Monday 30th March 1953.   For the start of the journey they had fair weather but, on 1st April, a southerly gale started to blow, which lasted for four days and nights.   The chain on the steering gear stretched, so the crew had to rig a tackle and remove to links to permit the chain to stay on the gypsy.   The galley flooded out and they spent 24 hours without hot food, a very unpleasant cold experience because a southerly gale originates in the Antarctic.

When the gale started to abate and they were again able to set foot on deck the ship appeared to be down by the stern, they found that the lazarete, aft of the engine room was full of water.   This space had been fitted out as a magazine and was also used to stow spare hatch boards. Everything was awash and the spare hatch boards, with their steel Cox's ends had smashed the ammunition boxes to pulp with the three tons of Polar Blasting Gelignite having been reduced to a liquid that looked like brown stew.   They first tried to pump the space out but the broken timber from the boxes and the shelving kept choking the pump.   They managed to get some of the foul mixture out using an airlift and baled the rest out with buckets. The mixture was giving off so much gas that all involved were sick for days with splitting headaches. The only option they were left with was to put a man in the compartment in standard diving dress, helmet and all and pump clean air to him, while he cleared the remaining timber.

They made landfall in New Zealand on Sunday 5th April, arriving at Auckland on the Tuesday morning.   Their first job was to gas free the magazine and trace where the water had entered, they found that the shipyard in Sydney had failed to replace a bolt on the steering gear casing and this was the cause of all their troubles. New equipment had been sent from Southampton, including their much travelled ASDIC set, additional grabs including one apparently ingenious 'grab within a grab' an "Iron Man" and a device for recovering gold coins – which was sent straight back to Southampton.

Yet again they had what seemed a long wait for new explosives to come from Melbourne, but by the 11th April they sailed to re-locate the **Niagara.** On the 12th the weather was too rough to work so they set about assembling the 'Iron Man' and the 'grab within a grab'.   Neither of these gadgets proved to be of any use.   They found that the only workable combination was: using the ASDIC to locate the wrecks, the observation chamber to deploy the diver and a four ton, eight tined cactus grab to both remove sections of the wreck, after they had been cut with SBG and recover the cargo.   For the rest of the company's life this was the combination that was used, whether for 400 ounce bars of gold or 2.5 ton slabs of aluminium.   The standard Westwood grab was so versatile that it could even be used to clear Sherman tanks, minus the turret, a weight of about 30 tons.

Tommy continues the story :

"Tuesday 17th April. Let go from buoy, 7.20 am, arrived at search area. ASDIC sweep continued all day (with) no sign of wreck. Tied up to buoy at 6pm.   An Auckland fishing boat came alongside. The skipper said "Are you looking for the "Niagara", "Yes" we said "Well you won't find her here, you are looking too far north". He indicated where to look for her. [We never found out why we had been given the wrong information as to the position in which the wreck lay, and whether this was just an error or was it deliberate. Even the depth of water we were given was 450 feet, which was correct for the area in which we made the fruitless search. The depth of water on the "Niagara" was 360 ft.]"

They recovered their first bar of gold on the 24th April and another in the first grab on the 25th.   Tommy summarises the technique:

"When the diver went down along with the grab he stayed down sometimes for up to four hours. When he ordered the grab to be closed we would then lift the chamber clear of the wreck. He would also at this stage be guiding the grab as well. When both diver and grab were clear of the wreck, we would swing the divers derrick away to one side, then take the grab up with whatever might be in it. Empty it and send it back down again. A mark put on the wire would tell the winch operator when the grab was at the desired position for the diver to take over. This only could apply if there were no lengths of scrap iron in the grab. If there were dangerous lengths iron in the grab, then the diver would have to be taken to the surface"

Mail, always important on a ship, could only be collected on their occasional visits to Auckland until once again local people showed their kindness:

"Saturday 9th May. Anchored inside Whangarei Heads. Ashore for an hour in forenoon, climbed hill and picked oyster mushrooms. Sunday 10th May. Hove up at 6.30am and went outside for a look. To much swell We came back and anchored off Reotaki, 8.30am. shore leave, 2pm. Launch went in with whoever wanted to go ashore. Just opposite to where we were anchored on the north side of the bay are three houses fairly near to each other. There were eight or ten of us who went ashore, and as we were going past one of the houses a man came out and spoke to us and insisted that we come in. we said that we would come another time when we were better dressed. But no, we had to come now, just as we were. He was a retired builder and had built this house to retire to because it was a beautiful spot. The house was like a mansion, carpets everywhere. All the people here were the same, they seemed anxious to speak to anyone, and were offended if you went past the house without speaking. All of them were retired couples. In one of the houses lived the Kennedy's, the others were Stanton's and Hughes. Mrs Kennedy asked how we got our mail, we said we got it whenever we went to Auckland. She said "why don't you get it sent to us, we will look after it". So when we got back on board we told the Old Man, and he thought that it was a splendid idea, and he went straight ashore and spoke to Mrs Kennedy. The arrangement arrived at was that if when we next came in to anchor, and if any mail had arrived she would hang a sheet on the clothesline. So next day the Captain phoned the office in Auckland and told them to send the mail up to Reotaki. Surely a gem of a person. Behind the houses the ground sloped upwards, terminating in a small hill with very rugged rocks. They had rules governing the taking of the oysters, you were allowed to pick and eat as many as you liked, but not to take any away. This rule was never enforced on us, as we picked many a bucketful. Further up and to the westward was a dairy farm. The only farm building was a milking shed. Only the cream was taken for sale. They kept pigs as well, and when the milk had gone through the separator, the skimmed milk went through a pipe into the pig trough. The cream was sold to the butter factory"[1]

They were in Auckland on Coronation Day (2nd June 1953), when all the flags were out, by now it was the *Foremost 17* that was also making the news in the Auckland papers and the crew were able to collect press cuttings to send home. The final batch of gold was landed at Auckland on the 25th July 1953, the intrepid team had recovered 30 out of the 35 bars that remained after the Williams salvage effort. By this time the story was being broadcast by New Zealand Radio and the divers were in demand to talk to the local schools about the project.

On the 11th August 1953 they left their ship cleaned and prepared for tow[2] and headed to the airport, this time they were returning via the Pacific and the USA. They landed at Heathrow on Friday the 14th August just six days short of eleven months since they left there. After leave the most of the crew rejoined their ship for work in UK waters, though at least one, Alan Martin, settled in Australia. Young Charles Cooper, who had sailed from the UK as a first trip cabin boy, later became a diver and then one of the company's Senior Salvage Officers.

Salvage Officer Rodney Paul was made an MBE in the New Year's Honours List 1957. After the *Foremost 17's* salvage, Captain John Williams was knighted for the original salvage work in 1942.

Charles Cooper and launch   Photo CEC   Foremost 17   Tommy Thomson via Bruce Benson

Divers Frank Higgins & Dick Youngs, with Frank Watts A/S

'Iron Man' Tommy Thomson

---

[1] MacLeods Bay, at the mouth of the Whangarei River, is named after a Scottish minister who left with his flock when the crofters were evicted from the Highlands of Scotland. They were sent to either Nova Scotia or New Brunswick, which they disliked; so they built two ships and, led by MacLeod, sailed to New Zealand. They settled the low lying ground on the south side of the bay..

[2] Alan Martin tells me that she was towed to South Africa by the Rode Zee, it is not clear what she did there. After much further work in the UK the Foremost 17 finally arrived at Passage West, Cork in September 1958 to be broken up.

Chapter Five – Expansion then Retrenchment 1946 to 1963

It was 1946 before the war work was completed and the ships were returned to their owners, sold, or, in the case of the war built tonnage, transferred to Admiralty management. The manager's accounts with the Bank of England were closed and everyone sought new opportunities in the post-war market.

The winter of 1946/7 was the coldest in recent memory. Everything was hard to get and was rationed, there were frequent power cuts and even home produced coal was in short supply. America had shifted its attention to the Marshall Plan to rebuild Europe and the British struggled on alone: this was not an unreasonable strategy because, whilst the British were hard up, many in Europe were starving and homeless.

In addition to general salvage work Risdon Beazley decided to concentrate on: - rescue and coastal towage, cargo recovery and sale & purchase. For a while this plan worked well but, with the re-emergence of the Continental towage companies who again sheltered their fleets behind a policy of cabotage, it became obvious that that part of the business plan was no longer viable; however the rest stood up well.

Cargo Recovery was becoming an ever more important part of the firm's activities. With the eclipse of SORIMA[1] and the equipment developed for war becoming available to commercial companies a new opportunity presented itself. Among the equipment that was available was ASDIC (sonar), and the Decca Navigator, a positioning system developed for D-Day that gave hitherto undreamt of accuracy.

RAB took full advantage of the new equipment, the availability of good tonnage at reasonable prices and the experienced staff[2] . In house there were the Masters: Captains Brackenbury (by now the Marine Superintendent), Hunter, Mackenzie, Young, Carlton, Dalton and Dent; as Allan Crothall was to say "fine seamen all". Salvage Officers included the RB stalwarts Percy Carrington M.B.E and Bill Robinson, who were joined by Rodney Paul, and, later, the former Admiralty Salvage Officers: - Captain J.B. Polland R.N.V.R. and the man who became Risdon Beazley's successor, Allan Crothall M.B.E. Maurice Woodward became their Senior Chief Engineer with Walter Watson, 'Bram' van Dintel; Reg Young and Ken Young. Divers included Frank and Pat Higgins, W. Bollard, and Tommy Bray: they were joined by successive waves of excellent divers – the first included Sam Dooley, Bob Mouncer, Lofty Yates, John Galpin, Terry Good, Fred Smith and John Butler. Because of the good relationship that had been built up with the Mackenzie family of Metal Industries many of the deck crews came from the Shetland Islands, via Captain Inkster the Lerwick Harbour Master[3].

During the late 1940s the **Lifeline** (Captain Hunter), the **Foremost 17** (Captain Charlton) and the **Foremost 18** (Captain Mackenzie) were all employed on cargo recovery work around the UK coast. The tugs, led by the **Twyford** (**HMS Warden** – Captain Young) were also active; much of **Twyford's** work was generated by the war built tonnage that was coming into commercial operation and being 'run hard'. Liberty ships seemed particularly prone to getting into trouble, they cracked easily at sea or if they grounded and were often demobilised when they shed their propellers. There was sufficient work for the British tugs of Overseas Towage, Metal Industries, United Towing and RBs; but by the end of the decade RAB decided that the market was too crowded and got out, handing **Twyford** back to the Admiralty.

---

[1] SORIMA continued to operate until 1955, then, after a series of misfortunes, that pioneering company closed down.

[2] Most of this list comes from Allan Crothall's book 'Wealth from the Sea'

[3] Charles Cooper believes that the original suggestion to recruit 'Shelties' came from Captain F Hunter.

RAB had decided that his future lay in expanding cargo recovery operations. Both RB and SORIMA had fitted vessels with ASDIC. SORIMA had more early success because they fitted their set on the former fishing trawler **Scalpay**, whilst RB fitted theirs to the tug **Ashford**, with a less suitable hull form. However RB soon overcame their early difficulties and fitted the next ASDIC sets to the **Lifeline** and the **Foremost 17; Lifeline** and **Help** were given false bows[1] to enable them to work in rougher conditions.

As usual RAB seems to have done quite a bit of lateral thinking, though the word would have probably been unknown to him. He realised that, whilst there were now many more wrecks with non-ferrous metals, these recently wrecked vessels were all over the world, many were in deeper water than those from the First War, and a completely new source was available – Japanese wrecks in the South China Sea.

He recruited Commander Thomas Pickford as the company's researcher; through him Commander Wilde worked in Japan, with assistance from former Japanese officers. Whilst Captain Enright maintained the contacts with the Admiralty. All were backed up by a strong team in the office led by Messrs Giddings and Lebburn, under the watchful eye of RAB.

In the early 50s the **Lifeline's** sister ship **Help** was chartered from the Admiralty to join her and the two former mud hoppers. A new ship also bearing the name **Twyford**, RAB's home village, was ordered from John Lewis in Aberdeen. John Lewis were probably chosen for two reasons, one, they had a reputation for building fine deep-sea trawlers and two, their prices were more modest that the South Coast shipbuilders. It is said that when the new ship arrived in Southampton she was 'shown off' to interested parties and the Thornycroft Shipbuilder's manager said "Risdon – we could have done a better job for you" to which RAB replied "Yes, but I couldn't afford your price".

The in house design team for the vessel included the company's naval architect Mr Lebburn, Captains Brackenbury and Hunter, Chief Engineers Woodward and van Dintel and draughtsman Eric Ralls (who was to become Works Manager when Lebburn died).

The vessel was to be built for World Wide operation to Board of Trade Class VII and to Lloyds Register Class + 100 A1 + LMC. The 220 feet long vessel had a gross tonnage of 1104 and had a range of 3,500 miles and was designed to work in 800 feet of water. As the emphasis was to be on reliability and ease of repair, possibly in out of the way places, steam was chosen, both for propulsion and deck machinery. At that time diesel machinery was still apt to require repairs at sea, which involved stopping the engine sometimes for hours in the worst of weather. During their careers the seagoing members of the design team would remember such stops, lying broadside on, sometimes in storm conditions.

In later years some self styled 'experts' ridiculed the choice of steam; but the writer, having spent two years on the **Droxford - Twyford's** successor, feels that it was the right decision for the time. Two steam winches were ordered from Clarke Chapman, these were bigger and faster than any winches that had been used for cargo recovery work and were capable of taking over a thousand feet of wire – non-twist wire that was specially manufactured for them in Italy and later in the UK using the same machines. The eight other winches were of the type used on Liberty ships so that spares and replacements were readily available around the world.

[1] See picture of Help alongside the casualty Neptunia

They also went to Roberto Galeazzi of La Spezia in Italy for the two observation chambers for the new ship, again these were capable of working in greater depths than any hitherto. So good were these chambers that one was used to inspect a contact, thought to be the **Glenartney** in 1420 feet of water. However the external lighting failed well before the chamber reached the bottom and the chamber itself showed some small indications of pressure stress.

To improve the mooring operation 28 foot launches[1] were designed and built in the RB yard – by the same men who had built Fairmiles and other boats for the Admiralty. Like the previous boats the launches were of double diagonal hardwood construction, with a further fore and aft planked skin forward for protection, and were launched by gravity davits. The design team were frustrated by some of the requirements of the Board of Trade. They applied to have the launches classed as lifeboats, but the BoT refused as the boats had transom sterns – so a set of lifeboats had to be mounted further astern, were they would have been extremely difficult to launch successfully when needed. The crews always said that, if disaster struck, they would head for the launches. Another problem was that the BoT insisted on the crew mess rooms being divided into a seaman's mess plus one for the fireman, the stewards and the petty officers. Only the seaman's mess was ever used, but the provision of the others caused the accommodation to be more cramped than the design team intended.

Twyford (2).   ***Photograph from Risdon Beazley collection***

On the **Droxford** there was talk that Mr Clifford Bennison had been a shareholder, but I understand that this was not so. RAB's sister Olive May Henderson Gray appears as a director at about this time, so may be additional funding came from that source? No doubt RAB paid the shipbuilders, 'cash on the nail'.[2]

Twyford was not blessed with early luck. After calling at Southampton, Captain Hunter took his new ship to South Africa where, though the gear performed well, she failed to find her target, the **Hannington Court**. She then crossed the Atlantic to search for the **Empire Manor**, this time they successfully located the wreck, but it was completely upside down and it was not possible to find the gold. Twenty years were to go by before RB completed this job [3]. By the end of the year the new ship had not recovered a single bar of metal.

---

[1] See photo in Down Under, a 24 foot class was made for the smaller vessels in the fleet.
[2] By the time the *Twyford* was commissioned, the **Help** was recovering cargo off of the Canadian coast and the **Foremost 17** was working off of Australia.. **Lifeline** & **Foremost 18** continued their work in north-west Europe.
[3] See Chapter on the Empire Manor

1954 brought a change in the ship's fortunes. Returning to South Africa, again the **Hannington Court** evaded them, but the **Klipfontein** had sunk off of Mozambique and **Twyford** recovered almost 1,200 tons of copper from this Dutch liner. Then she found the **Efstathios,** off the Spanish coast, and recovered 1,299 tons of metals from her.   After this there she made a succession of successful recoveries off the Canadian coast:- the **Mount Pindus** and the **Mount Taygetus** (at a record depth of 720 feet); the **Kaaparen** and the **Strathdene** near Nantucket.   Then it was straight back to South Africa, where, this time, they found the **Hannington Court**.

Allan Crothall described the circumstances:

"At the end of the Northern Summer of 1955, Twyford made passage back to South Africa to search again for the **Hannington Court**.   On this occasion Captain Brackenbury flew to Cape Town and joined the ship there, and has recounted, quite cheerfully, taking a temporary watch to relieve the Chief Officer, he was informed by Asdic Officer Frank Watts that a large shoal of fish had been heard.   "Not knowing much about Asdic at the time", he ordered Watts (who knew quite a lot and was very reluctant) to follow the shoal for several miles, and here a strong wreck echo was heard which turned out to be the **Hannington Court**, over ten miles from the position where **H.M.S. Dragon** was supposed to have sunk her.   False bearings must have been taken from the shore!"[1]

The **Twyford** recovered 916 tons of copper from the wreck, some of it fused together from the effects of the fire the ship had suffered. During this period **Foremost 18**, **Help** and **Lifeline,** were busy with a succession of targets nearer home that **Help** had previously located with her ASDIC.   They were **Ballarat, Cairmona, Calchas, Heddernheim, Juno, Kioto, Kong Sigurd, Ladywood, Medina, Parthenia, Port Nicholson, Seang Choon, Vedamore** and **Vinovia**.

When a BOAC Comet airliner crashed off the island of Elba in the Mediterranean early in 1954 the Admiralty recognised that "The observation chamber and grab method of cargo recovery used by Messrs. Risdon Beazley Ltd. of Southampton was likely to be the best and possibly only method of salvage". A personal telephone call was made to Mr Risdon Beazley, asking if the gear and a crew could be made available and this was promised. An appreciation was prepared for the Asst. Chief of Naval Staff.[2]

At a subsequent meeting of the parties who were to be involved, Mr Beazley offered his equipment and team asking only that the team's wages and their expenses be paid. Two days later the RB equipment was delivered to Bournemouth Airport crated for air-freighting.   It consisted of an observation chamber, a 10 foot grab, an Articulated Diving Suit plus spares and equipment. Captain Polland represented the company as salvage officer, he travelled with Tommy Bray, by now one of the company's top divers, John Galpin and Tom Allen, the last named being a boatswain.

When Captain Polland arrived on site he discovered that the Navy were attempting to moor the RFA **Sea Salvor** (formerly one of the RB wartime fleet) with a 'four point moor' Polland showed them how superior the RB "six point moor" was and the job proceeded.

All of this and much more was documented in the subsequent reports.   But the subsequent press release was typical, saying that "The British Salvager firm Risdon & Beazley have been of the greatest help" but suggested that the main credit should be given to the two RB divers who were ex-Navy, ignoring Capt. Polland and Tom Bray.

---

[1] From "Wealth from the Sea", this is a typical 'Brack' story – an intelligent man, he had a habit of playing down his successes.
[2] ADM1 25361 and 26051

When the medals were handed out none of the RB team were included; however Mr Beazley, whose war work had never been acknowledged, was made a Companion of the Order of the British Empire (CBE)

Following the **Help's** successful work in Nova Scotia, RB were invited back to clear the wreck of the **Trongate** in Halifax harbour, the **Trongate** still had a part cargo of ammunition. The tragic events surrounding the fire and explosion of the ammunition ship **Mont Blanc** in 1917 will never be forgotten there, large parts of the city were flattened and there was heavy loss of life.

Using the newly converted **Topmast 16** that had been towed across the North Atlantic, with the crew crossing on passenger ships; Allan Crothall's team succeeded in completing this delicate removal operation and then the **Topmast 16** was towed to Bermuda by the tug **Joseph H. Moran** where they then cut down the wreck of the **Wychwood** that had sunk after grounding in 1955. The work was contracted to Salvage & Shipping (Bermuda) a company formed to undertake the removal for the sum of £95,000. Presumably this was a joint venture between RB and local interests.

On the 8th July 1957[1] the **Topmast 16** was lifting her moorings after the **Wychwood** clearance had been verified, when the British liner **R.M.S Reina del Pacifico"**, the former flagship of the Pacific Steam Navigation Co., ran hard aground at speed on a coral reef. The **Reina del Pacifico** had 533 passengers on board and a cargo that included 2,770 tons of copper bars. Richard Farge, who lived on Bermuda, was on his way to the UK for a three-month stay; he and his brothers were in the bows of the ship enjoying the thrill of being on a liner that was threading her way though the coral reefs when the ship suddenly lurched and took an 11° list. The vessel had hit the Devil's Flat Reef and she was "sewed up and beyond self help" as Lloyd's Arbitrators say.

Tugs had failed to re-float the vessel when Allan Crothall arrived from his little salvage ship offering to do the work on a Lloyd's Form 'No Cure – No Pay'. There would have been many doubters when he said that he could succeed where tugs had failed.[2]. Tommy Thompson says that one of the tugs came within hailing distance saying "surely you don't hope to pull that great ship off the reef with that small craft?" Allan Crothall replied "I think we will, with our tackle". But his ship was equipped for wreck clearance work and that all-important tackle was in the yard in Southampton.

The Lloyd's Form was signed on the same day and the company chartered two aircraft to fly the 15 tons of equipment that were needed. They had the seats removed and the 1,260 feet of 6 inch circumference wire was flaked in the cabin of one, a Super Constellation chartered from BOAC. The second aircraft, from KLM, brought out the pumps and blocks etc. The equipment arrived in Bermuda on the Tuesday. Here it was found that no truck on the Island was big enough to take all of the wire; coiling half of the wire on the biggest available truck and reeling the balance on a transporter that the truck towed, solved the problem.

On Thursday afternoon, 'Davy' Crothall allowed his crew, and himself, to get a four hours sleep, their first since Sunday;

---

[1] Charles Cooper, who was at that time a diver on the **Topmast 16** recalls that it was on a Sunday – therefore the 7th.
[2] Wealth from the Sea gives Allan Crothall's account, Michael Davis sent his record of both the **Wychwood & Reina del Pacifico** salvages from Bermuda (and photographs that I did not have space to include); a letter that Tommy Thomson wrote sent by Bruce Benson; and the account of Richard Farge courtesy of Linda Abend at the Bermuda Maritime Museum

Whilst waiting for the wire the **Topmast 16** had laid out her ground tackles and the casualty had been lightened by discharging some of the cargo. On the evening of the 11th as High Water approached (2016 local time) the tackles were hove taut and the liner moved back so gently into deeper water that those passengers who had remained on board, were at first unaware that the ship had been re-floated. Well after the ship was afloat, an American male passenger was still telling all who would listen that the little Limey ship could never re-float such a big liner.

Once clear of the reef she was reloaded and resumed her voyage, with the only damage being a few sprung rivets. Ken Young, one of the **Topmast's** engineers sailed back to Liverpool with the liner to tend the two 6" pumps that the salvors had supplied; he remembered a beautiful old ship that was "on her last legs". Allan Crothall, every bit as modest as Don Brackenbury, said that it was "just a little matter of being in the right place at the right time".

Later the OTS tug **Marina** towed the salvage vessel back to Southampton, whilst the crew were flown back for a well earned leave, and the ship a much needed refit; she had earned over a quarter of a million pounds in the two and a half year voyage.

It would have been almost two years later the Arbitrator published his award and RB were paid for a job that they accomplished in only five days, but using know-how they had built up over many years[1]. Old age and a hard war caught up with the **Reina del Pacifico**, she only made one more voyage to South America, so she was in the scrap yard by the time that the award was made.

RMS Reina del Pacifico and Topmast 16   photo A C Crothall

On 11-02-1957, while entering the port of Cobh, Ireland, the Greek Line's **Neptunia** struck Daunt's Rock and was beached with major damage. Risdon Beazley were awarded the contract to refloat the vessel and make her safe for tow. RB allocated the salvage vessel **Help** (Captain Young), the work was supervised by the company's salvage officer Mr Percy Carrington. On 03-02-1958 she was towed by the tug **Gele Zee** to Henrik Ido Ambacht, the Netherlands, where she was broken up by Simons Scheepssloperij.

---

[1] I wrote to Lloyd's asking for a copy but have not received a reply

Neptunia after striking Daunts Rock Cobh Eire   photograph Charles Cooper

'Tommy' Young, 'Perc' Carrington   *Help at Neptunia (with false bow)*
& Major Gotto? (RB's son in law).   *photos Charles Cooper*

Late in 1956, on the back of all this success, RB placed a further order with John Lewis for an 'improved' **Twyford**, this ship was to be called **Droxford**. after another Hampshire village.   But before the new ship was delivered in 1958 the price of copper had plummeted to a level at which the ships could not operate profitably.   According to Tom Bennett's records this vessel cost RAB a total of £406,500 to build and cost £225 per day to operate (excluding depreciation), about the average price of copper at that time.   The UK Treasury contributed £25,000 towards the building cost.

On the 20th August 1959 the prototype Victor Bomber Mark 2 left Boscombe Down in Wiltshire for what was intended to be a routine test flight. A shore radar station was tracking the bomber when the echo on the display broke up and then disappeared. The coastal motor tanker *Aqueity* was passing the Smalls Lighthouse at the time and the Master and both members of the bridge watch saw a 'splash' on her starboard bow, this was followed by two sharp explosions. The Master, Captain Yendall, reported the incident to the Coast Radio Station and little more was thought of it until, several hours later, those on the *Aqueity* heard a news report on the BBC that an aircraft was overdue in the area. The Master again contacted Ilfracombe Radio and, this time the Admiralty and the Air Ministry were informed. Later Captain Yendall was summoned to London to explain what he had seen.

Early in September the Admiralty approached RB to charter one of the recovery vessels for three months, this must have been welcome work for the company as both vessels were laid up because of the depressed price of copper. The *Twyford* was offered and by mid September she arrived at Milford Haven to join a number of trawlers that were also on charter. In addition to her normal outfit *Twyford* was equipped with a TV camera. All concerned were expecting a straightforward operation rather like the recovery of the Comet wreckage. By the end of the year none of the searches by the ships had produced any wreckage[1].

At the beginning of 1960 only the two mooring vessels and the *Twyford* were gainfully employed.

It was not until late March that one of the trawler fleet recovered the first piece of wreckage from the ill-fated Victor Bomber, by this time they had searched an area the size of Greater London. At the end of the month the charted trawl lines of the small fishing vessels, which were marked in coloured inks, were beginning to show where the main concentration of wreckage appeared to be. On the 7th April *Twyford* moored in the middle of what had become known as 'The Splotch'. By late April *Twyford* had recovered one and a half tons of wreckage and the smaller vessels were being equally successful.

But in early August it was realised that the smaller vessels were better equipped to continue the recovery, now that the concentration of wreckage had been lifted and *Twyford* was off hired. She returned to Southampton where the crew were given leave and then dispersed among the diminishing fleet. On passing Plymouth a signal was received from the C in C congratulating Captain Young and his crew and advising them that the Master had been recommended for an OBE and Diver Don Jones for a commendation[2]. Captain Young, known to all as Tommy, went to the mooring vessels; he retired in 1962 and died five years later at the age of 68.

In October 1959 another military aircraft crashed in the Irish Sea – this time it was the first two seater trainer model of a Lightning twin jet fighter manufactured by English Electric at Warton Lancashire. The test pilot, J.W.C. Squier, ejected safely but suffered from exposure[3].

There were no reported sightings of the aircraft 'crashing' but calculations based on timing, flight path, altitude (~30,000 ft.) etc. put the likely crash site in the Wigtown

---

[1] Douglas A Koster tells the full story of the search in the book "Operation Victor Search". Mr Koster was serving as Second Officer of the Twyford at the time of the search..

[2] Captain Young had to wait until 1960 to receive his award and then it was an MBE. On the Droxford, Don Jones never said that he received an award, but then he also did not tell us that he was a crew member on an RN escort in Operation Pedestal either!

[3] This account is mainly from Charles Cooper's notes – Charles was a chamber diver on the operation; after this he resumed hard hat diving in the firm.

Bay/Solway Firth area; the undercarriage nose wheel had been found washed up on a beach in that area. The manufacturers and presumably the Government wanted the plane located and recovered to ascertain the cause of loss. **Twyford** was busy with the Victor bomber operation, so, when RB was contacted they sent the **Droxford.** **Droxford** went via Liverpool, where she embarked the English Electric and MOD personnel. On arrival she began a grid search with the ASDIC and the echo sounder. Later this was supplemented by towing the observation chamber near the seabed. This was a 'hairy' experience for the diver as, though the salvage ship appeared to be almost stationary on the surface, she was moved by the tide, a fact that the diver was all too aware of as he skimmed at an alarming rate just above the seabed. As it was winter underwater visibility was very poor, which added to the divers problems.

No contacts had been found after a couple of weeks and, with increasing amounts of weather downtime, it was decided to call off the search and the **Droxford** returned to Southampton to lay up..

In the spring the divers and the ASDIC Officers rejoined the **Droxford** to resume a search of the Western Approaches, this was to prove frustrating and unsuccessful. By September both recovery vessels were back in their home port for lay-up.

Twyford's lay up was short lived because RB were given the £320,000 contract to remove the wreck of the **Mitera Marigo** that had sunk in Falmouth Harbour. The two coastal salvage vessels might have been better for this work, but the **Lifeline** was on long-term charter on the mooring contract and the **Help** had been handed back to the Admiralty and was chartered elsewhere. So the wreck removal crew, which consisted of RB's best and ex Metal Industries men, found themselves on the **Twyford,** with good accommodation and the pleasure of working in one of the most beautiful harbours in the world, rather than out in the wild Atlantic. made this a most pleasant interlude. The wreck removal operation was similar to the work that a previous RB team had completed on the **Trongate** in Halifax N.S. again a minimum of explosives was used and, again, the salvage officer was Allan Crothall. The work was completed in October 1962.

Others were mostly the men from Metal Industries

Chapter Six - Recovery 1964 to 1965, Droxford

*By 1964 copper prices were recovering and it was decided to put the **Droxford** back to recovery work. Sadly Captain Frank Hunter OBE, the Master of the **Droxford** and before that the **Twyford**, did not live to see the new dawn of recovery; he had died on board the **Lifeline** during the previous year.*

*On 21 April 1963, the master of the M.S. **Helga Smith**, radioed that his ship had an uncontrollable leak and they intended to abandon ship 50 miles southeast of Cape Race. The US Coastguard Cutter **Campbell** answered the distress call. On arrival at the scene the **Campbell** illuminated the area with its floodlights as the crew of **Helga Smith** used lifeboats to leave their flooded ship and board **Campbell**. The Canadian salvage tug **Foundation Vigilant** attempted to tow the disabled vessel to St. Johns, but she sank about 10 ½ miles ENE of Cape Broyle, Newfoundland. Tom Pickford established that her cargo included 1,500 tons of copper. nickel and aluminium and had arranged a contract with the Salvage Association for RB to recover the metals. But the first problem was how to fund the considerable cost of a round trip to Canada.*

Helga Smith   **Photograph**   **Roy Martin**

Captain Brackenbury suggested that the best course of action was to locate and work the World War 1 wreck of the **Boniface** off of County Donegal in NW Eire. Another First War wreck, the **Oldfield Grange** also lay in the area, but this had been sought several times and had proved elusive. The **Boniface** had a cargo of war materials and 400 tons of copper ingots, if this could be recovered the mobilisation costs would be covered.

The **Droxford** was given her customary complete refit at Northam, just down stream from Clausentum, and the Marine Superintendent's Department set about crewing the vessel for yet another voyage to Canada, via the north of Ireland. Captain W A 'Bill' Ross, who had been Second Mate of the **Twyford** whilst she was in South Africa, was transferred from command of the **Topmast 16**. The engineering team under Maurice Woodward rejoined, as did many of the deck crew and the two ASDIC men who doubled up as Watch-keeping Officers. However a number of the former crew decided that they preferred the quieter life on the mooring vessels, with the possibility of getting a little summer leave – something unknown on the recovery ships. Captain Inkster was able to replace these men with a number from Salvesen's South Georgia whaling fleet as that activity had come to an end. The diving team was again lead by Don Jones and 'Brack' decided that he would sail as Salvage Officer.

At this point I contacted RB in the search for a short sea trade job sailing from Southampton. What I was offered was the job of Chief Officer/Navigator of the **Droxford**, anything but a short sea trader. I was invited to go and have a look at the vessel, which lay in the old Inner Dock in Southampton; in addition to the keys I was given a small screw driver and was told that, as Brack needed the Mate's cabin, I should pick the cabin that suited me and switch the tallys.

On that January day the **Droxford** was a rather forlorn sight with empty davits, no running rigging and a covered funnel. I had never been on a steamer before, though I had been on a cargo ship with steam winches. I claimed the Radio Officer's cabin as it was on the bridge deck and had two windows and was light and airy.

Whilst I was looking around two men came aboard the one introduced himself as Reg Butcher from Wimpey Marine and the other, an American, came from Brown and Root. They wanted to know about the owner and asked whether he would be interested in a new venture operating oil supply vessels in the North Sea. I knew no more about the company than they did, so I gave them the address of the yard.

It was many years before I heard how that meeting had gone, apparently RAB had listened to what they had to say and then said that he made a practice of doing business with those whom he knew and he didn't know them so - Good Afternoon. So RAB turned down his chance to be involved at the beginning of a new industry: he was now 61years old and had gone through six tough years and, if he made money again, he would have to pay a top rate of tax at 19/6 in the £1. With all this he could be forgiven for deciding that it was not the time for him to start something new.

I was put on weekly pay and worked by the **Droxford**. I started to realise how well organised the company were, when the ship's boats were towed down from the yard and I saw that all of the stores and equipment had been renewed. In the following couple of weeks new wires and ropes were loaded, as were newly overhauled grabs and observation chambers.

We sailed on the 1st March 1964, with the old hands grumbling that, as they had gone from weekly pay to monthly pay on that day, they had been 'done out of' two days pay. I was so homesick that I would have paid to get off the boat! I went on the focs'le for sailing, in keeping with merchant service practice but was asked to come to the bridge, Navy style. It was only when we sailed that I realised that I was the only person on the ship who could navigate.

We sailed to Falmouth where the launches went up to the small port of Mylor to bring back ten tons of Submarine Blasting Gelignite, this was loaded into the magazine – with all concerned ending up with headache. We were at anchor, loading the explosives, when the **Lifeline** passed us on her way down to Falmouth Docks to tie up for the weekend, we passed again when we set sail for Donegal.

Two days later we were off Bloody Foreland at the reported position of the sinking of the Boniface, Bill Ross took us through the outlying rocks into the outer part of Gweedore harbour as if he had done this all his life, I was amazed that we did not have a pilot on board – though I am sure that there would not have been one to employ even if he had wanted to do so. Over the next two years I was to develop a high regard for Rossie's ship handling, especially as this was a skill that I never acquired.

Once the ASDIC dome was fixed we started on the wreck search, without success. It was obvious to those who knew that the ASDIC beam was being deflected and was not reaching the seabed. Brack and Rossie went ashore to talk to the people who had seen the ship sink almost fifty years before. The three men agreed on the bearing but said that the sinking was 'a goodish way off'; the fourth person had been a young girl when the ship sank, she invited our two captains to sit in her chair and look through a certain pane of the window to get the correct bearing. Her evidence did not agree with the men.

After a few more unsuccessful days spent searching we invited one of the men, 'Charlie the Post', to come out with us to see if he could show us what was ' a goodish way off'. It soon became obvious that Charlie had never been that far out before and he spent much of his time marvelling at the ship "to be sure 'tis a palace.' We were a bit upset as we wrongly assumed that he was being sarcastic.

We widened our search area and then, with failure staring us in the face, we towed Don Jones around in the observation chamber; a hair- raising operation (particularly for Don) this had only been done twice before - once on the **Skyro** search and the other time on the search for the Lightning aircraft. Don was one of the most unexcitable men I had ever met, as a young man he had been on an escort ship on the Malta convoys and since joining RB had completed thousands of chamber dives. But you could detect a note of panic in his voice as it came over the bridge speaker shouting "up, up, for ***** sake up". We had almost towed him into one of the boilers of the wreck.

Once the moorings were laid and Don had surveyed the wreck we found that all that was left of the ship were the boilers, the engine a few steel plates and the cargo. Years afterwards when I was to be told by a lecturer that the effect of a wave is not felt at that depth I was able to tell him that the disturbance was so great that it would destroy a cargo ship and our diver could see the boilers and the plating being rocked back and forth even in moderate weather; he no doubt thought that this was yet another old sailor's tale. I went down on deck to see the first grab that came up – it contained a disgusting smelly pile of refuse and a bad tempered conger eel. During one of several spells of bad weather Brack and Rossie again visited the old lady and found that she was right and the men were hopelessly wrong about the bearing; that is what happens when men discuss things again and again in the pub!

Within four weeks we had recovered 340 tons of copper and it was time to start thinking about our trip to Newfoundland. Brack decided that the local meat was of good quality and we should load the several tons of beef that we required at Gweedore. Off we went to see the 'Flesher' to choose our beef and much to our surprise were taken to a field were a small herd were grazing contentedly, we were to choose our meat on the hoof, we felt like executioners. Several days later a group of us went back to load our beef, it took three days to freeze the meat, but the quality was unsurpassed.

We set off for Cork to land the copper. My wife flew to Cork to visit me, so this made a pleasant break. One evening when the two W.K.O.s were making their way back to the ship they saw two scruffy blokes with a sack that obviously contained a couple of bars of copper. When they asked these two what they were up to pinching copper they were told " well sirs, it is like this, we are from the Dublin Metal Exchange and we are taking these as samples"! Our recoveries were worth £68 to the W.K.O.s, and to me, as we were paid 4/- (20p) per ton.

I laid off a Great Circle course for Newfoundland and we sailed on the 25th May, we had exceptionally good weather for most of the passage, but ran into thick fog about two days from our destination. I was concerned about being set south by the

Labrador Current and on to the outlying Virgin Rocks. I managed to get a Noon Latitude by going down on the well deck to get a, rather lumpy, horizon, but was unsure of my Longitude. I asked the W.K.Os to sound for the hundred fathom line that runs almost North/South in that part. When I came on the bridge at 4 am the echo sounder was off and there was no evidence that we had found the line. I switched the machine on only to find that we were already on the bank. The excuse that was given for missing the edge of the bank was that echo sounder paper was expensive! Later that day we were still in fog and I went into the wheelhouse as the engines had stopped to find the same W.K.O. hailing a Portuguese fisherman to ask where we were; to be told that he, the fisherman, was a day and a half out from Saint Johns NF. Later I met the Navigator of the fishing fleet, he laughed and said that the fishing boat skipper would have no more idea of where he was than our man did

Again we made straight for the wreck site and, when the weather broke, we went into the port of Bay Bulls to anchor. I pointed out to Rossie that we had to go through customs at a port of entry, only to be told that they had never done that when he was in the Navy during the war. On one such stay a small iceberg found its way into the fiord like anchorage, by the time we wanted to sail it was starting to break up and was surrounded by brash ice. This was the only time that Rossie's ship handling skills failed him; he rang for an astern engine movement while we were in the ice, an easy way to lose the propeller blades. Eventually the agent heard where we were and we were instructed to come immediately to St. Johns.

Helga Smith was as difficult to find as the **Boniface** had been; our first find appeared to be a World War 2 vessel with a cargo that include prefabricated buildings. To start the search a plotting sheet was drawn on the back of an old Admiralty chart, this was scaled up from what ever charts we could obtain. Later the Canadians provided us with a book of tabulated Decca Navigator positions – this considerably reduced the work load when we were within Decca coverage. Often we would cover the whole search box without finding our target and it was necessary to glue an extra bit on. For hour after hour we plodded along at five or six knots with the ASDIC pinging away, if there was anything of interest Andy or Frank would put it on the loudspeaker for us to hear. One of the many shortcomings of the ASDIC was that, in the final few hundred yards of the approach they 'lost' the target; when that happened the echo sounder had to be switched on. This had to be done quickly, but if you were too quick and put it on before the ASDIC boys had chance to whip their earphones off there would be a howl of rage and misery from the ASDIC shack! The same thing happened if the 'sparks' started sending weather reports on the key while we were searching.

After two weeks we found our target, a cargo liner that had been built in Götenburg in 1944. A marker buoy was dropped and then, using the gyro and a range finder, four moorings were laid. At first sight this seemed to be a hair raising procedure. Each mooring consisted of a ship's anchor, weighing four tons or more, three 'shots' (270') of 1 ½ and 2"chain, a 'riser' wire and a steel mooring buoy. Like most things on the ship the mooring buoys were built to RB's own specification and could be pulled down to quite considerable depths without collapsing. The buoy was hung from the derrick, with a slip, the rusty anchor chain was flaked on the main deck and one of the deck crew had the unenviable task of standing on the forecastle with the buoy suspended by a substantial slip rope. Once the operator of the range finder decided that we were in position the anchor was slipped, the chain roared over the side and the bridge was covered in a cloud of rust and scale.

Four moorings were laid in this way and then the **Droxford** was positioned over what appeared to be the highest point of the wreck. Once this was done Don Jones or his number two would man the observation chamber, they would dress in warm clothes and have a Protosorb mask and a throat microphone, the mask was to absorb CO_2. Once everything had been tested, down he would go. At first there was ample light from the surface, but as it faded the lights above the chamber would be switched on and he would descend. This was a worrying time because he would be going through a 'snowstorm' of plankton, which would reflect much of the light and he knew that the wreck would be festooned in abandoned trawl nets which would float towards the surface.

When the chamber diver could see the wreck he was moved, a meter at a time, across the wreck. As he often could not see much more than that it was difficult for him to get the big picture. He would describe what he could see after each move and on the bridge we would plot the move and his report. He could be heard on the bridge through a loud speaker and each winch man and his linesman had head phones so that there was no delay in complying with each instruction. So it went on "three feet to starboard" - " I can see a bollard and a plate lap" - " three feet ahead ah! there is the corner of a (cargo) hatch" - " three feet to starboard" bump heard, "oh damn there is an overhanging deck" [1]. Generally the diver would work two hour stints, he would be told to use his oxygen when his breathing sounded laboured. If the wreck looked to be the right one the survey would take a day or more, on other occasions it would be rejected within half an hour.

On each visit to the surface he would bring his cup of tea to the bridge and look at the plot, pointing out where things differed from the drawing. The sketch of the **Alexander Macomb** on a later page is the result of one such survey. This was the first time I had been doing the plot, Don seemed impressed with my grasp of what he had seen; as I pointed out it ought to be, for the first eight months of my career had been spent on a Götenburg built ship of the same size.

Within a few hours we knew that we had the right ship, the next part of the survey was to decide where to cut the wreck. In this instance we had a cargo plan so that we knew we only needed to cut into two of the five holds to get to the metal: this may be why the casualty had flooded, the heaviest parts of the cargo seemed to be concentrated in too small an area. The moorings were lifted and a new pattern of six was laid for the recovery phase. We moored and started cutting the ship apart. In all we recovered almost 1,300 tons of metals from the ship. There were almost always icebergs in the vicinity, but they were often obscured by fog, so one of my many jobs was to track them in case they threatened to drift down on us. To add to our misery only two hurricane seasons in the previous eleven years had been worse than the one we worked through. My daily tasks included plotting the weather chart, a laborious business in those days, plotting the iceberg tracks, sending weather observations and tallying cargo. There was a Tropical Cyclone on the met chart for all but three days from 20th August to the 15th October, of these Cleo, Dora. Ethel, Gladys and Isobell headed in our direction.

One thing that did come alongside was a whale, I was in the bath, only a few feet above the waterline when I heard a bump and a scraping sound. I opened the port and was gazing at the blow hole of a full grown whale, quite a sight – and smell!

Our work continued until late October and, with the final recovery from the **Helga Smith** safely stowed in our hold we were looking forward to returning home, but that

---

[1] Sometimes the exchanges could be funny. Some years before, when the *Lifeline* was on a wreck called the **Benin,** Frank Higgins was in the chamber and Tommy Young was on the bridge. The conversation went - "I can see tusks" " you can see what?" all repeated several times ,until the exasperated diver shouted over the phone "Tusks, Tusks, like you get on a ***** elephant. **Benin** was a West African trader and was returning with ivory among her cargo when she was torpedoed.

was not to be. Whilst we had put the company back on it's feet RAB felt that we needed to at least, ensure the next season's work, so we were sent south to the George's Bank to search for the Liberty Ship *Alexander Macomb*. Looking back I can see that this was a sensible decision on the old man's part – but we felt very aggrieved at the time. There was also talk of us spending the winter in the Mediterranean recovering lead from a Bank boat that had sunk earlier in the year.

Fortunately the search for the *Alexander Macomb* only took a few days, we arrived on site early in the morning on my watch – the 4-8. At sunrise I took an amplitude to check the compass error and was swinging the ship to make a new deviation table in preparation for the homeward trip when one of the WKOs arrived on the bridge. I can't now remember whether it was Andrew Pope or Frank 'Dodo' Watts, whoever it was switched on the ASDIC and after a few minutes said "there is a contact a couple of miles (actually 3,200 yards) away over there".

After breakfast we were all on the bridge keen to hear the results, soon the contact proved to be a shipwreck of the right size: by sunset that evening we had four moorings down and Don Jones was down in the observation chamber. We were not right over the wreck so the moorings were relaid early on the following morning and by noon Don had confirmed that we had located a Liberty ship. As we could only get a position line from the Decca Navigator and the LORAN was not a great deal of use, I spent the two days getting a series of star sights to ensure that we could return to the spot. Over the next 24 hours we were able to prove that it was the *Macomb* and we were on our way back to Halifax to bunker and sail for home. We reached Southampton on the 27th November, I for one was very glad to be home! We paid off almost immediately, with a cargo bonus that bolstered my money by a quarter and we also got an extra week's money at Christmas.

But for me there was a disappointment, when I had signed on I had been promised a command on the UK coast; the ship, the *Topmast 18*, had already been converted, but a Master had been appointed. What I had failed to realise was that the new wreck removal ship, as she was, was under Allan Crothall's management (just as the mooring vessels were Commander Stamwitz's responsibility). The blow was softened when my money was increased to equal that of the newly appointed Master and I was told – we will call you Captain and you can sign on as Navigating Master. In fact, when I wrote out the Articles I decided that this was a pretty pointless exercise and signed on as Chief Officer again. I was glad of the extra money, but I still had to face nine months away on the Western Ocean, the 'old grey widow maker'.

At the beginning of March we were once again off on our travels; I routed the ship down to the Azores in a fruitless search for better weather and the trip took us an unpleasant 13 days. After entering in at Halifax we bunkered and, in addition to our weather observing status, agreed to make regular oceanographic readings for the Dartmouth Oceanographic Institute. In return the Canadians agreed to help us in our search for the wreck of the US ship *Collamer*, the RCAF had newly fitted an aircraft with a magnetic anomaly detector for submarine hunting and were keen to prove how effective they were: they produced excellent charts of these anomalies.

But the approaches to Halifax are full of natural magnetic anomalies and none indicated the wreck that we wanted. However on the 5th April Don, as observant as ever, noticed an anchor chain snaking away into the 'mist', we followed that and there was the wreck. We surveyed and identified the wreck and took samples of the brass, then it was back to the *Macomb*.

We relocated this wreck at 3,000 yards plus and dropped a marker: we also found another contact that I have since realised was the U-boat that had sunk the **Macomb**, this had in turn been sunk by a British Navy A/S Trawler.. While we still had the

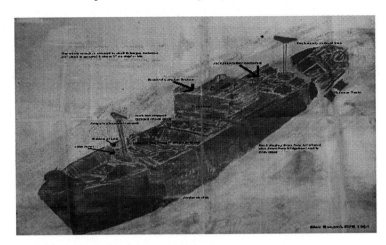

The wreck of the Alexander Macomb, with later notes   Roy Martin 1964

ASDIC dome rigged we went south to the Nantucket area to the reported sinking position of the **Maiden Creek**. We found two wrecks, neither was the wreck that we wanted , one proved to be a fairly large sailing ship constructed of softwood – probably a North American built vessel.

We started work on the **Macomb** and, as we were more than 300 miles further south than we had been on the **Helga Smith,** expected an easier job, but it was not to be. It is true that we were spared the icebergs and the weather was somewhat warmer but we still had to contend with the hurricanes and the quirky currents and poor underwater visibility that they caused.

The first casualty was our boatswain, Ted Gordon, like all the deck crew Ted was loath to cover the hatch and secure the gear at the end of a day's work.   During the night the weather blew up and the crew turned out to cover the hatch and secure, whilst at this work one of the four ton grabs 'walked' across the deck and trapped one of Ted's legs against the bulwark, crushing it.   I was called, I dressed the wound as best I could and administered morphine.   In those days the morphine supplied to British ships was in a paste – I can think of no better word for it – which was in a tube similar to a small toothpaste tube.   You used it by puncturing the skin with the coarse bore needle that was on the nozzle and rolling up the tube to inject the morphine, if the patient wasn't in agony before he certainly was by the time you had finished.   The first injection seemed to have no effect, so, contrary to the instructions in the Shipmaster's Medical Guide[1], I gave him another – still not much relief!   Whilst this was going on we were steaming towards Yarmouth NS and the Coastguard cutter **Rapid** was coming out to meet us, with a Doctor on board.

As I was in the ship's hospital I did not see the transfer take place but the brave doctor told me the story on our next trip into Yarmouth.   He was a Yarmouth GP and was on call when our PAN message was received, he had gone down to the harbour to board the **Rapid** for his first (and last I expect) long sea trip.   **Rapid** had been built for service in the Great Lakes and had for some reason been re-allocated to the

---

[1] The Shipmaster's Medical Guide was a most helpful book.   The first section was on 'First Aid to the Injured' and the final chapter was 'Burial of the Dead at Sea'.   We always joked that you went to see the Second Mate (the medic if you carried a Second Mate – which we didn't) with a splinter in your thumb and would end up being slid off a hatch board.   There were also a couple of pages on delivering babies. Sally Self has a copy and she says it should be called "How to commit manslaughter on the high seas"

Maritimes.   What everyone seemed to agree on was that they did not know what use she was in the Lakes but they were sure that she was of no use for Atlantic service. Long before the rendezvous the Doctor was very seasick.   He was told that the plan was for the **Droxford** to launch one of her boats to make the transfer. He asked the crew to tell him when to jump and was horrified to see that the **Droxford's** boat was even smaller than the **Rapid** and was pitching violently.   However he was given no chance to back out as, when the moment arrived, the cook from the **Rapid**, a big man, put his great paw between the doctor's shoulder blades and pushed him, saying "time to go now Doc".   I was most grateful to see him and I think he was thankful to get on a larger vessel, it took a while for him to recover but he started work immediately.   Ted got a decent shot of morphine and pain relief at last.

In his 'spare time' over the next few months a surgeon in Yarmouth rebuilt Ted's leg. On each subsequent call our first visit was to the hospital to see our bo'sun and thank the staff.   Ted was eventually flown back to the UK and, very sadly, the medical staff at his local hospital decided to amputate his leg.

Little more than a month later we had our second accident, this time to our senior diver, Don Jones.   It was customary for the divers to drive the two grab winches when they were not actually in the observation chamber, as they were grabbing material from an area that they had surveyed.   We were lifting substantial weights from the deck of the wreck, including Sherman tanks; during one such lift the heel-block carried away breaking Don's shoulder blade and several ribs, one of which pierced his lung.   He was moved to the ship's hospital and I started with the morphine.   One of the many helpful things the medical staff at Yarmouth Hospital had done was to make up our morphine stocks with a type that could be administered with a syringe this was much easier to use.   Don was still in a great deal of pain and after a radio conversation with the team I was authorised to increase the dose.   As there was little bleeding, it was agreed that we would go in to Yarmouth and land our colleague via the pilot boat.   We then went into port for a night.

That evening I was in the bath (again), this time there was no whale but instead I heard the rattle of bullets on the ship's plating.   Having been on a ship that came under fire before I was familiar with that sound.   I stuck my head out of the porthole – a foolish thing to do I know, but I don't think too clearly when I come under fire in the bath.   Local youths had collected some rifle shells from our deck and were lobbing them into a bonfire for a dare.   Ammunition is constantly being recovered when working on a wartime wreck both from the cargo and the magazines.   This is dumped at regular intervals, except for brass shell cases that are kept as 'spidge'. This time, because of the emergency, we had not had time to clear the decks.

There were two more incidents fortunately neither resulted in disaster, even though they were both very serious.   Because of the large amount of explosives on the **Macomb** the **Droxford** hauled off after the diver had placed each charge and the charge was fired from a launch.   This was a time consuming procedure and it was difficult to avoid breaking the firing cable so we then fired charges from the ship, but only after hauling out to the limits of the moor.   However even this slowed us down so for each successive firing we got nearer and nearer the wreck, much to the consternation of many of the old hands.

In the saloon we had the crests from the **Droxford** and the **Twyford,** listing the jobs the ships had done and one day these were decorated with a scroll saying 'Remember the **Artiglio**'. In 1930, the SORIMA vessel **Artiglio** was working on a wreck with a part cargo of explosives off the West Coast of France.   When firing a charge Alberto Gianni blew up his ship, himself and most of the crew.   The same fate almost befell us. There was a blue flash across the surface of the sea, followed by an upwelling and a fearful rumbling – we had detonated part of the cargo. Fortunately we were still some distance away and did not suffer serious damage.

The next time the jinx struck was shortly after we had landed Don with his injury. A storm had passed and this always set up a strong current across the wreck and bad underwater visibility. Billy Mason (John Cobb?) was in the chamber, as he went down past the open bridge front of the casualty he was suddenly sheltered from the current and shot into the midships accommodation smashing the lights and losing telephone contact, with the chamber ending up on its side. After some planning Rossie had the ship hauled across the moor so that he could drag the chamber out of the trap and bring it back to the surface; a typically skillful Rossie manoeuvre, by which he saved the life of our only diver.

By this time RAB must have been getting concerned about the amount of tax he would be paying so we were again sent off on location work. We were promised that we would be paid our bonus as if we had carried on recovery work until the end of the season, and we were, even though we had only recovered 900 tons.

Many years afterwards I heard that, at about this time, RAB had called a meeting of the Board to decide whether to order a 400 tons floating sheerlegs, similar to the **Magnus I** and **Magnus II** that had been built for Ulrich Harms. With some encouragement from RAB it was decided that the company would order this vessel. Later RAB called another meeting, basically to decide whose silly idea it was to order such a vessel and the whole project was canceled. After that Harms and Beazley cooperated in UK waters

We again went to search for the **Maiden Creek**, but conditions were not suitable and we were not successful, it was decided that we would return in the Autumn. Our next target was the **Empire Story** in the Bay of Fundy, we found the vessel off of Grand Manaan Island but the currents were so fierce that this recovery was not thought to be viable

Records show that we went to the Gulf of St. Lawrence, I have no recollection of this, but presumably we surveyed the **Mount Taygetus** or the **Mount Pindus**, which the **Droxford** completed two years later. October found us back at the site of the **Maiden Creek** and the **Coimbra**, but we were no more successful this time. We went back to the **Alex Macomb** to lift our light-buoy – always a difficult operation, and returned to Halifax for the last time that season.

We sailed for home on the 27th October, arriving on the 7th November. As we had been doing weather observation work for the Canadian meteorological office throughout the season and they kindly offered to weather route us homeward – they did their very best but finding good weather in the North Atlantic in November was a hopeless task. Their promise was 'you will not get an easterly gale' – a head wind. But that is exactly what we encountered as we got into soundings in the Western Approaches. In a force nine gale I saw a small trawler lying broadside on and, I assumed, in distress. We could get no reply to our Radio call so I asked Rossie if it would be OK to go over to see what help she needed. As we approached I was amazed to see that the trawler was broadside on because she was hauling her nets: a crowd of tough Bretons were doing this, up to their waists in the cold Atlantic water, tough men – or?

I decided, with great regret, that I did not have the stomach for the long trips and resigned, moving to Tate & Lyle's Sugar Line for almost two years.

Chapter Seven - The Empire Manor's Gold 1952 to 1973

SV Droxford   **Risdon Beazley collection**

The **Empire Manor** was a two- deck, six hold coal fired steamer of 9,700 tons deadweight, built in 1943 by Short Brothers Limited at Sunderland for the Ministry of War Transport.   She was managed by the Federal Steam Navigation Company, who in peacetime operated ships that mostly carried cargoes to and from New Zealand; the cargo on the return leg consisted mainly of refrigerated meat.   The **Empire Manor** was also equipped as a 'reefer' and two thirds of the cargo she carried on the voyage described below was stowed in her refrigerated holds.   Like most merchant companies, Federal Line had lost a considerable part of their fleet in the war; one, the **Dorset**, was lost on the Malta convoy 'Operation Pedestal'.   It was MOWT practice to allocate ships to managers in direct proportion to the losses of their own fleet.

Convoy HX 276 sailed from New York on the 21st January 1944, it was made up of 62 laden merchant ships; a further 17 joined from Halifax, including two merchant aircraft carriers.[1]   Six ships from the convoy turned back for various reasons and one, the **Empire Manor**, was sunk following a collision.

At the end of 1943 the British situation was dire, the country had started the war with a total of 8,977 merchant ships of over 100 gross registered tons.   This, the biggest merchant fleet in the world, was magnificently supported by Allied and Neutral merchant fleets; between them they sustained Britain.   But by the time HX 276 sailed over 4,500 vessels of the combined fleets had been lost and this figure did not include the British merchant ships that were lost on Admiralty service.

---

[1] Summary of information obtained by Roger Griffiths from The National Archives, (TNA) at Kew. HX convoys were 'fast' convoys (even though they were only expected to move at around 9 knots).   The even slower SC convoys sailed from Halifax with an intended speed of 7.5 knots.   Merchant Aircraft Carriers (MAC ships) were modified cargo ships that, in addition to their normal cargoes of bulk grain or oil, had a flight deck and were equipped with three or four Swordfish aircraft.   The vessels were commanded and manned by merchant seamen with their flight crews coming from the Fleet Air Arm of the Royal Navy.   Their names were prefixed M.V. not H.M.S.

Comparing convoy HX 276 with the smaller HX76 that had sailed from Halifax in September 1940 one can see the extent of the losses. The earlier 37 ship convoy was made up of 28 British ships, three Dutch, one Danish, one Belgian and four Norwegian vessels: the preceding convoy also included Greek and French ships. HX 276, twice the size, had only 18 British ships, including the two MACs, 50 American vessels, 8 Norwegians and one each from Iceland and Panama. Three of the British ships were Canadian owned and built, the naval escorts were also provided by Canada and manned by Canadian sailors. Neither the dedication of the British and Allied civilian merchant seamen, nor the contribution of the Canadians, has ever been properly acknowledged.

*The convoy Commodore's report on the voyage is not at The National Archives (TNA); but crew members from one of the escorts, **HMCS Wallaceburg**, remember that the weather was bad as the convoy approached the western edge of the Grand Bank of Newfoundland. At 1130 GMT on the 27th January the American Liberty Ship[1] **Edward Kavanagh** sheered to port and struck the **Empire Manor** in way of No.4 hold. As the American pulled away water poured into the hold and, later in the day, the **Empire Manor** caught fire and had to be abandoned. The **Wallaceburg** rescued all the crew. The next day the ship broke in half and the after part sank in 44° 05'N, 52° 35'W, whilst the fore-end remained afloat and on fire. Members of the **Wallaceburg**'s crew volunteered to join the Master boarding the casualty in an attempt at salvage, but it was decided that this was too dangerous. At 1300 on the 29th January the **Wallaceburg** sank the casualty with depth charges.*

Nine years after the sinking the new **Twyford** arrived on site. **Twyford** had been purpose built to recover metal cargoes after several years' experience using adapted war built tonnage. Risdon Beazley had concluded an Agreement with the Treasury Solicitor whereby RB were to receive 70% of the value of any gold recovered on success.

Twyford was under the command of Captain F R Hunter OBE, who had joined the company during the war. She was equipped with a large grab, an observation chamber and wartime ASDIC. The ASDIC operator was Andrew Pope; his opposite number, Frank Watts, was employed in the re-location of the **Niagara** off New Zealand, also to recover gold. Both of these men had been Petty Officer ASDIC operators and instructors during the war.

Conditions made the re-location of the wreck extremely difficult but it was eventually found in 320ft of water close to the reported sinking position. The observation chamber and the grab were deployed in the usual Beazley manner, but the fore-end was found to be upside down. Allan Crothall in his report says that **Twyford** blasted a hole in the double bottom tank at No.1 hold and removed several hundred ton of useless cargo and part of the 'tween deck without finding the lead or zinc that was stowed with the gold bullion[2]. At this point the attempt was abandoned.

In 1964 the **Droxford** was again on the Grand Bank, this time recovering metals from the **Helga Smith**, RAB's permission was sought to resume recoveries; however the Guv'nor said that the time was not yet ripe. The **Droxford** had been built in 1958[3] incorporating many of the lessons learned from the operation of the **Twyford**.

---

[1] Liberty Ships were a class of cargo vessel built in the United States to a British shipbuilder's design, 2,751 were built. The Empire Manor was built in Britain to another British design, whilst the Canadian built 'Fort' and 'Park' (and the US built 'Oceans') cargo ships were to yet another British design.

[2] Confirmed by Tom Bray who was on the Twyford on that voyage.

[3] The UK Treasury returned £25,000 of the payments that RB had made as a contribution towards the cost of this ship.

Allan Crothall had not been involved in the 1953 operation, but he had been closely involved in the research and had interviewed Canadian Naval Officers who had been present when the fore-end of the **Empire Manor** had been sunk. In 1969 he became the Managing Director of Risdon Beazley Ulrich Harms Ltd. **Empire Manor** was among the wrecks that he was determined to complete recoveries from.

In 1971 Mr Clifford Bennison of the Company's solicitors Messrs Ingledew, Brown, Bennison and Garrett had approached the Treasury Solicitor on the Company's behalf and an Agreement was made giving RBUH 85% of the 'official' value of any gold recovered.

Following successful operations on the **Hollington** and the **Harrovian** earlier in the year, the company had generated sufficient funding to send the **Droxford** back to the **Empire Manor** wreck site. The plan was to cut out the whole of No.1 double bottom, remove the cargo from No.1 lower hold, cut out the tween deck and recover all of the cargo that had been above it in the search for the metals.

In 1973 the ice situation, though not as severe as in 1972, was still bad and it was not until the 9th July that the *Droxford* could safely sail to the area. To give Capt. Ross a summer break, his first in many years, Capt. Terry McCarthy took the vessel to Newfoundland. Before Capt. Ross flew out to re-join his ship it was necessary to agree a simple code by which he could advise the office of success without alerting would be competitors. All messages had to be passed by radio-telephone through Cape Race Radio. Capt. Ross' suggestion was that he would report a problem with his donkey boiler, which had resulted in a number of furnace bricks becoming displaced, the number was to be the number of bars of gold that had been recovered: the **Droxford** did not have a donkey boiler.

The trip across the Western Ocean was fairly typical, a gale followed by several days of strong Sou-westerlies, with thick fog throughout the area where there were known to be icebergs. They arrived at St. Johns NF at 0900 on Sunday 15th of July. Capt. Ross resumed command on the 17th and the salvage ship sailed immediately for the search area, arriving at 1030 on the following day the A/S search began immediately.

Andrew Pope found that the conditions for operating the ASDIC were the worst that he had so far encountered. The surface sea water temperature jumped by 11° C as they approached the sweep area. They moored to a single mooring at the wreck position and lowered the bathythermograph; this showed the cause of their problem was, as they had suspected, a marked layering near the surface. The surface temperature was 18° C, at 10 metres depth it dropped to 8° C. At 30 metres it was 2° C and this was bottom temperature, though there was even a spot at 60 metres when the temperature was only 1 degree. Conditions like this reflect much of the sound beam back to the surface, the remainder can be bent sharply downwards.

Don Jones' journal records that, on the 20th July after three days search with the echo sounder, '1850 Eric Mace sighted wreck contact on the echo sounder, second run in gave a more solid and higher lift (of) 20-30feet'. That night they laid their six moorings around the contact which, when plotted using the Decca Chain that was now in operation, was very close to the position Capt. Hunter had obtained using star sights in 1953.

The double bottom of a merchant ship is an extremely heavy structure, especially in the forward part of the ship where pounding is experienced. Charges need to be placed first on the ship's bottom itself, the resulting cuts then need to be widened sufficiently to put a further set of charges on the tank top before sections of the several hundred tons of structure can be lifted clear. The lifts that they recorded weighed between 16 and 22 tons when lifted out of the water.

Once in the lower hold they were faced with the removal of the about 800 tons of cargo that was stowed there. This included 8 x 4' bundles of waterlogged plywood and field telephone cable, a very troublesome combination[1]. Bundles of rotten plywood either disintegrate whilst being pulled up, or jam the grab open, whilst the telephone cable becomes entangled with the sheaves and all the working parts of the grab. This boring, smelly, work continued until the 29th August at which time Captain Ross reported that the fore holds were "as clean as a whistle" and he was 100% sure that the gold was not there. He also reported that most of his explosives had been used. All they had to show for their efforts were some ingots of lead and zinc, which they knew had been stowed near to the gold.

To get to this point the company had spent almost £100,000, in addition to what had been expended on the 1953 operation: this together amounted to about a third of the maximum possible return on a 'No Cure – No Pay' operation. With shortening days, the probability of worsening weather and a ship costing £1,500 per day Allan Crothall could have been forgiven for telling the ship to return and save the cost of more fuel and explosives. Like Risdon Beazley before him ACC was not a gambler in the accepted sense, but he was also not faint-hearted, so the **Droxford** was to go to St. Johns NF for the necessary stores during the next Spring tide period around the 14th September. In the meanwhile they had to contend with this set of springs and gale force winds from the 5th to the 7th September.

In the days before they left the site on the evening of the 11th the divers placed most of their remaining explosives on the forecastle area of the ship and around the anchor chains and windlass: if the heavy bars of gold were still in the ship this was the only place they could be. **Droxford** entered St Johns harbour at 1745 on Wednesday the 12th September; as usual she would have moored alongside the Harvey Pier at Water Street. Harvey, Beazley's agent, had made all of the necessary arrangements, despite a transport strike. The ship loaded oil, stores and fresh water on the Thursday; she sailed at 0945 on the Friday after loading a new supply of explosives. The only available explosives were supplied through the Canadian government the material had a lower velocity than that which the Beazley ships normally used, but it proved to be effective.

The Canadians were always most helpful to the Beazley ships, but even they could not control the weather; by 1700 on the Saturday, after only ten hours work, **Droxford** was on her single mooring riding out a gale. On Sunday the 16th even the single mooring was slipped as the beam sea made it increasingly uncomfortable, the vessel steamed slowly into the severe southerly gale throughout the night.

The following morning dawned sunny and warm with an easing wind and a moderate tide, this allowed the moorings to be re-positioned and re-marked after which diving resumed. They then started lifting the wreckage of the forecastle of the casualty; this was 'badly concertinaed' indicating that the vessel had indeed hit bow first. As gold is even heavier than lead there was a real possibility that the ingots could have ended up among the forecastle wreckage. Six dives (dips) were made on the Tuesday, in worsening weather, by early on the morning of the 19th another severe gale was blowing with 'very bad' sea conditions. Those moorings that could not be slipped had to be chopped or burned through, 'gas axed' as those in the oil industry now call it.

---

[1] A cargo list is attached.

There was some improvement on the following day, which was spent recovering and re-splicing mooring wires. It proved to be 'quite a job getting the launch down and up'. The Beazley launches were 28 feet long and double diagonal planked, they had been built in the yard to the company's own design, launching and recovering them required superb seamanship by both the Master and the launch crew. It was a measure of their skill that there was only one boat accident within the recovery fleet throughout it's history, this was on the **British Prince** and after that accident all boats were fitted with buoyancy material.

The weather was overcast by Friday 21st and only one dip was managed before the moorings were slipped at Noon after the ship received a hurricane warning. This was hurricane Ellen, one of only two tropical storms to become a hurricane when North of 38° Latitude. Ellen reached her maximum intensity, Category 3, that day. By the 22nd Ellen had accelerated to a forward speed of 50 knots and became extra tropical. This last change was of no interest to those on the **Droxford**, here was a severe storm with reported winds 117 knots (135 MPH) and this was to be avoided – especially as the little salvage ship's speed was only 10 knots.

Droxford entered her temporary home port of St Johns at 0730 on Sunday 23rd September and secured at the Oil Jetty. Also sheltering in the harbour were the last ships of the Portuguese 'White Fleet'. For over four hundred years these brave seamen had fished the Grand Banks from their dories, returning to their homeland at the end of September. 1974 was to be the final *'Campanha'* (campaign) for them, whilst 1980 was to see the end of Beazley's Worldwide search for metals.

In the Southampton offices of the company, and on board the **Droxford**, the prospect of the failure of their particular *Campanha* was being contemplated. It seemed to those given to wilder flights of fancy that the Grand Bank of Newfoundland felt that it's claim to the gold was stronger than that of the Bank of England and the weather gods were on the Grand Bank's side.

A very subdued **Droxford** crew loaded yet another two tons of explosives and sailed on the evening of Monday 24th, Ellen having continued her course out into the Atlantic. 24 hours later the ship was again on her moorings with a very cold northerly wind blowing. Again on the 26th the weather deteriorated, the spring tides and the bitterly cold water caused a further suspension of operations that continued throughout the 27th. With lighter winds on the 28th and a heavy confused swell only 'rough grabbing' was possible. Then at around 1120 the first gold ingot came up in the grab with the second diver, Dick, on the main winch, seven more followed before the main grab wire parted. The £45,000 of gold was stowed in the bullion room and work ceased for all to enjoy a well-earned bond issue.

There was one last task for the watch-keeper on the evening 8 to 12 - to let the office know. "Cape Race Radio this is the **Droxford** – Mike Yankee Bravo Yankee, I have a message for Topmast at UK Telex Number 47505". As always Cape Race responded promptly, knowing that these boys were not given to idle chatter. The message used the code that 'Rossie' had devised almost four months before "We have a collapsed furnace in our donkey boiler, eight, repeat eight, fire bricks have been displaced, repairs being made".

The message arrived on the Telex machine at the Beazley office at Clausentum Yard, Southampton in the early hours of Saturday morning when all of the office staff were sound asleep; none more so than Roy Martin, then the Operations Manager, whose birthday falls on the 28th September. The following morning, before setting off early for a meeting, he made his usual call to the on site Security Officer to check on the overnight messages – there were three.   The last message, which Mr Jones reasonably felt was the least important, was to the effect that **Droxford** had a boiler problem that they could fix.   Martin was part way up the A31 trunk road before the meaning of the message dawned on him, he turned the car round and was able to get to the office as the others arrived for their half day Saturday work.

Work on the Grand Bank continued to be hampered by wind (up to 55 knots), tide and swell, but by the 5th October a further 24 bars had been recovered.   Saturday the 6th October dawned overcast, with light rain and wind, but a gale warning was received and the ship slipped and went to a single buoy.   There the crew repaired damage to the hatch that had been caused when the casualty's anchor chain had 'taken charge' whilst it was being recovered and stowed – fortunately no one had been hurt.   The full force of the gale was not felt until the 8th and no further work was possible until the 12th when they started 'rough grabbing' and recovered a another 24 bars.   On the morning of the 13th another five bars were recovered, making a total of 61 bars on board the ship.   On the 14th another gale warning was issued and the **Droxford** again went to St Johns, by this time the value of the gold on board exceeded the book value of the ship.

At St Johns a police guard patrolled the ship and the quay and identity cards were issued.   After all the wild tales that had circulated about the **Droxford**, and the **Twyford**, seeking a copy of the 'star studded gems of Omar Khayyam' that had supposedly been in the **RMS Titanic**, here was a real tale of treasure.   Canadian radio and television networks had run the story by the 17th but strangely the tale did not seem to be picked up by the British networks.   **Droxford** was back on the moorings by the 19th fully fuelled and stored with the intention of recovering the remaining nine bars.   On the 21st one more bar was recovered, after being sighted by the diver, this proved to be the final bar.

That night the **Droxford** again had to slip her moorings and was steaming into winds of up to storm force with a very heavy swell, which continued for two days. Quieter weather arrived on the 24th and the diver made a thorough search of the whole forecastle area seeing nothing but a few zinc slabs and lead bars.

The crew were weary as is shown by the note in Don Jones' journal 'we did not move to dump wreckage' – they knew there was no point.   The next morning Captain Ross sent a message to Southampton saying, in effect, 'have we done enough?' the reply was 'yes and more than we could reasonably expect – come home'.   By 1615 that evening the moorings had been recovered and the telegraph was rung 'Full Away'.

But even then the battle with the elements was not over, the Noon positions were:

October 26th, 1973,	Lat. 43° 55' N, Long. 47° 50'W,	Dist. 183'	Av. Spd. 9.28K
October 27th ,1973	Lat. 44° 06'N, Long. 42° 33'W,	Dist. 228'	Av. Spd. 9.54K
	Under the influence of Hurricane "Gilda"		
October 28th ,1973	Lat. 43° 24'N, Long. 39° 50'W,	Dist. 123'	Av. Spd. 5.23K
October 29th, 1973	Lat. 43° 06'N, Long. 35° 50'W,	Dist. 176'	Av. Spd. 7.35K
October 30th, 1973	Lat. 43° 39'N, Long. 30° 42'W,	Dist. 225'	Av. Spd. 9.57K
October 31st, 1973	Lat. 44° 51'N, Long. 25° 46'W,	Dist. 233'	Av. Spd. 9.71K
November 1st, 1973	Lat. 45° 43'N, Long. 22° 26'W,	Dist. 154'	Av. Spd. 6.55K
	Hurricane conditions, winds maximum gusting to 93 Knots.		
November 2nd, 1973	Lat. 46° 28'N, Long. 19° 43'W	Dist 128'	Av. Spd. 5.33K
November 3rd, 1973	Lat. 47° 09'N, Long. 15° 35'W	Dist. 174'	Av. Spd. 7.73K
November 4th, 1973	Lat. 48° 44'N, Long. 10° 16'W,	Dist. 229'	Av. Spd. 9.72K
November 5th, 1973	Lat. 49° 57'N, Long. 04° 56'W,	Dist. 226'	Av. Spd. 9.41K

Revolutions were adjusted to arrive at Southampton at 0800 6th November. At 0552 the **Droxford** passed the Bridge Buoy at the Needles, Isle of Wight and at 0605 the Pilot was embarked. The Dock Pilot took over at 0805 and at 0835 the tug **Willanne** assisted the vessel port side to alongside No.68 Berth Town Quay.

As with everything that Risdon Beazley had ever done, this was a low key affair. There were no onlookers when a security van pulled up alongside the ship. Though the van was unmarked and painted an unexciting dun colour, the fact that the three people in the cab wore bowler hats and suits somehow set it apart. They started to unload their empty bullion boxes but were told that this was not necessary, the ship's carpenter had made boxes during the homeward trip. So good were the ship's boxes that the Bank staff jokingly offered the Chippy a job. Allan Crothall and Roy Martin took the opportunity to have their photograph taken with their feet on a carpet of gold bars. At 0915 the 25,301.969 fine ounces of gold were loaded into the Bank's van, the job was done.

Risdon Beazley Marine Ltd, as they now were, received the Bank of England's cheque for £313,638.27 later that month. On the 20th December 1973 Mr E M Cockburn wrote a short letter to Mr W Just at the Treasury saying:

"SALVAGE OF GOVERNMENT CARGOES

I thought you would like to have a copy of the enclosed note of a meeting I recently had with Mr Crothall, Managing Director of Risdon Beazley. It gives you an interesting account of their work. I think they do very well out of these contracts but then so do we, and I need hardly tell you how well we have done out of the gold from the EMPIRE MANOR. Risdon Beazley are apparently having trouble with the Department of Trade and Industry and the Salvage Association and you might like to know their side of the story (see paragraph 8)."[1]

Allan Crothall ends his 14 page report to the Treasury with the following paragraph:

"Thus ended a cargo recovery operation that broke no records for depth (330 feet against 894 feet for the wreck of the "HOLLINGTON") or for value based on the official price of gold, but which for sheer persistence in the face of every difficulty including below average open Atlantic weather conditions, would be difficult to surpass. Even after completion of the operation, the "DROXFORD" was almost certainly the only salvage vessel in service that would have survived the appalling conditions of the return voyage to make a safe delivery of the recovered material".

---

[1] On one visit the representatives of the SA asked who's Rolls Royce was parked in the yard, they were told that it was Mr Beazley's. They replied that he did so well out of the cargo recovery contracts that 'they' had bought the car. This was nonsense because the SA were often unaware of the existence of the cargoes that Tom Pickford brought to their attention and therefore the 10 to 12.5% that they were paid was money out of the blue. The bad feeling continued and culminated in the saga of HMS Edinburgh' gold..

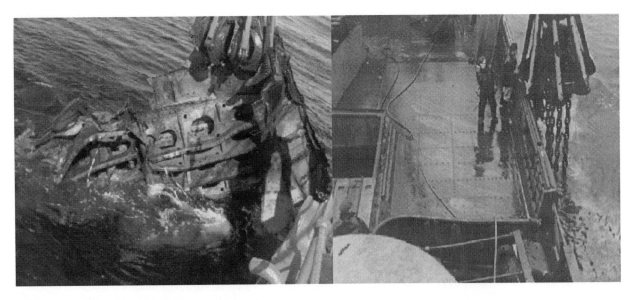

Empire Manor The double bottom　　　　　　　*The first gold bar*
Photographs W A Ross

Empire Manor cargo - New York for the Mersey

Cheese	191
Lard	295
Powdered milk	78
Dried egg	90
Refrigerated fruits & hams	1263
Citrus pictrine	8
Seeds	9
Dried fruit	475
Refrigerated meats	1429
Asbestos	16
Lead	524
Machine tools	15
Photographic goods	12
Hand tools	10
Copper	78
Plywood	218
Machinery	99
Radio equipment	6
Zinc	413
Graphite powder	3
Spool wood	17
Nickel	7
Ball bearings	12
Sundries	71
Trucks	26
Aircraft parts	11
Mobile Units	58
U.S. Army refrigerated cargo	1013
Total	**6447** tons

Chapter Eight – Salvage of S.S. Great Britain 1970

The launching of the S.S. Great Britain at Bristol by the Prince Consort in 1843.

Early in 1970 Leslie James Collingwood (Bill) O'Neil, the senior salvage officer of Risdon Beazley Ltd, was sent to the Falkland Islands to look into the feasibility of salvaging the historic ship **S.S. Great Britain**. As with most of Beazley's projects, it was kept fairly quiet until it became a reality.

The **Great Britain** was a technical innovation designed by Isambard Kingdom Brunel, and launched at Bristol on the 19th July 1843. The ship was credited with many firsts; she was the first ocean going ship to be built of iron, the first large vessel to be fitted with a screw propeller, double bottom and watertight bulkheads. These plus many other innovative features make her one of the most famous ships of all time. Her hull measured 322 feet, beam 50 feet, main deck to keel almost 33 feet, weight 3,270 tons. The 4-cylinder engine weighed 340 tons and developed about 600 H.P. and she actually achieved 12.5 knots on trials.

The vessel arrived in Liverpool during February 1876, after the completion of voyage number 44 to Melbourne, and was laid up at Birkenhead, only to emerge again as a fully rigged sailing ship in 1882, having had all her machinery taken out by her new owners. The final voyage of the **Great Britain** began on 6th February 1886, sailing from Penarth to San Francisco with a cargo of coal. She had made this voyage a few times before, and the return cargo was usually of wheat. She ran in to a fierce gale off Cape Horn in mid-April and a month later she had made no headway when a fire broke out in a cargo hold. The captain decided to head for the Falkland Islands for repairs to the fire damaged hold and leaking decks. Due to the limited repair facilities in the Falklands, the marine insurers declared her a constructive total loss and she was sold to the Falklands Islands Company. She was used as a floating storage vessel, mainly for coal and wool. She contributed to the victory of the Battle of the Falkland Islands by supplying coal to **HMS Inflexible** and **HMS Invincible**.

In 1933 she was no longer required for her present role, and was stripped of her tween deck planking, which was used in the construction of a bridge. Some of her yards were used as horizontal supports on a jetty that still remains to be seen today. In 1936 it was decided to scuttle the **Great Britain** in deep water but many people, led by a local police constable, Mr Doley Williams, complained that she deserved a better end than that. Eventually the Falkland Islands Company relented, and she was towed to Sparrow Cove about 3 or 4 miles North of Port Stanley. Holes were punched in her hull and she sank upright in shallow water. 'The Britain', as the locals called her, was largely left in peace except for the occasional visit from crew members from naval ships that were anchored in nearby Port William. These were usually cruisers and battle ships that preferred to anchor in Port William as opposed to the normal anchorage in Port Stanley Harbour, due to restricted draft and manoeuvring room. Also, during the summer months, the local inhabitants from Port Stanley used Sparrow Cove as a favourite spot to picnic if they or a friend owned a boat. I can certainly remember getting very excited as a young boy, and being able to scramble onboard the old ship. Even in those days, (early fifties), she was quite dangerous due to rotten decking, old iron ladders, and the slippery mess caused by many years of cormorants using her as a roosting place.

Bill O'Neil returned from the Falklands and reported to Mr Risdon Beazley that there was absolutely no chance of the vessel being able to float on her own for any length of time, so the question of refloating her then towing her all the way from the Falklands to England was absurd. However, he believed the vessel could be refloated. It would not be 'a piece of cake', but if she was able to stay afloat for a few hours, she could be floated over a submersible pontoon. Such a large vessel had never been salvaged this way, and the tow would be the longest of its type ever under taken. An associated company, Ulrich Harms of Hamburg, had used this method to transport dredging equipment such as small workboats, tugs, bucket dredgers etc. to remote places. The usual method was to tow such plant and equipment but this has always been a very laborious method, and bucket dredgers used to be a tug captain's nightmare to tow over long distances. When all the interested parties had agreed, and permission from the Falkland Islands was granted, (and not without some local opposition), the salvage plan was formulated.

Ulrich Harms at this time was delivering dredging equipment to Boke in the Republic of Guinea on board one of the company's large submersible pontoons, **Mulus 3** (2,667 tons gross). She was being towed by the **Varius 2**, which has been described in many references to the epic salvage project as a tug, but in fact the **Varius 2** hardly resembled a tug at all, she was in fact a stern trawler. The Captain of **Varius 2**, Hans Hertzog from Heligoland, was instructed to tow the **Mulus 3** to Montevideo, where the British salvage team would join them and prepare for the salvage project. Ulrich Harms purchased 3 x 724 tons gross identical stern trawlers from the German Government. They had been built specifically as fishery research vessels and had had little use. They were the most comfortable ships one could ever wish to sail on. The two large trawl winches were ideal as towing winches. However there were problems manoeuvring whilst on a short tow, as unlike tugs that have a central towing position, either direct from a winch or tow hook and gog eye, these ships towed from the large gilson blocks on the quarters normally used for towing fishing nets. The salvage team from Risdon Beazley was hand picked by Bill O'Neil and taken from the company's various salvage vessels to prepare for the mammoth project ahead. Pumps, diving and rigging equipment was prepared and then transported by air to Montevideo.

Bill O'Neil was no stranger to the Falklands. During World War Two he had been billeted ashore from **HMS Exeter** after she was badly damaged during the Battle of the River Plate. He maintained a close friendship with the family whose house he had stayed in, and in his words they had "treated him like one of the family". The other salvage team members were Bob Light from a family of well-known 'Hard Hat' divers. Bob's speciality was as a shipwright, having trained in the Royal Navy. Stuart Whatley, also ex-Navy, was one of the new breed of divers known as 'Clearance Divers'. His technical diving knowledge was very important in case we were called to go on deeper jobs before returning home. But besides that, Stuart was a great guy to work with and had "arms like legs". I will always be very grateful to Stuart, as he taught me that there was much more to diving than just getting wet and cold. Don O'Hara was also an ex-services diver. He specialised in carpentry and his skills were used to the full on the **Great Britain** job. I was the last member of the team to be picked, no doubt because I was a Falkland Islander and my local knowledge might come in useful. My speciality was diving and rigging, a trade I had been taught in the various merchant vessels I had served on prior to joining Risdon Beazley Ltd.

We arrived in Montevideo a day or so before the **Varius 2** and **Mulus 3,** to give us a chance to get acquainted with the Uruguayan agent and to assist him with tracking down scrap steel and some labourers. As soon as the **Varius 2** arrived we moved onboard and were shown to our accommodation, which was very clean but right down in the forepeak, where even the most seasoned seafarer could not help but feel a bit queasy in a very heavy head sea, especially after a couple of Schnapps.

The following few days were very busy, preparing the **Mulus 3** for the salvage job ahead. First we obtained two jumbo derricks taken off a scrapped British cargo ship. These we welded together, with a very heavy plate at the top and the base welded to the bow end of the pontoon, making a sheerlegs for lifting the masts out of the **Great Britain**. In addition to this, we had long vertical pipes or tubes, about three feet in diameter, welded to the deck to form supports for the ship (dolphins) to be braced against. Also, keel blocks similar to those found in the bottom of a dry dock were fastened by welding to the pontoon's deck for the bar keel to sit on. Other loose steel and equipment that would not get harmed by seawater was sea fastened to the **Mulus 3**. **Varius 2** was topped up with fuel, stores etc. We sailed from Montevideo cheered on by a surprising amount of people who were taking an enormous interest in our forthcoming adventure.

After leaving the main harbour, our Uruguayan pilot took us quite close to the wreck of the **Calpean Star**. This is the ex-Royal Mail ship **Highland Chieftain** (14,131 gross tons) built by Harland & Wolf, Belfast, in1929. **Highland Chieftain** was constructed to the requirements of H. & W. Nelson Ltd for the emigrant and meat trade between the River Plate Ports and the British Isles. In 1932 the identity of the Nelson Line was changed to Royal Mail Steam Packet Company.

During World War Two the **Highland Chieftain** was used for trooping, and also her meat carrying capacity was put to good use. She did suffer some considerable damage on the 11th October during an enemy air raid whilst in Liverpool. I mention this ship mainly because she had strong links with the Falkland Islands in the days before air travel took over. Many Islanders took passage on the 'Highland Boats' (as they were known) from Montevideo to England to visit relatives in the U.K. or with children going to England to further their education.

The 1,000-mile passage to the Falklands was quite rough, however the **Varius 2** offered a lot more comfort than a normal tug. We took a more westerly route than would usually be taken to keep us closer to the Argentine coastline. We averaged something like 4-5 knots, which is a reasonable speed for a tug and tow in the stormy seas of the South Atlantic. The trip itself was most useful inasmuch that it gave us a good chance to get to know the crew of the **Varius 2**.

Many of the crew were able to speak passable English and the Captain, Sparks (radio officer), and Horst Kaulen spoke faultless English. Horst Kaulen, (nicknamed Mini by the Germans due to his short stature), was in charge of the ballasting of the pontoon and all matters concerning the **Varius 2** and **Mulus 3**. I kept the 1600h to 2000h bridge watch for the captain so that he could attend to the multitude of chores that required his attention. One such chore was overseeing the removal of a lot of the fish processing machinery to gain space for the ship's comparatively new role as a multi purpose salvage vessel.

We found that the Germans had a similar sense of humour to our own, so at no time did we feel as if we were unwanted but necessary guests. I remember the Sparks purchasing a new pair of khaki drill trousers from the slop chest, and as he was fairly short he had to shorten the legs by about four inches. Whilst doing this, he kept me company on the bridge, and turned up the four inches and tacked them ready to cut off and sew properly. The captain presented Sparks with a huge amount of reports and other paper work to be sent to the company office in Cuxhaven by morse code.

Whilst Sparks was away in his radio room, the captain turned the trousers up a further 6 inches. When Sparks returned to the bridge, he took the scissors and cut off the unwanted hem and sewed the legs up neatly. Somehow there just happened to be a large audience present when Sparks put the trousers on, and needless to say the bottoms came to about the middle of his thigh. He did look at me a bit suspiciously, but had to concede amid the laughter, that even Radio Officers could make a mistake.

Horst Kaulen was an ex-diver with the appropriate scars to prove it. One of his thumbs had been almost severed when he was diving in the Port of Hamburg on a ship's bottom in pitch-black water. Horst had not noticed that the ship had made contact with the seabed as the tide ebbed. His air hose was trapped under the ship and he could not surface. He cut his armoured air hose with his diving knife, after closing the escape valve on the helmet, and had enough air trapped in his diving dress to surface. He was able to cling to the side of his diving tender, but rather than pull him onboard, the diver's linesman tried to remove his faceplate. Fortunately Horst was still clutching his diving knife and managed to strike the unfortunate linesman a hefty blow, that made him realise that with the face plate removed the diver's air would escape, and with all the lead weights and boots he would sink like a stone. After getting onboard Horst felt pain and soon discovered that whilst cutting his air hose in the black water he had almost severed his thumb.

Another amusing anecdote concerning Horst was that I had told him that Penguin eggs were rather nice to eat, and of course he wished to try one. Even though it was too late in the season, I did manage to get him a Gentoo penguin's egg from a friend, and asked the cook to fry it. As luck would have it, Horst was having his morning visit to the toilet, so undaunted he opened the cubicle door and I gave him the enormous breakfast common to the German seamen, but topped with a Gentoo egg covering the entire plate. He said it was his best breakfast ever. It's just a shame I didn't have a camera handy. Horst was very photogenic, and was more than happy to remove his 'Elbsegler' hat and jump on it if something had gone awry or not according to plan, and a camera was handy.

We passed Cape Pembroke Light House very early in the morning of the 25th March 1970 and began shortening in the tow. When we were roughly abeam of York Bay, the **Mulus 3** pontoon was transferred alongside the **Varius 2** as a 'hip tow' so that we could pass safely through the 'narrows' and into Port Stanley Harbour. But in doing so the captain, Hans Hertzog, got the two tow wires crossed somehow. I think the fault really lay with poor communication between the bridge and Horst Kaulen, who was supervising the towing winches on the after deck. As is usual in the Falklands the wind increased, and we were closer than was healthy to a lee shore.

After getting sorted out, which seemed to take forever, we were able to get underway again. I had explained from memory regarding the leading marks to steer by on entering the narrows, only to find that both the vertical black and white painted leading masts, known locally as the 'Land Marks', were no longer in position. (Later I was to find they were both still there, but had rotted and blown over and lay partially covered with diddledee bushes). The sun was shining on the town making the red, green and silver corrugated roofs on the houses look very picturesque, and on our port side the iron barque **Lady Elizabeth**, complete with masts and a yard arm, reminded me that I was really home again after an absence of some 10 years.

The **Lady Elizabeth** was built at Sunderland in 1879, and arrived in the Falklands on the 13th March 1913, making passage from Vancouver to Mozambique. She experienced a terrible storm off Cape Horn, and on approaching the Falklands for repairs struck the Uranie rocks and, like so many other vessels from that era, was condemned. She was put to good use as a floating warehouse for over 20 years before being beached in her present location in Whale Bone Cove, better known as 'the bottom of the harbour'. **Varius 2** and the **Mulus 3** berthed alongside the Port Stanley public jetty, which is very close to the Falklands Islands Company jetty. This jetty incorporates another hulk from a bygone age, the **Egeria.** She had put into Port Stanley on the 12th September1872 after failing to round Cape Horn. She was over 90 days out from London with a cargo of coal and cement on passage to Callao, and being considered unseaworthy was allowed to sink in her present position. The **Egeria** is still in use as a warehouse, preserved no doubt by the sheets of corrugated iron that cover her as a roof. **Egeria** was built in New Brunswick as a barque rigged vessel in 1859 of 1,066 tons.

It seemed very strange to arrive back home after such a long absence and the quiet nature and helpfulness of the people was a nice surprise to both the Germans and the salvage team. My mother still lived in Port Stanley at that time, in a typical stone house on Davis Street with tremendous panoramic views of the harbour and beyond, over the ridged stretch of land called the Camber. On clear days Port William could be seen. Sparrow Cove, the resting place of the **Great Britain** could also be seen with binoculars. I decided to see my mother during the lunch hour, and on walking up the steep Philomel Hill, I was stopped by a young boy of about 6 or 7 years old. He said "Are you from that square boat at the jetty"? I replied, "Yes, I was" which seemed to satisfy him, and he continued messing with his cycle. It struck me how unusual it was to hear a child talk without shyness or being warned off about talking to strangers. On reaching our house my mother came to the door, totally composed and said "Hi Lyle, I thought you would have arrived yesterday, was there a heavy sea running?" It was just as if she had seen me only a couple of days previously, rather than 10 years!

My mother told me of an elderly lady who had a chair that was part of the **Great Britain's** original furnishings when the vessel arrived in the Falklands. The old lady let me have the chair for £5, and it is now on display with other artefacts in the **S.S. Great Britain** museum in Bristol. I remembered that at a sheep station (or camp settlement as they are locally known) called Goose Green, a large bell inscribed "**Great Britain**" was mounted on a type of gallows. It was used daily to summon the shepherds and other workers who lived in the large building called the 'cookhouse' that meals were ready, or as a fire or emergency warning to all the inhabitants living in the various houses on the settlement. This did prove to be the bell from the **Great Britain**, and the Falkland Island Company kindly donated it to the project.

After all the formalities had been completed, and we had taken on fresh water and some other stores, not to mention a hangover after a couple of evenings in the Globe Hotel, we left the jetty for Sparrow Cove to see what the **Great Britain** really looked like.   Although it was many years since I had last seen her, my initial reaction was of extreme dismay as to her condition, and I was certainly not alone with my feelings. With not too much trouble we managed to put the **Mulus 3** end on to the **Great Britain's** port side, and the **Varius 2** alongside the other end, with a couple of anchors down to help steady the pontoon and ship from the blustery conditions.

When I had been on the vessel as a boy, I doubt if I realised the importance of the ship, and certainly would have thought very little about the decay and structural damage. We found that the main or weather decking where it existed was completely rotten, and the only safe places to walk, with extreme caution, were on top of transverse and longitudinal beams or the large box section that ran fore and aft each side. The Tween Decks had no decking at all; so placing equipment such as pumps etc was a bit hairy. The focs'l was reasonably intact and the ancient anchor winch was still operable, even after all those years of neglect. Inside the bottom of the ship there was at least a couple of metres of mud and debris that had accumulated over the years. Prior to scuttling, she had been used for storing junk from other ships. During pumping and mud removal we found many interesting artefacts, such as the ornate blue and white porcelain toilet pan that had been the throne for first class passengers many years previously. There was also a small steam compound engine from a tug or large launch, which was discovered well preserved due its immersion in mud for a long time.

The most obvious and ominous structural damage was a huge split in the starboard side. This had been caused by cutting openings in the sheer strake to make a kind of gun port door to enable passage from ships tied alongside in the years that she was used as a floating storage facility. It was also used as a loading or discharging opening. This opening had weakened the hull considerably, and after several years of sitting on the seabed, and with the scouring action of the seabed caused by wave surge in stormy weather, the vessel had twisted slightly. On diving and clearing a way under the ship's hull we found the split extended right through the bilge strake, also the garboard strake, and only stopped at the keel. This really meant the hull was only hanging together by the port side, and no doubt sometime in the future would have broken completely in half. We continued our diving survey with a thorough inspection of the lower hull, and found her to be riddled with wastage holes caused by the action of the weather and sea. This was a swathe of about one to two metres wide and extended the full length of the ship, with the starboard side slightly worse than the port side.

One of the first jobs was to bring down a yardarm that was still swinging precariously from the main mast. Luckily a detachment of Royal Marines stationed near Port Stanley generously assisted us with some of the fetching and carrying whilst setting up the operation. A sergeant volunteered to climb up the mast and attach rigging for us so that we could bring the iron yard down. It was about 100ft long and weighed about five ton. The masts had to be removed for two reasons. The first, weight, and the second that it would assist with stability, not only in the refloating but also for the long tow back to England. The mizzenmast was the first to be lifted. Unfortunately, our home-made sheerlegs was not long enough to attach a lifting sling as high as was required for the centre of gravity, and on hoisting it pulled out of its bed very easily and fell on to the weather shelter we had on deck. Luckily no one was inside, otherwise it might well have resulted in a severe headache for several days.

An amusing thing happened within minutes of removing the mast. At least three Germans and two of our team (including myself), found ourselves delving into the thick mud where the mast had been stepped, hoping to find the coin of the realm that was often placed there before inserting a mast to "bring the vessel good fortune". We never did find a coin; neither was one found after the other two masts were removed. We had never discussed the possibility of a coin, but obviously German sailing ships must have followed a similar practice. To avoid a repetition with the fore and main mast, we hired a local carpenter, Willie Bowles, with his petrol driven chain saw, and cut the masts at the weather deck level. Both these weighed in the region of 20 tons and 4 feet in diameter. It took quite a while to cut through the masts, as they were not from a single tree but made up from about eight tree sections, pegged and strapped together. The mizzen was landed in Port Stanley and put on display in a waterfront area known as 'Victory Green', surrounded by old cannons and a more modern gun that is fired on ceremonial occasions. The mast was not erected, but laid on concrete plinths. During a visit to the Falklands many years later, I was disappointed to see that the mast was quite rotten, because rain and snow over the years had not run off as it would have done if it had been standing.

Stuart Whatley and I started plugging the smaller wastage holes in the hull and making patches for the larger ones. The patches were made with 3-ply with a bolt to go through the hull with a strong back or 'T' piece to secure it in position. We used rubber strips to make a seal, and in some places we followed the practice, used for hundreds of years, of oakum and tallow to help seal the patches. At a rough estimate we must have covered at least 200 holes. In some places the ship's side was so thin we had to be very careful not to enlarge the holes whilst pushing the plugs through. After this task was completed, our attention turned to the vertical damage in the starboard side. We put a call out through the local radio station saying that we could do with some old mattresses to help seal the massive split. The response was staggering. Foolishly, we had not specified that we only wanted flock or stuffed hair mattresses, so although we did receive many of the type we requested, we were left with lots of interior sprung mattresses, that we did eventually find various uses for.

We stuffed the mattresses from the keel to well above where the Salvage Officer said the maximum draft should be. It was quite hard going, pulling the mattresses under the ship, as it took ages before the air would escape, particularly with a few mattresses that were of the rubber foam variety. We put plywood over the mattresses, and similar to the holes in the ship's side, we used hook bolts to hold everything in position. Whilst this was all going on, the other two men from Risdon Beazley's salvage team, with assistance from the crew of *Varius 2*, were drilling holes with a rather antiquated air driven drill through strips of steel over one-inch thick by 30 feet long and three feet wide. These had to be bolted to the longitudinal stringers near the deck edge bridging the split. This was done on the weather deck and both of the tween decks. On drilling the ship's stringers, it was noted that the *Great Britain* was far from a rusty heap of scrap, as the drill bits had to be sharpened dozens of times before the holes were finished. The workers who so many years ago had cut the opening in the ship's hull must have had a terrible job, as it was long before gas cutting was possible, and we could see all the jagged edges where they had used drilling as the method to cut the opening. The engine room bulkhead appeared to be very wasted and we did start applying patches to the numerous holes but very soon realised that it was a pointless exercise, so that meant that there was no compartments at all that could be sealed sufficiently to aid refloating. We then turned our attention to putting a couple of mooring ropes to the shore. This was also difficult, as apart from large boulders there were no good anchoring points. Bill O'Neil decided against digging large holes on the beach to put in some anchor points, due to a shortage of time and resources.

On Sunday 5th April we started up the pumps and as all looked well the *Varius 2* manoeuvred the *Mulus 3* into deeper water and gently let her sink on the seabed, after all the air hoses and bottom valves had been prepared. The pumping actually took many hours before we could see any difference in the water level inside the *Great Britain*. We encountered the usual problems of blocked suction inlets and the difficulty of keeping the engines topped up with fuel. The most exhausting part was having to shift our large pumps. Even though they were mounted on steel wheels we had no firm deck to pull them along, and had to use a multitude of rigging to get them in a better position. When the water did start to go down many more holes appeared that required patching. It was blowing a gale non-stop and the business of getting into the water with patching gear was not at all easy or pleasant, especially on the weather side (starboard) of the ship. At one stage the rising tide actually started to lap over the top of the mattress patching, and Bill O'Neil began to show concern, as this meant if nothing else, she was going to be of a deeper draft than had been calculated.

We had been working very hard and had continued without sleep for two nights or even a decent meal break. It was laborious, to say the least, to get out of our diving suits and scramble on the *Varius* to a sit down meal, so the five of us made do with sandwiches and as much coffee as they could bring us from the ship. The situation was looking quite bleak. The water level inside had gone down considerably, but no movement on the *Great Britain* at all, plus a raging gale was blowing. Bill O'Neil suggested that we should go back on board the *Varius 2*, have a decent meal and a shower, then split into watches in order to keep an eye on the pumps. But he warned us the *Great Britain* should have been afloat by now, and that all our work and efforts may well have been in vain.

We had just sat down to a very welcome German breakfast (enough to keep a family going for a week), when there was a shout that the *Great Britain* was moving. Breakfast was abandoned. We got back on the *Great Britain* via our workboat, to see that not only was she floating, but also was starting to get blown off shore. Our mooring ropes were restricting her movements, but would not hold for long. The *Malvinas*, a standard built 75 foot MFV, fortuitously had appeared with several people armed with cameras. We quickly got her skipper, Chris Bundas, to nudge the *Great Britain* with his bow to check the drift. Our workboat also did its best, plus the small tug *Lively* from Port Stanley was luckily on the scene. All together, with clouds of diesel smoke, we were able to stop her drifting. The *Varius 2* had been unable to assist quickly as she was at anchor close to the submerged pontoon.

Due to the atrocious weather, which was gusting to storm force 10, we couldn't attempt to dock the *Great Britain* over the *Mulus 3*, so the pumps were stopped and we let her take to the seabed again. She was about 30 feet from her grave of over 30 years. The suction on the sea bed must have been broken with the slight rocking movement caused by the gale, and with the ship now in a light condition, was sufficient to help her to float. Had we not been able to respond quickly, and without assistance from *Malvinas* and *Lively*, the *Great Britain* could have gained momentum, and almost certainly would have been wrecked on the rocky outcrops nearby, or drifted completely out of Sparrow Cove to meet her end in Port William. At the time this happened, and probably not until reading this, few people, including some members of the project, were unaware just how near to disaster the salvage of *S.S. Great Britain* had been. To fail on refloating was a possibility, but to float her and then to lose the ship was unthinkable. As the gale did not abate, we decided to take the chance of some rest, and two men would keep a watch (4 hours on and 4 hours off) and service all the pumps. At least we felt confident that we would be able to float her again, and that in itself was a tonic. As is quite usual in similar situations, we were unable to sleep, so we all returned to the preparation of floating and docking after a hot shower and a hearty meal of curried Falkland Island mutton.

We had two days before the wind abated sufficiently. We started up the pumps again on the evening of the 9th April. *Varius 2* had made a day trip into Stanley to replenish her tanks with fresh water and to get a few sundries. The following morning the *Great Britain* was floating nicely. The pumps were coping well with the amount of water that still seeped in from various places that we had so far been unable to trace. With assistance from *Malvinas* and *Lively* we moved without incident to the *Mulus 3*, and manoeuvred between the dolphins, only to find that our draft was too deep to get further than 30 feet over the pontoon. There was no time to argue or try anything else as we had to get back clear of the *Mulus 3* before the ebb tide caught us. This would have been quite a serious situation.

The *Mulus 3* had to be refloated and moved into deeper water. This was done with the minimum of fuss and some nice ship handling from Hans Hertzog and Chris Bundace with the *Malvinas*. We managed to get back to the pontoon early the same evening, but once again the weather had another go at us. This time it was recorded as gusting force 11, even stronger than on the three preceding days. We had no choice but to keep all the pumps running, with mooring ropes on every conceivable protrusion, and ride the storm out. Had we not been so tired the experience would probably have been very exhilarating, to say the least. Strangely, the rudder that was stuck fast with rust at 30 degrees to port freed itself and assisted in keeping a reasonable heading throughout the worst of the storm.

The following morning the wind had dropped sufficiently enough to try again. This time we did manage to get completely over the *Mulus 3*, but we had to shift more mud and debris from inside the *Great Britain* just to get that couple of extra inches of draft. A great deal of diving followed to position the ship's keel exactly over the wooden docking blocks, and to make sure that the bilge keels would meet the side blocks. With the aid of pulleys and chain blocks from the weather deck to the tops of the Dolphins, we held the old ship firmly in position while the tide ebbed, and she settled nicely upright on the deck of the *Mulus 3*. Sometime not long after midnight, there was a frightening sound of a couple of very loud bangs like the reports of a firearm. On investigating, we found that the plates that had been bolted to the stringers to reinforce the area over the split had buckled and a couple of the bolts had sheared. This was particularly encouraging, as it indicated that as the pontoon was taking the 2,000 tons weight the ship was straightening herself back to her original form.

Early on Sunday 12th April the Germans started deballasting the *Mulus 3*, with the divers in full attendance, assisting with the air hoses and operating all the valves that had to be opened and closed to keep everything on an even keel. These valve wheels were not exactly diver friendly, and our arms ached for some time afterward. One end of the pontoon was kept on the seabed as long as possible to aid stability. By mid-day we knew that we had succeeded, as the bow of the *Great Britain* started to rise above the surface, and as she emerged more and more we began to realise the enormity of our achievement.

I doubt if anyone could fail to admire the lovely lines of this old lady as she rose above the water. To me she looked like a clipper or yacht, and to enhance her appearance great sheets of scale coated with mussels fell off. This revealed iron that looked as good as new, especially before it was exposed to the air for long as it then took on a more rusty appearance. Pumping was finished the following day. The historians then reminded us that it was exactly 33 years to the day since she was scuttled in Sparrow Cove. We still had mounds of work to do securing the ship for the short trip into Stanley, as we did not want to take any chances at this stage. We moved several of the Dolphins firmly against the *Great Britain*'s sides, and put a couple of runs of weld at the bottom to hold them in place. There was yet more water that we were able to pump out as we now managed to get inside the double Bottoms. It was very pleasing to note that the split had closed as well as if it had been done mechanically. All that showed was tufts of mattresses protruding. Very little water had seeped through our patching during floating, but of course many holes had appeared that we could not have seen whilst she was sitting on the seabed.

From the distance, and as many photographs show, when the *Mulus 3* was fully pumped out the **Great Britain** totally dwarfed the **Varius 2** and all that could be seen from the port side was the top of the large stern trawler's funnel. On the morning of 14th April all was ready to take the **Great Britain** into Port Stanley in order to complete sea fastening for the long tow back to England. Sadly, what followed was a show of very poor seamanship, and hopefully went unnoticed by all the spectators in the flotilla of small boats and people on every vantage point.

The **Varius 2** had coped well with towing the **Mulus 3** alongside previously, but now, with 2,000 tons sitting on the **Mulus 3**, the draft had increased plus the high sides of the **Great Britain** caught every gust of wind like an enormous sail. Bill O'Neil did not wish to interfere with the towing, as there was a sort of truce between him and the Germans to stick with the tasks they both specialised in. I suggested to both Horst Kaulen and Hans Hertzog that they move the **Varius 2** astern by about 10 metres so that she would be in the best position for this type of operation, which tug masters call a hip tow. The idea is that the stern of the tug is clear of the pontoon or whatever it is handling, giving it the ability to make full use of the rudder and be able to steer. I was told that there would be no problem and they would be able to steer okay.

I went on board the small antiquated wooden tug/launch **Lively** and took a rope from the bow of the pontoon. The **Lively's** sister tug, **Clio**, made fast to the pontoon and we got underway without mishap, and passed through the narrows into Port Stanley Harbour. I doubt if any of us involved with the project, or any one else present in Port Stanley, will forget that special moment with all the cars (or rather Land Rovers) blowing their horns, and the bells from St Mary's and the much bigger Christ Church Cathedral ringing us in. However, we could hardly manoeuvre at all and spent several hours getting no closer to the jetty. All we could do was drop anchor in the middle of the harbour, as the wind had increased to gale force again.

What followed was a scary night. We dragged anchor, and Hans was unable to do much with the main engine due to the fact that we were yawing through 180 degrees, and we were all very pleased to see daylight. Fortunately the wind decreased and we weighed anchor, attached the **Lively** and the **Clio** to the fore end of the pontoon and put the **Malvinas** alongside the port side

Then, albeit terribly slowly due to our restricted steering, we were able to edge our way alongside the Falkland Islands Co. jetty. Had we not had this short lull in the weather the general opinion was that we might well have to head back out to Port William until weather conditions improved. Over the next ten days the **Great Britain** was firmly secured to the **Mulus 3** pontoon. For all this work we had to take on several welders from Port Stanley, some labourers to help with the heavy work cleaning loose scale and debris, driving wedges between the hull and chocks and also to assist us move most of the dolphins again to better positions for bracing.

We were not very popular with the project management team because we had to use cutting equipment to cut fairly large holes through the shell plate at the upper tween deck and weather deck levels to enable us to pass heavy wires and chains round the big stringers. Turnbuckles were used to fasten the chains and wires securely to the deck of the pontoon to help prevent any movement on the long trip home. Whilst the preparations for the lashings were being completed Bill O'Neil, Stuart Whatley and myself spent a full day inspecting and diving on the **Lady Elizabeth**, plus survey dives on the other hulks in Port Stanley Harbour. As the Risdon Beazley salvage team were required for other work in Europe and someone was required to remain with the **Varius 2** in order to report to the Risdon Beazley office if required, I suggested taking on a local seafarer. Kenny Thompson a Falkland Island able seaman and ex-shipmate /school pal of mine suited the role just fine. Kenny was about to return to the U.K.

anyway to resume his seagoing career, and the idea of the long trip appealed to him. Nearing the end of the preparations the **Great Britain** management team organised a cocktail party in appreciation for all those who had assisted in salving the famous ship. The party was held in the bar of a local Hotel, and was a great success. With great difficulty I managed to persuade my mother to attend. I noticed at the beginning of the evening she was trembling and on asking why, she admitted that it was the first time she had ever been in a pub! I guess I had forgotten that Falkland Island ladies did not go in the pubs as a general rule. It didn't mean they never drank alcohol, just that to do it in a pub was not the thing to do many years ago.

Lyle dwarfed by the Great Britain

Great Britain at Sparrow Cove
Both photographs Lyle Craigie-Halkett

We finally sailed on 24th April at about 0900 hours. A large gathering bade us farewell from the jetty and the faithful **Lively, Clio, Malvinas**, and the Royal Marines hovercraft escorted us, plus a flotilla of small private launches. The local air services aircraft made some very spectacular passes over us as their final tribute. In many ways, in spite of the success of the job, it was a very emotional time for the locals, as a great slice of history was shortly to disappear forever from the Islands. For me the strange feeling of elation of a good job, and that I was on my way back to Southampton to my wife and son, mixed with sadness at leaving my birthplace, mother, childhood friends etc, as I doubted very much if a chance to return would ever present itself again.

We cleared the Cape Pembroke Lighthouse at about midday, and the tow was paid out to the satisfaction of the **Varius 2** captain. The sight of the great ship wallowing slowly in the South Atlantic swell is something I will never forget, as at times the pontoon would scarcely be visible, but the **Great Britain** really looked as if she was going it alone.

With perhaps a touch of seamen's superstitions, we all agreed that we thought the old lady really wanted to get back to her birthplace, as during the whole of the operation we were constantly amazed that most things turned out for the best, rather than having enormous set backs as so often happens in the realms of salvage. After four days the gale that had accompanied us died away, leaving a fairly heavy swell, but at least the sea was quite calm. So we took this chance to check on the pontoon with its strange load, so some way was taken off the **Varius 2** and the tow wires adjusted a little.

Being manoeuvred onto the pontoon at Sparrow Cove

Moving from Sparrow Cove to Port Stanley   Both photographs - Lyle Craigie-Halkett

Three of us, with a German coxswain, took the small steelwork boat and hung on fiercely as it was launched through the stern ramp (normally used for hauling trawl nets). After clambering on to the deck of the **Mulus 3** we checked all the lashings, braces etc and found every thing to be in perfect shape. Nothing had moved at all, except a few more tons of mussels and rust had fallen down and was starting to smell quite foul. After being accustomed to the throb of engines, it was very strange and peaceful.

We were now convinced that there was no foreseeable reason why the tow all the way back to England would be anything other than a normal towing job albeit a long one. On returning to the **Varius 2**, we realised it was perhaps a bit foolish to have used this method of launch and recovery in the open sea.   As we approached the stern we could see the rudder at times, and of course the wash from the propeller was not helping. The bottom of the ramp was lifting five to six feet above the surface. Amid much shouting, we attached a hook over the bow gunwale, and then waited until the stern dropped in a trough. The winch driver had to heave full speed on three-ton winch and pull us up the ramp to safety, followed by a stiff drop of rum.

We reached Montevideo on 2nd May 1970. The average speed for the trip was just over five knots, indeed much faster than the trip down to the Falklands. The following two days were spent with further cleaning, lashing, and bracings. We also put in a few more cradles to help support the hull for the other 7,000 miles or so to go. On the 6th **Varius 2** and **Mulus 3,** with the **Great Britain,** left Montevideo for the final and longest leg home. The Risdon Beazley salvage team returned to the U.K. to work on other projects during the time it would take for the **Great Britain** to near her final resting place. Historians had calculated that on her last and fateful trip to the Falklands, the **Great Britain** had averaged 4.5 knots, but on her return piggyback journey the average speed was actually 5.3 knots. The tow was mainly uneventful until the 1st of June. As they approached the Cape Verde Islands, stormy conditions slowed them to almost no headway at all, but most importantly, no damage was done to the **Varius 2** and her charge. The 14th July saw them making good speed again, and passed Madeira on the 18$^{th.}$ They were abeam of Cape Finisterre. Shortly after entering the Bay of Biscay, a RAF Nimrod with a press photographer on board took dramatic photographs, which very soon appeared in a newspaper with the headlines "Grandmother of them all".

S.S. Great Britain, towed by the salvage tug Varius II . Photo Lyle Craigie-Halkett

The **S.S. Great Britain** Project Management team had a very difficult time with various authorities in respect of bringing this type of vessel into the United Kingdom on a pontoon - not to mention all the insurance required to undock her in Avonmouth graving dock, plus the risk of floating her on her own bottom for the last leg tow up the river Avon to Bristol. All this was not really the concern of Risdon Beazley Ltd, but what did concern us was the seemingly silly attitude of the Immigration authorities when they got wind of the fact that there was a Falkland Island seaman on the **Varius 2** (Kenny Thompson). Kenny was being paid by Risdon Beazley and was to leave the **Varius 2** on arrival and then continue in the employment of Risdon Beazley Ltd on their salvage vessels. As Kenny was born in the Falklands, he required a work permit if he was to remain in England, but as that had not been applied for, and he was on a German ship, he was refused entry. Kenny had been to the U.K. several times before on vessels belonging to the British Antarctic Survey, and whilst those ships were in the U.K. for the Austral winter the crews signed off and could go wherever they wished. It was pointed out that Kenny had family living in Oban, Scotland. Also that his ancestors were born in the United Kingdom two generations previously. This did improve the situation a little, but nonetheless he was on a German ship entering British waters. I am not sure who came up with the ludicrous solution, but as the small convoy neared the Pilot Station the work boat from the **Varius 2** had to take Kenny, complete with his kitbag and personal effects, and put him on the pontoon. He then had to climb on to the **Great Britain** and thus he was allowed entry to England, as a British seaman on a British ship. It took several months before Kenny Thompson managed to see the funny side of his entry into Britain, as he could be credited with being the first able seaman belonging to Brunel's famous ship since 1886! Captain Hans Hertzog had a bit of a problem as he had been requested to slow down so that Jack Hayward, who had financed the project, would be able to take aerial photos of the convoy passing Lundy Island. This was not at all easy, due to a following wind, and the **Great Britain** acting like a great sail, not to mention that the Bristol Channel has one of the strongest currents in England. However I think the outcome was satisfactory.

The small Risdon Beazley diving/survey vessel **Queen Mother** had met the **Varius 2** in the South West approaches with equipment that would be required for the next phase of preparing the **Great Britain** for her last trip on her own bottom. **Queen Mother** seems a very strange name for a salvage boat, the reason for this was that she had previously been a pilot boat, and was actually launched by H.M. The Queen Mother, and one of the conditions of her sale was that the name would not to be changed. It had caused a few funny moments, such as when one of the crew was returning to the ship in Gladstone Dock Liverpool after a pub-crawl. The dock police on the gate asked the usual question "What ship do you belong to?" "**Queen Mother**" was the reply. He was told there was alternative accommodation available for smart asses, and had to wait until a list of ships in dock had been studied before sending him on his way. Not long after acquiring the **Queen Mother**, we were searching for the wreck of the Elder Dempster ship **Apapa,** which had been torpedoed on November 28th 1917. A Panamanian registered cargo ship pestered us for several hours requesting a pilot for Liverpool. They had obviously looked at an out of date Lloyd's entry, and seen that the **Queen Mother** was a Pilot Vessel.

The **Varius 2**, **Mulus 3** and **Great Britain** arrived at Avonmouth during the morning of 23rd June 1970. The tow was released and a local tug, the **Sea Challenge**, took over the responsibility of bringing the pontoon and load into dock. As we entered the Royal Edward Dock, the **Great Britain** was welcomed back by all the ships in dock sounding their hooters. I doubt this was pre-arranged, as for the couple of minutes it continued the noise increased until it was just about deafening. In spite of the docks being closed to sightseers, every vantage point was packed with press photographers, reporters and the general public trying to get a photograph.

We moored the **Mulus 3** in a lay by berth as a ship was currently occupying the graving dock. We had quite a lot of work to do preparing for floating her off the pontoon. The major job was to cement over the patch covering the split in the Starboard Side, so Bill O'Neil requested a large amount of quick setting cement, which was promptly delivered. The trouble was that we had to hand carry the cement across a gangway and then down almost vertical ladders to the bottom of the ship, and then had to really go like fury as the cement was setting so quickly. On completion of our job, there was more than half the load of cement still tumbling round in the lorry. When we told the driver we didn't require any more, he said we had to have it all as he had no place to take it, and it must not be allowed to set in his lorry for obvious reasons. After a few heated moments he just tipped the lot on the quayside and sped off. The following day a couple of workers had to be hired to remove the mound of cement that had set solid, using jack hammers, which took several hours. On July 1st all the loose equipment, such as the masts, were removed from the deck of the pontoon. A further strong steel plate had to be welded over the split at the insistence of the people responsible for the tow to her final destination in Bristol.

Horst Kaulen had flown over from Hamburg to oversee the floatation. We had quite a fright during the operation, caused by a sticky valve in the *Mulus 3* due to trapped air, and she suddenly took a Starboard list, causing the *Great Britain* to rear over to Starboard. Meanwhile the trapped air was rushing out from the port side bottom valves of the *Mulus 3*. The press photographers just about caused a stampede on the dock edge, trying to get a good shot of the air escaping, but as soon as the compressor was stopped so did the escaping air. I dived and managed to free the faulty valve and after a few hours the *Great Britain* was safely afloat without assistance, except for occasional pumping to keep her totally dry inside.

Two of us split the night between us by keeping a close watch on the ship, and of course keeping a keen lookout for new leaks. But I am proud to say that she was reasonably sound; the small trickle of water seeping in was no more than on many ships I have worked on, but we had to keep alert. Additional portable pumps had been placed throughout the lower hold, and our big salvage pumps were primed and ready for any eventuality. A platform was erected with scaffolding from side to side to act as a bridge so that the pilot would be able to keep a good watch on the tugs and bends in the river. Once again the weather took a hand in the schedule, and in spite of the riverbanks being lined with photographers and sightseers alike, the tow up the Avon had to be postponed due to the wind gusting force five to six. It was a great disappointment to the many people who had travelled a long way to see the spectacle of the *Great Britain* being towed to her final resting-place. British Rail had organised a special train from London that was to be stopped at the Avon Gorge as the ship went past. Whether they had time to cancel the bookings I never heard.

Even though our main concern was to watch every nook and cranny for any sudden inrushes of water, we took furtive glances of the world outside, and could not believe the great numbers of people everywhere watching our progress. It was later revealed that many people had slept in their cars overnight in order to see the spectacle, and it was later estimated that 100,000 people turned out to watch the *Great Britain* being towed to Bristol. It was quite an emotional trip, especially passing underneath the Clifton Suspension Bridge, another of Brunel's masterpieces. In 1844, outward bound from her builders, she had of course passed the same place, but that was before the bridge had been built. The foundation stone of the bridge was laid on August 27th 1836, but the bridge was not completed until December 1864.

On arrival in Bristol we berthed in Y Dock to await the next suitable spring tides, which were just about two weeks away. This was to make sure that the *Great Britain* could pass over the sill into her permanent dock, which incidentally is the same dock that she was built in. We had to trim the *Great Britain* by the head to bring the stern up enough to clear the sill. Using a rubber water filled bladder, giving a weight of about fifty tons placed in the bows, did this. We finally squeezed into the Great Western Dry Dock during the evening of the 19th July 1970. By chance it coincided with her being launched from the same dock on the 19th July 1843, for no other reason than that it was the only suitable predicted high water.

Prior to the tow from Avonmouth through the river Avon on Saturday July 4th, Bill

O'Neil had been told by the Southampton office to ensure that all the Risdon Beazley team were suitably attired in clean Risdon Beazley coveralls etc, as there would be a good deal of press coverage. Bill did not have coveralls so he gave £20 to a person closely associated with the team (although now deceased and should remain nameless), to buy him a white coverall. It was several hours before the person reappeared, obviously having had a very liquid lunch, clutching a plastic carrier bag and being assisted by a taxi driver, who was demanding his fare. The following morning was still a bit windy, but the dock the great ship occupied was required that day for another vessel, so the decision was taken to proceed. Shortly after leaving the dock, Bill O'Neil put on his new white coverall and commented "Not too bad, but a bit short in the leg." However, on turning his back to us, everyone burst into laughter as 'Kellogg's Cornflakes' was emblazoned across the back. Needless to say, he had to keep a jacket on for the remainder of the day.

The Duke of Edinburgh visited the ship during the final docking. We found it rather disappointing that he said little to Bill O'Neil, the salvage officer, and gave us the impression that he thought it was only German Salvors who had salvaged Brunel's vessel and brought her back to Bristol. (Perhaps he had not been sufficiently well briefed). The Risdon Beazley involvement was now at an end, and after the ship settled on the chocks we gathered our equipment together and returned to Southampton.

The S.S *Great Britain* was credited with many firsts, and she now has a few more to add to that list. The first vessel having failed to round Cape Horn to be salvaged from the Falkland Islands. The first ship of more than 1,000 tons to be salvaged on a submersible pontoon. The longest tow with that type of load by a Stern Trawler (this record still stands). The actual salvage was achieved in nothing short of record time, unfortunately no one other than professional salvage operators would appreciate this fact. I pay a visit to the *Great Britain* practically every summer, and it is very gratifying to see how she is sympathetically being restored to her former glory.

I would like to dedicate this as a tribute to Bill O'Neil who sadly passed away several years ago.

Lowering the mast and 'that' crack   *from Lyle Craigie-Halkett's collection*

Chapter Nine   The Varne Wrecks 1971 - 1973

During the second week of 1971 a maritime disaster occurred in the English Channel near the Varne Bank. The people of Folkestone and Dover, who witnessed wreckage being washed ashore, plus the sad remains of seafarers who lost their lives in the cold and treacherous currents of the English Channel, will remember it for a very long time. The newspapers, quick as usual to award a morbid title, named it 'Death Alley'.

The Panama registered Texaco Petroleum Tanker **Texaco Caribbean,** 20,545 tons and 175.21 metres long, was built in Kiel by Kieler Howaldswerke in 1965. It was outward bound in ballast from Terneuzen in the Netherlands to Trinidad to load her normal cargo of clean oil for a return trip to Europe. During the night of the 11th January 1971, the **Texaco Caribbean** was in collision with the Peruvian registered motor cargo vessel **Paracas**. The **Texaco Caribbean** exploded violently, no doubt due to her not yet being gas free in the cargo tanks. The severity of the detonation caused many windows to shatter in Folkestone. The tanker sank by the head, causing the fore end to shear off after coming in contact with the seabed. The remainder of the vessel was still buoyant, with the stern well out of the water. It had a crew of 30, of whom eight lost their lives, including the Captain. 19 crewmembers were rescued by the Norwegian motor vessel **Bravour**, and soon after transferred to the Dover lifeboat. Other ships in the area saved three others. All 22 were taken to hospital.

The last sight of the Texaco Caribbean   photograph Charles Cooper's collection

The **Paracas** was not badly damaged in the fore end and did not sink, nor were any serious injuries reported. The casualty was towed by the 1940 built Tug **Heros** belonging to the West German Salvage Company Bugsier-Reed und Bergungs A.G. to Hamburg for discharge and repairs. The Netherlands Dock and Shipbuilding Company in Amsterdam built **Paracas** during World War Two. She was launched in 1940 as a motor ship of 9,481 tons, 520 feet long and a beam of 63 feet, but due to hostilities was not completed until 1943. When peace was restored in 1945 she began trading for her owners, Nederland Line, under the name of **Celebes**, and continued to fly their flag until 1966. Naviera Maritima Fluvial S.A. of Callao purchased the ship and put her under Peruvian registry with the new name of **Paracas**. At the time of the collision, **Paracas** was on passage from Peru to Germany with a cargo of fishmeal and fish oil.

The following night, 12th January 1971, a second calamity occurred. The motor cargo vessel **Brandenburg**, outward bound from Bremen to Jamaica with a general cargo, struck the stern section of the **Texaco Caribbean** and ruptured her port side, causing a gash that was eventually found to be about 30 metres long. The **Brandenburg** quickly foundered about two miles away. A fishing boat fortunately rescued 11 out of her compliment of 32 crew. Seven bodies were taken from the sea and the remaining 14 were unaccounted for. **Brandenburg** was built in Lubeck for the Hamburg-Amerika Line in 1951 as a general cargo vessel G.R.T.2,695 tons length 110.37 metres. The company had recently merged with Nord-Deutscher Lloyd and **Brandenburg** was operated under the banner of Hapag-Lloyd.

On the 14th January 1971, the Risdon Beazley Marine diving/ survey vessel, **Queen Mother**, sailed from Southampton for the site of the recent shipping disasters. She was under orders to survey the wrecks with divers and to plot the positions correctly, but most importantly, get accurate depths over the top of each piece of wreckage. Being January, the winter weather quite often prevented us from leaving the shelter of Dover Harbour to continue with the work. As with most areas not far from sandbanks, rough seas stir up the sand/mud, making underwater visibility virtually non-existent. The owners of the **Texaco Caribbean** awarded Risdon Beazley the contract. We were to enter the accommodation and watch keeping areas of the tanker to search for and recover any human remains. On enquiring why we were to concentrate on the Tanker and not the cargo vessel, we were informed that it was probably due to the fact that Italian insurers were reluctant to award life insurance benefits unless a body was produced. It all sounded a bit gruesome, but may well have been true.

Initially we were groping round in visibility reduced by the recent storms to less than one metre, and some days it was absolutely black. We tried using a thermal cutting lance that had recently been developed for use underwater; it was called a Kiri Cable, closely resembling a coil of 12mm wire rope without a rope heart. Oxygen fed through the centre kept the flame going, which in ideal conditions could pretty well cut through anything.

We only had part of the equipment, so it meant igniting the lance on the salvage ship and as the diver was descending the shot rope to the wreck, this 'thing' was fizzing and spluttering like a malfunctioning Catherine Wheel. Needless to say, it had to be continuously fed so that us divers arrived on the wreck complete with the limbs etc we started out with! The lance quickly proved impossible to use in black water, not only because of the danger of getting severely burnt, but also to get maximum bottom time, we had to leave the surface in the last run of the current before it stopped completely. After a short stoppage the current then turns to run in the opposite direction and increases velocity. The diver must surface regardless of what he is doing before the current builds up too strongly. We reverted to taking lump hammers down to the wreck, and the big accommodation windows of the Tanker could be shattered with a good bang. With surface demand diving equipment, minus bale out bottles or inflatable lifejackets, we could wriggle through the windows to grope around the interior whilst the second diver could tend the air hose and telephone cable from the outside.

It is difficult to describe the sort of feeling one gets when searching in black confined spaces for bodies. A part of you hopes that you don't locate any, whilst the other part of you knows that that is what you are being paid to do, and that there are bodies unaccounted for and every effort must be made to locate them sooner rather than later before they become decomposed. I found one body in the tanker mixed up with his bedding and other debris in his bunk, so at least his death must have been instantaneous. We found two further bodies in the wheelhouse, one of which was actually trapped behind the ship's wheel. We were unable to get into the lower accommodation due to lack of space caused by internal fittings such as carpets, cupboards, jammed doors etc. Also the portholes were too small to gain entry. Over the ensuing weeks a few of the victims' bodies were washed ashore from the wrecks.

During a break for bad weather we were sent to survey a wreck on the Goodwins, off Deal. For once it was an easy wreck to locate, as the masts were still standing high above the surface, in fact the masts were used by the local fishermen as navigational mark, also it was used as a subject of interest to boats taking out day trippers in the summer months. We were not surprised when a bit of a fuss erupted after our salvage officer instructed us to cut one of the masts down during our short time on the site, but as the wreck and contents belonged to our company there was nothing that could be done. The wreck was the American ship **North Eastern Victory**. She had run aground on the Goodwin Sands during Christmas Eve, 1946 and broke her back in the process.

The Risdon Beazley converted hopper **Foremost 18** salvaged more than 1,200 tons of lead from this wreck in 1950. Two shallow drafted landing craft were used with massive airlifts to remove the sand. The other cargo of grain was also vacuumed away to expose the lead, which was then lifted by divers. As there is a considerable balance of lead remaining, we surveyed the wreck to find out if another attempt was worthwhile. Needless to say, the water was totally black, and the wreck was covered with marine growth, including some very tasty mussels. It was decided not to work the wreck again as the lead price was very poor, and there was even more sand to remove than there had been 21 years earlier.

We returned to the Varne Bank as soon as the weather moderated sufficiently for diving. The underwater visibility was excellent, and we were able to complete the body search and recovery within a reasonably short time. We were also able to make very detailed survey dives on the **Texaco Caribbean** and **Brandenburg**. The missing bow of the Tanker was located at this time. In good visibility, diving on the **Brandenburg** was very interesting as her deck cargo of Ford County Class Tractors were still in position on the main deck lashed with chain. She also had many cars; the majority were Ford Capris.

Working on cargo ships is always much more interesting, as one is never quite sure what will be found next. Whereas Tankers are very repetitive, and apart from the usual ship's fittings, there is nothing much to keep both divers and topside crews excited in anticipation of what may appear next.

We stopped work on the 26th February due to foul weather and spring tides that made diving time so short it was hardly worth remaining on site. I was able to return to my home in Southampton for a few days. On the evening of the 28th February, whilst listening to the radio, I heard that at about 20.00 hours another ship had sunk in the vicinity of the Varne Bank. I sensed that the ship had strayed inside the wreck buoys and struck one of the wrecks.

Early next morning I was on my way back to Dover to prepare for another wreck search. We quickly learnt that the recent sinking was a Greek registered cargo ship called the **Niki**. She was going down the Channel with a cargo of railway lines from Dunkirk to Alexandria, and was presumed to have run into one of the submerged wrecks. 10 bodies had been recovered from the water by the Dover and Dungeness R.N.L.I. lifeboats and landed at Dover. The **Niki** had a crew of 21, plus the wife of the chief Engineer. There were no survivors from this latest tragedy.

Niki was built in 1956 by A.G.'Weser' Werk Seebeck, Bremerhaven and was named **Carl Meetzen** for the shipping company of Carl Meetzen Schhiffahrt und Handel G.m.b.H. of Bremen. She remained under that ownership until about 1969. Her length was 292 feet, beam 42 feet, depth 24 feet 7 inches and her gross tonnage was 2,425 tons. Her new owners were Compania Anomima Naviera Orinoco'Cano' who renamed her **Perija**, and she then flew the flag of Venezuela. She did not remain in that ownership for long as by the beginning of 1971 she was flying the Greek flag and her port of registry changed to Piraeus. It was quite a strange coincidence that the three casualties were all German built.

The weather was still very bad on the 1st March, however we sailed to the wreck site from Dover to see what the conditions would be like out there. On arrival we could see the top five or six feet of the **Niki**'s mast; she was clear from the other wrecks, but not far away. I dived down her mast and as we guessed, she was perfectly upright. The visibility was nil, and I couldn't even see if my lamp was switched on or not. There was nothing that could be done further. Judging by her being upright and fairly close to the **Texaco Caribbean**, there was no doubt that she had ripped open her bottom on the shallowest part of the wreck, which was the stern of the tanker, and sank very quickly.

The following six days were unworkable, due to blizzard conditions combined with rough seas and the anchorage in Dover was quite crowded with small vessels seeking shelter. As soon as the weather abated sufficiently we sailed to the site but were unable to moor over any of the wrecks due to the rough seas. Another diver and myself jumped from the survey ship, the **Queen Mother**, into the sea near the stern of the **Texaco Caribbean**, as this was the safest place to dive, and with the water being so shallow over the wreck the visibility was reasonably good.

It didn't take us very long to prove that the **Niki** had struck the tanker within a couple of metres of where the **Brandenburg** had also ruptured herself. There was absolutely no doubt about this, as by this time we were very familiar with the **Texaco Caribbean**, especially the after section. It was a bit hairy getting back on board the **Queen Mother**, but the captain was an ex-tugmaster, and could handle our little ship better than any of the other captains in the company.

Risdon Beazley Marine was then awarded the contract by Trinity House to disperse all the wrecks to give at least a depth of 21 metres at low water spring tides. At that time it would have been impossible to salvage the wrecks intact. The costs would have been prohibitive, with the unpredictable weather, strong currents and short diving times.

Cutting wrecks in liftable sections with chains from floating sheerlegs was a proven method but only feasible in sheltered waters. The method used for cutting the Russian Submarine **Kursk** with subsea winches and cables studded with Tungsten Carbide Chips was not developed at that time, and may have been too costly to use anyway.

The personnel of Risdon Beazley Ltd were not novices at cutting shipwrecks in a clinical fashion rather than just blasting. This was thanks to many years of working on shipwrecks in both deep and shallow water to recover valuable commodity cargoes, plus dispersing wrecks that had been sunk in estuaries or harbour approaches as blockships, or by enemy action, and occasionally from normal shipping disasters.

Risdon Beazley Ltd mobilised two of their coastal salvage vessels to commence work on the wrecks, besides the survey diving ship, **Queen Mother**. The two nominated ships were the **Topmast 18** and **Topmast 20**, both identical ships. They started life as Naval Mark 2 L.C.T.'s (Landing Craft Tanks), and later converted for Risdon

Beazley Ltd to perform a multitude of salvage jobs. Risdon Beazley also owned a third similar craft, the **Topmast 16**. She was on permanent contract work with their coastal salvage vessel **Lifeline**, servicing heavy moorings for the Ministry of Defence.

Both the **Topmasts 18** and **20** had reasonable accommodation for a crew of about 16. The tank deck had been converted into a focs'l space with the decompression chamber and diving stores. There was also an explosives magazine that could hold about three tons of submarine blasting gelatine. Abaft that was a very good-sized cargo hold that stored spare moorings, grabs and other hardware. An additional engine room had been installed aft of the hold to supply power for all the winches, diving equipment and domestic requirements. When the vessels were under way, rather than working over a wreck, small generators in the main engine room supplied electricity.

The crew's accommodation was between the new engine room and the original engine room, plus the officers had very acceptable cabins above the main deck in the bridge section. Both ships had a six point mooring system and very sturdy workboats for towing out the mooring wires to the Risdon Beazley style conical Buoys. A heavy derrick was situated amidships, enabling the ships to operate an excellent grabbing system, which was operated totally by one person.

Most of us preferred the **Topmast 18**, as she always seemed to be a happier ship. It may have been due to the fact that all her winches were electric, whilst the **Topmast 20** was supplied with low-pressure hydraulics and was very noisy indeed. So much so that it was impossible to communicate normally whilst the system was running.

It took a very special shiphandler to get the best manoeuvring out of the **Topmast**s, mainly because they had retained their original propulsion, which was fixed pitch twin screws both turning in the same direction, unlike conventional twin screwed vessels. The business of screwing the vessel round by one astern and ahead on the other just didn't work. Several captains used to conventional vessels never really got the hang of it, but there were a few who could handle the ships very nicely. It was pointed out that the ships were really designed to make one important voyage only, and that was to get tanks and trucks across the English Channel and ashore as quickly as possible.

The **Topmast**s **18** and **20** laid six-point moorings round the **Texaco Caribbean** and **Brandenburg**. The **Queen Mother** laid a pattern of four moorings round the **Niki**.

The first task was to remove bunkers from the wrecks. Only the **Brandenburg** had fuel remaining of any quantity. We tapped into the Docking Plugs and let the oil float to the surface through a 6-inch hose, then assisted by a pump, loaded the oil into bowsers placed in the holds. During the early weeks we did inadvertently release trapped oil, and by today's stringent standards would probably have caused a fuss, but I believe it was generally known that we were working in congested shipping lanes, and to a certain extent a blind eye may have been turned towards small oil slicks.

The salvage vessels then commenced cutting the wrecks with explosives. Slack water periods are generally of a short duration, except on the very best Neap tides in the Dover Straits, so the three ships had to work in complete harmony. Rivalry existed of course, but that only enhanced the work that was being done. Divers, usually working alone from each ship, would commence diving as the current eased and performed their predetermined tasks. Generally, the dives would be to lay explosives and return to the surface in order that the ship could be pulled clear of the wreck by at least 200metres before detonating the explosives, and to be as far away as possible from the strongest shock waves.

On arrival at the safe distance from the wreck, the vessels would all liaise with one another to make sure that other divers were clear of the water before detonating the explosives. The ships then heaved themselves back into position for 'another run'. In good conditions three 10 minute dives were possible in a slack water period, but as the work progressed and we had to go to deeper depths, only two runs of explosives were possible. Several miles away a vessel from a small salvage company was working on other wrecks. We were unable to communicate with their ship, and quite often we felt the thud underwater when they detonated their explosives.

We later found out that the other ship was using an enormous amount of explosives at one time, attempting to squash the wrecks into the seabed, rather than our method of cutting into sections and removing with lifting gear, followed by laying the sections on the seabed nearby. In fact, we later got the job of completing a couple of the wrecks that they were unable to complete, simply because of our different methods of working and the fact that the *Topmasts* could lift very big sections of wreckage, and the ship they had had no lifting gear to speak of at all. The other advantage that we had was that, unless it was spring tides, we could continue working with our three ton cactus grabs removing scrap and debris all day, whilst the other operators could only work at slack water periods with divers. During spring tides we generally took the ships into Dover, as the slack water periods were too short to do any meaningful work, and those who were able went home for a couple of days break.

A strange phenomenon occurred not long after starting blasting on the *Brandenburg*. One evening as dusk was approaching, we had pulled clear and detonated the explosive. As the usual water disturbance appeared (usually about a minute in that depth), something large appeared to jump clear of the surface of the water. Unsure of what it could be in the approaching darkness, we launched a boat to investigate. Some thought it could have been a dolphin whilst others thought it was some part of the wreck. The current was quite strong by the time the launch was able to get clear of the mooring wires and chase after the object, but not long afterwards returned to the ship with a large inner tube from one of the tractors. The gas from the explosive must have somehow released the inner tube from the wheel, and of course it would expand quickly as it surfaced, causing it to appear to leap out of the sea. This happened several times over the next few weeks but did not give us the same kind of surprise.

Over the ensuing summer months we had several near misses with ships. The most significant was a U.S. Aircraft carrier **USS Forrestal**, launched in 1954 displacing 59,000 tons and 331 metres long. She was heading directly at our location at full speed. Our three ships were all sounding 'U' on the foghorns (you are standing into danger). The two light vessels nearby were also sounding their horns. Eventually she did veer off, but we believe only because we were on her course heading. The Americans gave us a good wave as they passed, no doubt thinking that we were wishing them 'Bon Voyage'. Had this enormous ship struck either of the wrecks, the only solution would have been to build a lighthouse on the top of it!

Another strange incident occurred during an afternoon dive on the *Brandenburg*. We were alone, as the other two ships had been sent to other jobs. I was working in quite poor visibility on the seabed, laying explosives alongside the hull, when I could hear a ship approaching and asked my linesman if he could see a ship fairly close. He replied that on the surface the visibility was perfect and it was flat calm and no ships were to be seen. I questioned him again, as the noise was increasing. He informed the bridge, who confirmed that there were no ships anywhere near our location. By this time the noise was so great that I could feel the vibrations through the water, and the linesman could even hear the noise on my telephone. I was a bit nervous about what to do exactly, but realised there was nothing I could do, except finish my task and return to the surface. By the time I arrived on the surface the noise had just about diminished. The only explanation was that without doubt it was a foreign submarine, as the Royal Navy would observe notices to mariners and would keep well clear of our area. I expect that if we were detonating a charge just as the submarine passed the Hydrophone or Sonar operator would have had a severe headache for a couple of hours.

Brandenburg was also responsible for giving me quite a fright during a dive in very bad visibility. I had finished my task and was making my way back to the shot rope (the line from the salvage ship to the wreck), when I found that my diving hoses had become fouled. I had to trace them among the loose scrap, and by this time the current was starting to run. Eventually, I found that the hoses were tangled in a large piece of shell plate that was standing up unsupported, and was quivering with the current against it, plus a slight surge from the swell above. With my lamp I was able to see that somehow the air hose had passed through a rivet hole. I really thought I was imagining things, but as I was studying it the rivet hole sprang open via a hairline split to the edge of the plate, and I quickly jerked my hose out. As the tide was running so strong by this time I had no choice but to let go from the wreck and make for the surface, without returning to the shot rope.

I surfaced on the opposite side of the ship to the diving position, and was streamed out like a flag. The linesman had to get assistance to pull me against the current, and then with my help, keelhaul me under the ship and back to the diving ladder. He then had to quickly remove my diving harness so that I could run to the Focs'l and climb into the decompression chamber. On the Varne wrecks the dives were often deeper than 100 feet, so surface decompression was required on most working dives, depending on the deepest depth recorded during the dive, plus the all important time factor of leaving to arriving back at the surface.

My personal favourite was the early morning dive. If the tide was due to be slack, it was a bit of a shock to the system to plunge into the cold waters of the English Channel at 0400 in February or March with a very thin wet suit and ordinary plastic working gloves. After the dive was finished, a couple of hours in the decompression chamber dressed in the old fashioned Naval submarine style woollens, with a mug of coffee and a bacon sandwich put through the medical lock, usually followed by a doze, was better than working on deck in the early mornings, especially if the weather was dismal.

In the decompression chambers, the sound of the explosives was quite loud, but it was always a relief to know that it had detonated. A misfire is a problem, because the position where the explosives are placed must be avoided until the reason for the misfire is known. We were very proud of the fact that our team never had one misfire. If there was not too much other noise on the ship, the grab could be heard working in the wreck. It was a strange sound, something like rattling ball bearings in an empty can.

In Risdon Beazley Ltd we always used the British Naval diving tables and procedures. These had been in use since the company was formed, and in all the time the company operated no serious diving accident had occurred, with the exception of a fairly serious bend (decompression illness) not long before the final days of working wrecks in the waters of the United Kingdom.

Contrary to what many people thought, the Varne wrecks were not blasted to pieces (this would be impossible anyway). The wrecks were cut systematically into large sections. Practically all our explosive cutting charges had been removed from the boxes, then formed into sausage shapes and tightly sewn into hessian. In this manner they could follow the contours of the material to be cut. Generally, if the underwater blasting gelatin we used was not in direct contact with metal it would not cut. To enhance performance it was better, if possible, to make sure that the charge was laid on clean plate rather than debris. Also, if possible, it was better to lay scrap on top of the explosive to help force the blast into the steel or material to be cut.

On some wrecks we did use boxes lashed together, but this was for a totally different reason. It was to help weaken the wreck before opening the decks for cargo recovery. Our opposition used to lay large amounts of explosives in a heap on top of the wreck, then use a rubber boat to detonate. The result was generally a big mess of tangled metal and occasionally we had to go to those wrecks to complete the clearance with our grabs. We found it a more difficult job, rather than working on the wreck from the outset.

After cutting, the sections were lifted with the grabs or slung with lifting chains, and laid as flat as possible on the seabed. Legislation existed as to the amount of explosives to be used at any one time, because the shock waves travel along the seabed and can cause damage to harbour installations and buildings near the shore. But we had no need to exceed the amount agreed on, otherwise the salvage vessels would have to completely leave the mooring pattern before detonation, rather than heave a couple of hundred metres clear of the wreck on our moorings. In this way, we could return for the next run of explosives within minutes. In the movies any underwater explosives always erupts into a gigantic geyser. This should never happen unless the explosives are sitting on top of a very shallow wreck. In actual fact, the less evidence on the surface means that the explosives have done a good job and the gasses have been concentrated in a confined area, rather than just coming to the surface.

When working the **Brandenburg**, our first cuts were on the seabed against the hull, and the same on the deck side. Cutting was then concentrated on the uppermost shell plate (Port side). The wreck was lying on her Starboard side. The ship's Port side was removed, then the decks were cut from internal bulkheads and, with explosives on the underside of the deck, they were then forced outward to lay with the beams uppermost on the seabed. For most of the ship's length the ship's bottom was treated in the same manner. Sometimes, if the current was running in a direction that would help, we would wait until the velocity of the current built up before detonating the charge; this would also help push the cut material over.

The stern section was still standing in one piece, and I took down a double length explosive charge, measured carefully by the salvage master. This was inserted through a porthole and dangled through a cross alleyway in the crew's accommodation. The porthole was then closed and hooked with a welding rod to keep it as tightly shut as possible against the electric firing cable.

After I surfaced, the ship was then pulled clear on the moorings, and the charge detonated. There was practically no sound transmitted into the decompression chamber (where I was by this time), and the guys on deck said there was hardly even a ripple of shock wave on the surface. It was not until the following day that I was to inspect my handiwork. The result was that the stern was completely opened like a sardine can and practically flattened, thus not requiring any further work. All this was thanks to the many years of experience by the salvage master.

Cargo also had to be removed from the **Brandenburg**; most of it was never brought to the surface as it was ruined by immersion. We grabbed and then released it clear of the wreck to make space for working inside. The cars looked in pretty bad shape after a few weeks, but the tractors still looked as good as new. They could quite easily have been cleaned and the electrics renewed. The engines could have been running within hours after flushing the engine blocks with a special dispersant and lubricant that we used if a ship was refloated not long after sinking. We were told that because of insurance the County Class Ford Tractors were not to be recovered.

On one occasion a loaded 10-foot container had to be removed. We had no idea of its contents, so it was brought to the surface and heaved clear of the water too quickly, making the doors burst open with the water still trapped inside. The contents were millions of T-shirts. Hundreds drifted away and we learned later that many beachcombers in Folkestone had no need to buy T-shirts for a very long time. All the crew of the three salvage vessels took as many of the T-shirts as they wanted. The remainder were dried and used for wipes and rags for a very long time. Unfortunately, due to the washing machines working overtime on the ships, we ran out of fresh water in a couple of days and had to go in to Dover to top up again, much to the despair of the Salvage Officer.

One other thing I remember about the cargo was the large amount of Bols products. Plastic cans full with sweet smelling liquor, boxes of labels, and bottle tops, even the bottles all going to Barbados to be bottled and presumably imported back into Europe. It was tempting to sample the liquor, but for sure it was contaminated, and even if not it would not have done us divers much good, not to mention the other crew members who mostly came from the Hebrides and the Shetland Islands, who have been known to enjoy a drink at times.

We had been asked to look out for the safe from the master's cabin, and we did manage to find it, quite a long time after cutting open the bridge section, and brought it to the surface. Apart from a small amount of mixed coins and some documents that were ruined, a load of Deutschmarks still in bundles fell out. I have forgotten the value, but certainly several thousand pounds worth. The bundles were put in our boiler room on pipes and ledges to dry out for several days, and not a single note was taken by any of our crew. The money was eventually returned to the ship's owners, Hapag Lloyd, who as far as we were aware never even bothered to thank us.

The centre castle of the **Texaco Caribbean** was upright, and we cut the whole bridge section, lifted it with a bit of a struggle and then placed it on the seabed. As I unshackled the lifting chains I thought what a perfect haven for fish it would be, as it resembled a large bungalow. I would love to see it after all these years as I expect many species, including conger eels, will be occupying it.

Apart from the vast size of the tanker, it was relatively straightforward to disperse the wreck to the required depth of 70 feet, at the lowest astronomical tide or L.A.T. The usual method of charges on the seabed was first used, and then vertical cuts in the shell plate to meet up with the bottom cut. We soon found that the bulkheads did not require as much explosives to cut them, so we sliced the explosives in half lengthways and were then able to cut twice the length in a single dive as we could when cutting the hull. The main difficulty was recognising one part of this ship from another, especially in poor or zero underwater visibility. If near superstructure it was easy, but on the tanks or the ship's side everything looked or felt the same.

If we had been away from the wreck for some time for bad weather, or our moorings had dragged, it was impossible to quickly tell which side of the wreck you were on. She was an all-welded vessel, unlike riveted ships with plate laps and plate butts that you can feel, and get a good idea of exactly where you are, or which way to go. We devised a simple but perfect solution, and that was to have knotted tails of polypropylene rope placed on the deck edge over the tank transverse bulkheads. The tails of polypropylene floated, and the number of figure eight knots corresponded to the number of the transverse tank bulkhead you were on, plus, just to make it even easier, we used red 32mm polypropylene for the port side, and of course green for the starboard but of 16mm polypropylene to give a different feel. If it was totally black then only the feel of the cordage would let the diver know of his whereabouts on the wreck.

Generally on the first dive there would be at least one-metre visibility, but needless to say, after the explosives had been detonated it was usually black, unless the work was taking place high on the wreck rather than internally or near the sea bed. Sometimes the visibility near the Varne Bank could be fantastic and the diver would be able to see up to 20 feet, but as soon as poor weather approached, causing a swell, it stirred up the shallow sandbanks and would remain black until the weather subsided.

We removed the propellers from all the wrecks, including spares. The **Texaco Caribbean**'s propeller was cast of some strange composite material that I am unable to recall the name of, making the value, in spite of the size, rather less than the normal manganese bronze of the other two wrecks. It was quite unusual for Risdon Beazley Ltd to remove ship's propellers, and certainly the company's salvage vessels working cargo recovery from shipwrecks worldwide never removed the propellers. This was simply because Risdon Beazley would have a contract with the underwriters to recover a certain cargo from a wreck and the wreck's propellers remained the property of the hull underwriters.

The **Niki** was dispersed in a similar manner to the other wrecks, but firstly the mast and Samson posts had to be cut away to enable the salvage ships to moor over the top of the wreck. The national press printed a photograph of our workboat tied to the top of **Niki's** mast, just as I was about to dive with the explosives. The seabed explosives were laid first alongside the hull, just above the double bottom, then the decks were removed. The accommodation block followed this. Internal bulkheads were cut to allow the ship's shell plate to fall out onto the seabed and lastly the bow was cut, allowing it to roll on the seabed, and then sliced with explosives. When the **Niki** was finished all that remained was the engine block and a pile of railway lines laying on the tank tops. This made easy pickings for other diving companies. Within a short time of completion of the Varne wrecks dispersal and our departure a ship working out of Folkestone had recovered the railway lines and landed them in France. It was doubtful if they had a contract from the cargo underwriters.

Wreck Clearance is worth a mention, as it is a very important feature in any wreck dispersal operation. The wrecks were cut to a predetermined depth, previously agreed between Trinity House and Risdon Beazley Ltd. This was known as the clearance depth. Whilst cutting was in operation we would have several points on a wreck that were measured exactly for depth and then used by the divers as a reference for cutting other portions.

Our instructions were not to cut more than three or four feet deeper than was required, as this usually meant extra work, not only in cutting but also more material to remove. Most importantly, if a wreck was dispersed, for example, 15 feet lower or deeper than required, it was quite possible that the wreck would never have to be touched again. If the wreck was required to be cut down some more in the future for deeper drafted vessels to pass safely over the top, the contract would be for tender again, and we may well get the job. Also the company would have all the records of work done previously.

When the Divers and Salvage Officer were satisfied that the wreck had been dispersed to the required depth, we would make a check ourselves by having a cargo derrick salvaged from one of wrecks slung horizontally beneath the salvage ship and then move the ship over the moorings. Normally two divers would be sitting on the derrick, and if it came into contact with wreckage a marker buoy was tied to the offending piece and would have to be dealt with later. The derrick had to be adjusted every 20 minutes or so in accordance with the tidal range. This was painstakingly done by an ex-naval hydrographer and in some instances the captain.

Dover was used as the standard port for tidal references, and the ship would be in touch with a representative ashore, who would in turn be watching a tide meter on one of the harbour walls. Trinity House would be informed that the wreck was ready to be officially swept for clearance and one of their ships would appear, usually on spring tides if it coincided with flat calm conditions. Trinity House vessels used chains hung vertically over the ship's side and the bottom of each chain had spun yarn (tarred marlin) attached.

The vessel would then go up-tide from the wreck and be allowed to drift over the wreck site, with constant adjustments to the chains in accordance with the tide gauge at Dover. After passing over the wreck the chains would be pulled up, and if the spun yarn was intact the wreck was declared as cleared to the required depth. If, however, the spun yarn was broken, the wreck would be declared as 'foul' and the contractor would have to find the part of the wreck that was still standing too high and remove it. The French used a similar method for the wreck clearance we did off Le Havre and Dunkirk, except they used seizing wire rather spun yarn.

The Varne wrecks took about 18 months to complete, but during that time some divers would have to go to different locations for other important salvage work. Accordingly, one of the salvage ships would be employed elsewhere for a time, but the main work on dispersal never stopped, except for spring tides and adverse weather conditions. We had become regular visitors to Dover, and if the weather was poor all three salvage ships would be either in the anchorage or, if the weather was particularly bad, we would 'lock in' and moor alongside. We had a very good relationship with all the Port Authorities and people associated with shipping, in fact the Harbour Master was an ex-Risdon Beazley captain.

Our association in Dover was marred by a stupid event that could have been averted by the Master of one of the *Topmast* vessels. The Captain and Chief Officer had been together on the bridge late one evening and had seen one of the crew members return to the ship, obviously under the influence of drink. Instead of going to the accommodation, he went to the foc's'l, and after several minutes reappeared and was seen to be throwing some objects from a box far out into the harbour. On inspecting the focs'l, after the seaman had gone to the crews' accommodation, they noticed that the magazine lock had been forced open. The next morning, when informed about this incident, we checked the magazine and found that several sticks of submarine blasting gelatin were missing. The explosives were perfectly safe, and could only be exploded with electric detonators, but the dock police had to be informed, and quite a fuss emerged. I spent two days diving before all the sticks had been recovered, none the worse for their immersion, thanks to the waxy cardboard packaging. The ship had to land the explosives and the seaman was sent to jail.

The seaman, who had only been employed by the company for a couple of weeks, was tried at Canterbury Court. He was Irish, however no political motivation was apparent and it was disclosed that he had some kind of a grudge against the captain. He pleaded guilty but was let off because the evidence given by the witnesses was conflicting. This episode did sour our relationship with the Harbour Port officials for a time and no Risdon Beazley Ltd ship ever entered the inner basin again with explosives on board.

During November 1972 we were contracted to assist the Drill Ship, **Wimpey Sealab**, which was a converted Bowater's cargo ship. Her task was to drill test bore holes for the Channel Tunnel. The work did not go at all well for a start, mainly because it was the first job for the ship and most of the crew were unaccustomed to this type of work.

Her first location was very near to the shore, not far from Shakespeare Cliff. Shortly after getting moored up the weather turned to gale force and she started to drag her anchors. I was requested to dive in a near gale down one of the mooring pennants to see if the anchor was dragging. This was a very silly request, but being on charter we had to do what was requested. The weather was too bad to take our ship, **Topmast 18**, out of Dover's western entrance, so we took one of our heavy launches. The swell was quite bad, with spray blowing over the top of the mooring buoys. I'm ashamed to admit I did jump over the side of our boat, but there was no way I was going to dive down a large wire that was flexing with the weight of a ship on it during a gale. As the gale increased they decided to leave the moorings, but in doing so fouled their single propeller in a mooring wire, and for a time the ship was moored to an anchor by her propeller. The Bugsier Salvage Tug **Hermes** was on station in Dover Harbour, and received an emergency call from the **Wimpey Sealab**. The **Hermes** then towed the **Wimpey Sealab** to Sheerness for repairs.

After the return of the **Wimpey Sealab** we used the small powerful tug **Argus 5,** belonging to our associate Germany company Ulrich Harms, to assist with running moorings further out in the Dover Straits. I was sent to work on the tug initially but after several days returned home. Within a few days the **Argus 5** sunk. She had been towing a heavy mooring wire for the **Wimpey Sealab** when, for some reason, the mooring winch stopped paying out and the tug got beam on to the wire as they had not been using a gog rope to keep the wire in line with the stern. Consequently she was pulled over and remained afloat, laying on her side long enough for the three crew members to abandon ship by life raft, without even getting wet.

With the survey salvage vessel **Queen Mother**, we located the **Argus 5** in 120 foot of water on the 16th January 1973, during a lull in the winter gales. She was sitting upright with the offending wire still fast in the Blake Slip (now called a pelican hook). The visibility was perfect and the German Ensign was fluttering in the current. It seemed rather surreal, as it was only about a couple of weeks since I was actually working on the tug and enjoying the banter with the Captain and crew. With the assistance of my diving buddy we released the mooring wire and retrieved some personal effects from the wheelhouse, to be returned to the crew. Several months later the **Argus 5** was lifted by a salvage sheerlegs and refitted for further service.

Chapter Ten South China Sea Recoveries 1978 - 1980

In April 1978 we had just completed a contract with the Seaford as emergency towing vessel (ETV) on the tow out from Leirvik to the North Sea with the new "Cormorant A" production platform. I was called into the Southampton office and interviewed about the possibility of going to the Far East to survey some Japanese cargo vessels that were sunk during the second world war by American submarines. Extensive research from Risdon Beazley's specialist researchers showed that there was evidence of Malaysian and Indonesian tin having been carried in large quantities on these vessels. The value of tin at that time was the staggering sum of £10,000 per ton, a figure that to date has never been equalled.

On June 10th the Risdon Beazley Hydrographer, Fergus Hinds, and I left Heathrow for Singapore. In Singapore the first task was to visit the vessel **Smit Malacca** to evaluate whether she would be up to the job of searching and mooring over shipwrecks for short periods of time. On first impressions she appeared rather small, but would be capable of mooring with some innovations. The accommodation was quite cramped, however the fact that she had a Simrad hull mounted sonar put her a long way above other possible candidates.

Smit Malacca

Smit Malacca was fairly long in the tooth. She was of Dutch construction and had been built as a small North Sea stern trawler in 1964, and her original name was **Clearwater.** From 1969 The Nederland's Salvage Company of Smit Tak used the ship for survey and diving /salvage work and renamed her **Orca.** In 1977 she was sent to the Far East to do similar work for the associated company of Smit International in Singapore.

Whilst I was concerned with getting a safe diving spread and moorings sorted out, Fergus was busy getting acquainted with the navigational equipment that was hired to assist with accurate positioning. This was known as Decca Pulse 8. Normally one or two operators would be taken to operate the system, but as ours was a fairly secretive mission, Fergus took on the operating himself, so had to be shown the procedures before fitting the gear on board. To complicate matters even further, Fergus entered a permanent error, so that on the off-chance someone decided to copy our positions, they would end up being quite a distance from where we actually were, and have no chance of finding whatever we found and surveyed.

I met the Smit Singaporean divers who had been nominated to join us for the trip and found them to be nice guys and most importantly, very safety conscious. I have remained firm friends with one of these divers ever since. The crew destined to sail with us was very friendly, but a bit concerned that they could cater for us, as we obviously differed quite a lot from the local people they generally had on board.

The captain, Chris Masapatala, was from some remote Indonesian Island and was quite a character. He spoke perfect, if somewhat antiquated English. Chris had a habit of worrying about wearing out equipment if used too much, so consequently he would switch on the 'Hughes Radar' just long enough to take a bearing and switch it off again. Fergus did point out that he was probably reducing the life of the Radar by so many 'on and offs', but it made little difference.

The cook (the most important guy on any ship), was recruited because he had looked after British Naval officers at some time. This guy, although Singaporean Chinese, was about 6 foot 2 inches tall, and wore a proper chef's hat. I am about 6 foot tall and could not stand upright in **Malacca's** tiny galley, so it was no surprise to see this poor guy frequently flexing his back muscles on the deck. As to his cooking, 'impeccable' was the only word that could describe it. It took quite a bit of polite banter with him to have Chinese style meals occasionally, as we could have English style cooking any time.

The other chap I would never forget was Soon, the Chinese engineer whom I had the fortune to sail with again several years later. At that time, Soon spoke very little English, but had quite an unusual sense of humour for a Chinaman. He used to get engrossed when we played Monopoly, as it appealed to his knowledge of money matters. From start to finish of the game he would prompt everyone to 'Buy Hotel' even if the player did not have the means to do so. Another feature of Soon was the fact that he had an extra thumb on his right hand. This was considered to be very lucky for him and his family.

After loading light moorings, diving gear, consumables and fuel, we left Singapore on 16th June for the estimated position of the Japanese shipwrecks. Being a small tug like ship, **Malacca** was a bit jerky, and it took some time to get used to the movement. Both Fergus and I are quite big men, so we had to make sure that only one of us at a time was occupying the floor space of the small double cabin we had been allocated. After getting our sea legs, and having gotten rid of the queasy feeling of a strange motion, I would have lengthy meetings with the divers to explain what we intended doing once the wrecks were located, but omitted telling them what exactly we were looking for, and as usual, the word 'survey' covers a multitude of sins in the salvage industry. The divers did not find out what the main reason of the project was, or at least, not until several months later.

I was quite concerned (and interested) as to what I could expect to find with relation to marine life on the shipwrecks, as my previous diving experience had been limited to Europe and the Falkland Islands, and generally in poor visibility. Sharks bothered me quite a lot as I had never seen one, so I asked what was the best possible thing to do if I encountered one. The divers told me that a shark has a very tender underbelly, and if I went inside the wreck I would not be followed. I took this as being fair comment from people far more experienced in shark infested waters than I was. A few days later I was to question this gem of advice.

The passage took about 48 hours, and we arrived in the approximate position on Sunday 18th June about 1400. The wreck as usual was not in the position that had been recorded, but by 1700 the following day we found a contact by sonar that appeared to fit the size of vessel we were searching for. I wanted to dive as soon as possible, but the chief diver said it was not a good idea because it was getting late in the evening, and by the time we had moored ourselves over the wreck it would be too late. He proclaimed at that time of the day the fish are very hungry, thus creating a dangerous situation, so I took his advice. I dived the following day and confirmed that it was indeed the correct wreck; ' **Engen Maru'** a 6,968 ton no frills cargo vessel sunk by the U.S. Submarine '**Pampanito**' on February 6th 1945. Her position was recorded as 150 miles off the Malaysian coast.

The wreck was broken in two amidships, with the stern section laying on its Starboard side, and the forward portion upright. During this 120 foot dive I encountered more sea creatures than I would have believed possible to congregate in one place. Within 10 minutes of diving on the stern I could actually see the tin ingots, which was the first and only time I have ever seen the cargo that is being sought laying there ready to be salvaged. I was accompanied by the Smit chief diver, but I managed to keep him away from the ingots so that he would not see them and realise that this was what it was all about.

On the following dive to the wreck I took a video camera, wired to the surface to give a picture on the ship which would be recorded, plus I could communicate through a connection on the camera. This all sounds rather sophisticated now, but in actual fact it was an absolute pain to manage because it was very cumbersome, plus the cable was heavy and as stiff as bamboo to try to coil or manage.

The **Malacca** was moored directly over the stern of the **Engen Maru**, my task was to go to the forward section and survey/record what I found. On this dive my companion was a rather nervous Singaporean/Malay guy. He was tasked to look after the heavy camera cable to lessen the drag for me. About 400 feet is quite a long way for a diver to swim with a heavy cable, time was of the essence, as the longer I stayed in the water the longer I would have to spend in the decompression chamber with my companion. We were using a one man chamber, designed to be used in an emergency rather than for every day use, therefore it was very humid and rather sweaty.

The visibility was excellent, and without doubt, the best I had ever encountered diving on a shipwreck. For this reason I was able to stay about 15 feet above the wreck, which gave me a much better field of vision. Plus, the shallower I was able to stay, also reduced the time I would need to decompress. I was well past the point of easy return to the shot rope (rope that was attached to the wreck from the **Malacca**). At no time should divers working on shipwrecks surface freely, as it is a very dangerous thing to do, as the possibility of being swept away is very real, or worse still, to get tangled in the dive ship's underwater protrusions.

I had just passed No 2 hatch when I felt a sharp tug on my camera cable, and looking round to the other diver (about 20 feet behind) I noticed that he was gesticulating wildly and pointing to the deck of the vessel below me. As I turned to look, two or three sharks were lounging on the wreck watching me (so much for sharks do not go in or near wreckage). I thought there is damn all I can do now, if they are hungry and eat divers that will be the end of me. So I had little option but to carry on, much to the obvious dismay of the other diver, who promptly let go of the camera cable and disappeared out of site back to the shot rope. With the extra weight of the cable I had great difficulty in staying above the wreck and its attendant sharks that seemed mildly interested. I completed the survey and noticed about 6 of the same specie of shark laying on the Forecastle deck. On returning to the shot rope my friend was waiting there to help once again with the cable.

There was little point in saying much about the episode after the dive, because the diver probably thought I should get help from the 'men in white jackets'. Over the next few days I broached the subject, only to be sheepishly told that none of them had ever actually seen a shark underwater, and genuinely believed (until now) the advice they had given to me was sound, as they had been told the same story at some time. (In spite of it sounding very nice to be a salvage diver in Singapore, Malaysia and Indonesia, the majority of diving would be in very muddy waters, or in recent shipwrecks that sea creatures tend not to investigate or inhabit for some time).

We started searching for wreck No 2 on Tuesday 20th June, but were rather hampered by poor weather, making life uncomfortable to say the least. Another contact was found on Friday, due to the unsettled weather the current had started to run quite strongly, so diving was out of the question. However we did manage to put a couple of moorings down, and with some difficulty was able to lower the camera in a cage that had been purpose built for the job. We soon found the wreck was far too small, and it had fresh blue paint on it, so possibly a large Vietnamese fishing vessel that may have been a refugee vessel.

We had suspended a weight below the camera. This was to give us an indication of the size of any objects and distance from the lens. The weight was an old chipping hammer head that I had painted white, and it was amusing to see barracuda actually taking a bite at it. Because of the increasing wind and current we dragged our moorings into the wreck and lost both stern anchors.

We resumed searching for four days, and eventually found a large echo caused mainly by the dense column of fish above the wreck, rather than the wreck itself. By this time we were getting low on fuel, water and stores, and besides we needed more anchors, so we proceeded back to Singapore, rolling heavily until we arrived in the Straits of Malacca on Sunday 2nd July. We loaded everything required and sailed again the following evening, and found the weather had vastly improved. On Wednesday 5th the new target had been relocated, and we managed to get moored over it before nightfall.

The first dive to the new wreck was quite difficult as the current was still very strong, plus this wreck was 40 feet deeper, making the seabed over 160 feet. At times it was difficult to actually see the wreck because of the concentrations of marine life, including a few sharks, but mostly barracuda with their seemingly sinister grin. The average size of the barracuda would be near two feet.

During the dive the following day, I confirmed that we had found *Taigyo Maru*, because of a similarity to the other wreck that was a near sister vessel, plus measurements of the hatch coamings. Also, this was a composite vessel as she had been used to transport fuel. *Taigyo Maru* 6,889 tons, was listed as being owned by the well known Osaka Shosen K.K. company. She had been torpedoed by U.S. Submarine *Guavina* on 7th Februrary 1945 about 40 miles distant from *Engen Maru*.

The wreck was standing upright and quite intact. I was able to get inside the dark spooky confines of the after hatches and did notice many blocks or bales of rubber, still buoyant, and trapped beneath the decks. However, on this occasion was not able to find any tin because of overburden (other cargo). As usual I had the camera, and from the bottom of one of the holds looking upwards towards the natural light, I could see a giant Manta Ray, seemingly flying unperturbed about the 'tween deck level. This was probably the most beautiful thing I had ever encountered whilst diving inside shipwrecks, and luckily the guys on the ship could also see it on the monitor as it was recorded. Some time later in Singapore, the film was taken ashore to show to the Smit directors, but on switching it on, unfortunately, most of the film had mistakenly been recorded over with a Malaysian news broadcast!

On our very last day whilst preparing to have a final dive on the **Taigyo Maru**, a fair sized fishing boat was seen approaching from the East. Because of the sun, it was difficult to see. As the boat neared us, we realised that it was a Vietnamese refugee boat, something we were very aware of, but never actually thought that we would ever see. The boat was typical of the thousands of fishing boats seen in Vietnamese and Thai waters, it was about 40 feet long with a central cabin. The difference with this one was the fact that from ever aperture in the cabin (oblong openings rather than portholes) either a head or several arms was protruding, waving bits of rags.

We desperately tried to keep the craft from coming too close, and most of our crew was instructed to get food, canned goods, fresh water, fuel, cigarettes and anything that could help these unfortunate people. The boat hit our Port Quarter heavily, but we would not allow any of the people to come on board as they would easily have overwhelmed us. There must have been at least 100 people on the boat, plus many children and tiny babies; the noise was horrific and distressing.

We passed over everything possible to help with their plight. Unfortunately they were not really grateful, as all they wanted to do was to transfer over to us, and this we simply could not do, even though it goes against every code of practise with saving life at sea. Through very broken Malay/English, one, seemingly more calm than the others, told us that they had been attacked by Thai fishermen, who had robbed them of everything visible, even the boat's compass; we gave them a spare compass.

What really saved the day was Fergus, who has a very good authoritative voice (no doubt from his Naval days). Fergus bellowed to the people to stay where they were, and this made them pause a little. The men on the boat were turning rather nasty by now, and became threatening. One of our divers panicked and ran to the wheel house and engaged the clutch on the main engine. All this did was to create turbulence, because we still had one stern anchor down. This caused mayhem with the refugees, who thought that we were leaving them to their fate.

The mothers threw about 5 or 6 babies into the sea, then jumped in themselves, and not long after this, the husbands jumped in too. While all this was going on, I was slowly recovering our stern anchor, and once free from the seabed we moved clear from the unfortunate refugees. Once we had seen that they had rescued all the people from the sea we took our departure and headed back to Singapore.

Needless to say, this episode shook us all up considerably, especially Fergus and I, but we had no alternative. Had we taken all the refugees on board our little **Smit Malacca** would have been dangerously over crowded. Furthermore, we would not have been welcomed into any country with these people on board. We had to console ourselves that we had given them everything possible from a compass, charts, food, water and fuel to a degree that we had only about 4 days supplies remaining for ourselves.

This gave us a bit of an insight as to what we should expect in the future if we brought a salvage vessel from England to recover the cargo from the two wrecks. We arrived back in Singapore Tuesday 12th July. All our equipment was off loaded and two days later I was flown back to England.

After a break of several days I was sent to Loch Striven to spend some time on the **Lifeline**, and give my opinion as to what could be done to enable her to be suitable for cargo recovery in the South China Sea. **Lifeline** had been deployed on cargo recovery many years earlier round the British Isles, using an atmospheric observation chamber, and if the water depth did not exceed 160 feet, standard diving dress was used (the heavy Siebe Gorman equipment with copper helmet etc).

Risdon Beazley's divers working on shipwrecks had now progressed to using the more mobile method of S.C.U.B.A. Diving with wet or dry suits and surface demand breathing equipment, or for dives of short duration, twin bottles with a regulator. This latter method was only used in good conditions with relatively good underwater visibility and calm seas. A launch or Zodiac type boat would be in the water in case the diver was forced to surface unexpectedly, or became disorientated.

The **Lifeline** had new diving equipment installed in Southampton, which included a Twin Lock decompression chamber with low and high pressure supply. A medical lock that was intended for passing through tablets, dressings or other medical supplies. This lock was also quite useful for passing hot drinks and snacks to the diver. Larger meals had to be passed through the outer or small chamber lock. Medical oxygen plus every available safety device was purchased and put onboard. We would be operating far from a Port with diving medical facilities, and we really had to be covered for most eventualities. At least two divers would have Paramedical certificates.

The **Lifeline** had recently been used to service the Ministry of Defence moorings around the British Isles with her team mate **Topmast 16,** a converted L.C.T MK 2. Most of the work was done over the bow of the vessels in a very similar method as used by anchor handling tug/supply ships that are employed in the oil industry to-day, except that the modern method is to work over the stern. Luckily the heavy derrick on **Lifeline** was still in place but had to be re-rigged for her new role. The slewing had to be mechanised with a winch to pull the derrick in board, and a counterpoise or weight sliding up and down the mast in a guide to pull the derrick out board. For grabbing we utilised the two main hoist winches, normally used on that type of ship for heavy lifting over the bow. The two stern anchors were removed and stowed with other salvage equipment in the hold. The aft winches then had the 36mm mooring wires replaced with 22mm mooring wires spliced into 44mm polypropylene, that in turn would be attached to the mooring buoys with riser wires and anchor chain connected to large stockless anchors, weighing in excess of 3 tons.

The forward moorings were polypropylene. Only these were turned round the twin capstans because of the great length of 44mm braided polypropylene required (roughly 300 meters on each capstan). Storage bins had to be made, otherwise with the ship rolling, coils could fall into the water and lead to a fouled screw.

This method of mooring over a wreck was perfected by Risdon Beazley, and is the only safe way of mooring over a shipwreck or obstruction of any size. Other methods of wires direct to anchors generally fail, as it is extremely difficult to avoid the wires becoming fouled in the wreck or in the debris that generally surrounds a shipwreck. A typical Beazley 6 point mooring pattern was as follows. Each individual mooring consisted of 1 x 3-5 ton stockless anchor, 3 shots (45fathoms) of 2-3 inch anchor chain connected to about 27 fathoms of 32mm internal wire core riser wire, and this in turn was attached to a short length of 2 inch chain with a swivel shackled beneath a conical mooring buoy, that on end would measure about 12 feet with a centre diameter or girth of about 5 feet.

Risdon Beazley had the buoys manufactured in-house to the company's own unique design with internal stiffening. Tests had showed that these buoys could submerge to 100 feet without damage, whereas other buoys of similar size would crush long before reaching this depth.

It is worth mentioning at this point that Risdon Beazley also had two different types of mooring hooks that had been designed and perfected over the years. These would not have been used anywhere else in the world. The hooks were rather heavy, but designed not to become detached if the mooring wire was broken, no matter how heavy the swell may be. The difference in design allowed one type to be slipped by the work boat, tugging a short pennant that released a pin. The other type was very similar in design, but had a small pad eye welded to the crown of the hook with a 14mm wire of about 6-7 fathoms spliced into it. The hook was tripped from the buoy by attaching the end of the 14mm wire to a cleat or bollard and slacking off quickly on the main mooring wire.

The second method was mostly used by the coastal salvage vessels, and the former was always used by **Droxford** and **Twyford**, generally in deeper water depths. To moor the ships to the buoys required good ship handling skills, not to mention the skill of the launchman and bowman, plus attentive seamen on the winches.

The ship would be steaming at about 1 knot with sufficient steerage way and the launch would grab a mooring hook and then go very quickly to the intended buoy. The winch operators had to be very experienced, as the wire was to be let run as quickly as possible so as not to impede the manoeuvrability of the launch. It also had to be kept at an angle, as it was quite easy to snag the wreck, and if this happened there would be a long delay, re-splicing wires if the snagged wire was damaged or lost.

Briefly one of the ship's launches would be lowered over what would be the lee side after the ship was moored. These launches were built very stoutly by the shipwrights of Risdon Beazley and had about 45h.p. Engines. This did vary slightly, depending on what ship the launches were intended for. The weight of the launches was about 4 tons.

To 'moor up' the salvage vessel would have sufficient 'steerage way' to manoeuvre and generally be head to current or wind, the launch would run alongside the vessel grab the mooring hook that was attached to the mooring wire then speed off towards the designated buoy. Very experienced winch operators on the vessel were required to prevent the wire running off the winch too quickly which would easily become foul in the wreck or rubbish on the sea bed close to the wreck, and also not to restrict the launch pulling on the other end.

Normally the head buoy would be the first to be attached quickly followed by the other five. As the ship was being centred over the wreck's position the winch operators would be under instruction from the wheelhouse. With experienced crew this operation could be completed within an hour however I have seen other ships and crews and some using different methods take several hours even the best part of a full day. **Lifeline** could roll on a wet lawn, however it did not take very long to become accustomed to it, unless the weather was particularly bad.

After having seen sharks in the South China Sea, I thought a very important addition would be a shark cage to give protection to the divers. I asked Mr Ralls, who was the engineering superintendent for Risdon Beazley, if the shore fitters could make a suitable cage, and I would supply a drawing similar to one I had seen in Singapore. Mr Ralls answered that there was no need, as he knew exactly what was required, and would see to it personally. Meanwhile, I attended to the other items that needed addressing to load on board the ship before she left the U.K. When the cage was completed, Mr Ralls sent for me to go and look at it and advise the fitters if it was to be painted and if so what colour..

I was dismayed at the construction of the cage. It was at least 3 times heavier than I would have wished, as I only had a 1 ton air winch designated to lift it; and this contraption must have weighed well over a ton. I mentioned that it was very much stronger and heavier than I had expected. Mr Ralls replied that safety for divers was paramount, and if a shark entered the cage there was 'no way it could escape and harm a diver'. I did not have the heart to tell him that the object of the cage was for the diver to be able to seek refuge, should sharks become a problem.

The cage was later reduced in size by the ship's divers, and proved to be very useful as we used it as a lift to and from the shipwreck. Many ingots of loose cargo were recovered inside the cage. In fact one diver, Ken Matthews, would seldom surface after a dive without loading several ingots into the cage. Luckily, the cage never had to be used as an escape route from aggressive or hungry sharks.

Lifeline was slipped at Thornycroft's in Southampton for a bottom clean and paint, plus to have all the alterations required for her new phase of work. I recall talking to a boilermaker who was drilling penetrations through the steel bulkhead below the bridge. He remarked that he had broken just about every drill he had trying to get through the tough steel. I mentioned this to Reg Young, the chief engineer. His reply was that he was not surprised as she was built nearing the end of hostilities, and many plates were armoured. *Lifeline* sailed with mainly a run crew about mid August 1978 for the longest journey of her busy life.

I picked a few divers who I thought would be best suited to work in the South China Sea and, in my opinion, had the best knowledge of ship construction and diving safety procedures. As I recall, the divers consisted of Graham Mann a young fit and hard working diver whom I made diving supervisor, Dave Davis who had been a Beazley diver for quite a long time and Ken Matthews who is probably the best wreck diver I have been fortunate to work with, plus a couple of newcomers to the company.

We took about another 4 divers from Smit in Singapore. These were the most suitable of the divers who had been with us on the *Smit Malacca*. It was quite amusing to note that the Singaporean divers only now realised why we had surveyed the wrecks a few months earlier.

Graham really wanted to use American decompression tables, but I had to insist he use the standard decompression tables as devised by the Royal Navy. The American tables at that time were based on research by the U.S. Navy for the oil industry. I had heard of several accidents with these tables, besides, I was not at all sure that if an accident occurred Risdon Beazley's insurers would be happy with the fact we had suddenly started using American decompression tables without informing them.

The ultra safe Royal Navy tables that we in Risdon Beazley's had used for many years, meant that the divers spent ages decompressing after a deep or very long dive. I personally did not see this as a problem, as we had no shortage of divers, and having a twin lock chamber meant that in the case of an emergency, decompression space was always available, and if both inner and outer locks were in use, diving would be suspended until one became free. This seldom happened, as after each dive a prolonged period of grabbing or the detonating of explosives took place.

As far as I am aware, *Lifeline* had an uneventful trip to Singapore, with two or three stops to take on fuel, water and fresh provisions. *Lifeline* was certainly no ocean greyhound, but plodded along at about 8 knots. However the least headwind or head swell could slow the old lady to 5 knots quite easily. The master of *Lifeline* was Ronnie Bell, who became a friend, and we worked together many times afterwards.

Ronnie was a Scot, and had served his time with S.A.F. Marine, a subsidiary of the British & Commonwealth Line.

Ronnie gave enormous assistance with his excellent navigational skills, and his interest in the type of salvage that we were embarking on. Ronnie was my back up as grab operator, and we shared the use of a German type seaman's cap "Elbesegler". Being a bit superstitious, like most seamen, we had the idea that if the hat was not worn by the grab operator, the recovery rate would be dismal. I am not sure if this was ever proved to be the case or not.

Quite often Ronnie would appear to be getting a bit fed up with the routine, so I would ask if he would like to have a dive. He had taken diving lessons at some time, and never refused. He would very happily remain in the shark cage watching whatever activity the diver would be performing. On completion of the decompression Ronnie would be full of enthusiasm about our work, and often came up with clever ideas to enhance the recovery rate. Needless to say, it was highly irregular, and I expect I would have been severely reprimanded if the directors of Risdon Beazley got wind of the fact that the ship's captain was also diving. Bill O'Neil (Peggy) sailed with us on our first few weeks trip as salvage officer. On our return to Singapore I took over the responsibility.

Reg Young was **Lifeline**'s chief engineer. Reg was a Southampton man, and had spent most of his working life with Risdon Beazley. At least 20 of those years he had spent on **Lifeline**. There was nothing about the ship he did not know; he was able to repair the radar, keep other machinery operating by deftly making pieces on the ship's lathe. Reg was very much of the old school that is sadly no longer with us. Equally at home on a steam vessel (**Lifeline** had been a steam vessel) as on a motor ship, and if I needed a hand to splice wires, that was no problem either.

Although Reg knew the **Lifeline** better than any other person in the world, new rules dictated that the certificate Reg had was no longer valid, and he would have to attend college if he wished to continue with his career. The second engineer, Geoff Colclough, did have a full up to-date chief's endorsement, so that was taken into consideration to allow Reg to maintain his post on a temporary basis, at least. I remember Reg saying if he had to go to school at sixty plus years of age to keep his job he would rather not bother.

Our Bosun on that first trip was Rob Roy, another long term employee of Risdon Beazley. Rob hailed from Leven in Scotland, as his name would suggest. He was a very nice character, not adverse to sinking a whisky or two off duty or ashore. He was a first class rigger, and by virtue of the fact that he had worked for so many years on the salvage and mooring vessels, every conceivable type of wire grommet or lifting wire that was used would be coiled and stored for immediate use. The cook's name escapes me for our first trip, except I recall he was a Geordie coastal cook, and his cooking and baking were first class.

Most of the remaining crew came from the Southampton area, and after the first voyage we did employ more Singaporeans, mostly from Smit International.

Early in October Bill O'Neil, the divers and I flew to Singapore, and after a night in a hotel joined the **Lifeline**. It took us five days to store the ship and get all the equipment ready for cargo recovery. In fact we spent the full time on the passage to location running on the grab and mooring wires. We also resumed a practice that was quite unique to Risdon Beazley, and one that I was very much in favour of.

In those days, all divers had a second string to their bow, inasmuch as they were either able seamen or had engine room experience. While on passage, the divers that had able seamen certificates or similar would work on deck or help out with watch keeping. **Lifeline** did not have automatic steering, so a helmsman was required at all times, usually doing one or two hours at a time. In a similar vein, the mechanical orientated divers would help the engineering staff. This really worked very well, and helped bond the crew together as a unit. Needless to say, if any large scale diving maintenance was required, the divers would attend to that first. The diving supervisor would be permanently attending to diving gear.

On Wednesday 11th October we loaded 3 tons of submarine blasting explosives, about 100 electrical detonators and sailed from Singapore for the South China Sea. These days if 3tons of explosives was required anywhere in the world, I can only imagine the problems and red tape to acquire it. Three tons of explosives was a rule of thumb amount required to remove hatches, decks and shell plate of an average 5 hold cargo vessel, to have it opened sufficiently to expose all the cargo that had been stowed safely for ocean voyages.

I often wondered in later years why it had been decided to mobilise in October for work in the South China Sea. At that time I was not really aware of the seasonal conditions in the Far East, however in the ensuing years when I worked for Smit International South East Asia based in Singapore, I soon realised that the South China Sea is no place to work during the North East Monsoon, roughly September through to January.

The weather generally starts by having quite fresh North East winds of force 4-5 and occasionally 6. When the wind has been blowing from the North East at force 6 over several days, the current will become very strong and the seas quite rough. We experienced very bad weather at times with very rough seas, with high swell no doubt caused by the relatively shallow water.

We arrived at the **Taigyo Maru** area on Friday 13th. The weather was borderline, but we did manage to locate the wreck and drop marker buoys. The following day was slightly better with less wind and swell, but with very heavy rain squalls. We laid our pattern of 6 moorings round the wreck so that we would be facing the North East, and stemming the prevailing weather and current.

The first and most important task on **Taigyo Maru** was to confirm that tin had been carried on the ship. I had actually seen tin on the **Engen Maru** when I dived from **Smit Malacca,** and this was only possible because the stern of the wreck was very broken up either by bottom impact on sinking, or caused by the U.S. Submarine.

The early dives on **Taigyo Maru** was to get **Lifeline** positioned over the stern section of the wreck, so that we could commence removing overburden (unwanted cargo), and look for tin. The tin would probably be on the tank tops in No 4 hatch or either side of the propeller tunnel in No 5.

On practically all wrecks worked by Risdon Beazley, the exact detail of all cargo carried on each particular wreck was known long before a recovery operation was carried out. However, in the case of the Japanese war losses, it was more a result of painstaking research over a very long period. This entailed finding out how much tin was produced by Indonesia and Malaya; how much was thought to be purchased by the Japanese; but more to the point, how much had just been taken. The best our researcher could do was to confirm that in all probability tin was carried on a particular homeward bound Japanese ship, but quantities were very vague.

All available shipping movement records would then have to be checked and cross checked with tin movements to get an idea of which cargo vessel could have been carrying a substantial tin cargo. Research found that even tankers carried tin if required.

I personally recovered tin from the tanker **Eiyo Maru**, built in 1929 by the Yokohama Docks Co. She had been sunk about a mile off the South Vietnamese Coast having been torpedoed by the U.S. submarine Guavina on February 20th 1945. The tin had been carried two ingots deep right around the after accommodation block on the poop deck.

During my work on this tanker a strange but funny story was related to me through a translator. **Eiyo Maru** was reasonably close to shore and out of sight of any lighthouses or largely inhabited areas. At some point local fishermen had found the wreck, and I expect like many of the second world war wrecks near the Vietnamese coast, they were observed by locals as they sank. These fishermen had been able to dive to the wreck (presumably on a single lungful of air) and as the ingots were not stowed inside the ship, many would have been quite visible. I am sure that with difficulty they did managed to recover over 1 ton. Then came the problem of how to sell the ingots. So what they eventually did, was to cover the floor of a fishing hut with ingots and eventually informed the local authority at Vung Tau, whom I believe confiscated the ingots rather than pay a small amount to the poor fishermen who had certainly risked their lives recovering them.

I dived on the **Eiyo Maru** a couple of times to position the small salvage ship. It was amusing to see so many pieces of light polypropylene just appearing out of the sand, like some kind of Indian rope trick. These pieces of rope had been attached to ingots, and then I guess another fisherman diver at a later stage would connect a further rope to the surface, for pulling the ingot up by hand.

We removed the main hatch beams using a grab, guided by a diver, then the grab penetrated through loose general cargo, consisting of many different bagged items such as flour, that was like a very thick paste, fruit, rattan and other produce that was difficult to identify.

The tween deck was reached after several hours grabbing through the narrow confines of the hatch coaming, until the tween deck hatch beams appeared. Apart from the divers checking periodically that the grab was well placed, there was nothing that the divers could do, as by now the underwater visibility was reduced to zero, caused by the activity of the grab.

We continued removing overburden with the grab, but now no chances were taken in case the grab contained tin. In other words, each grab was brought all the way up to the surface to have the contents checked. Previously only random grabs would be brought to the surface for inspection. The grabbing cycle at this depth (surface to surface) would be about 15 minutes.

The first ingot of tin appeared on Tuesday 17th October. Basically, this was enough to alert Risdon Beazley that there was indeed tin in both vessels. Diving was very difficult as a North Easterly current was running all the time. No doubt a product of the prevailing North Easterly wind.

We commenced laying explosive cutting charges to remove the hatch coamings and complete main deck. A normal explosives charge on the top of the decks would be about 100lbs, and if placed correctly, would cut about 20 feet. On strong structural places like corners of the hatch coaming, it was usual to place about 50 lbs, but in a clump rather than a long line, as used for the decks.

I had never seen so many fish killed on any wreck. The sea was literally white with many different species, floating belly up, and of course many other species without a swim bladder, would just remain on the seabed or the wreck.

I was photographed with a giant grouper that had come up with the explosives. It was more than 2 meters long, and the girth had to be over a meter. The mouth was so large a football could easily be put inside it. I am sure we all felt quite sad that so many fish would be killed on a shipwreck with the first few runs of explosives. Most specie of crabs seem to be unaffected by explosives, unless of course they are very close. Because by the time the visibility clears after explosives, crabs will usually be feasting on dead fish and often accompanied by lobsters as well.

Many times in the ensuing months, when the current was not so fierce and the dead fish would float near the *Lifeline*, we witnessed a feeding frenzy by sharks, turning the sea red with blood. All one could see was turbulent water being whipped up by the sharks, and often a black shape would rear right out of the water. We certainly never contemplated diving whilst this kind of activity was going on.

Sea snakes and squid were in abundance, especially on calm evenings when they were probably attracted by the ship's lights. Most of the sea snakes had very attractive markings, which were coloured yellow, red and black. I did catch quite a few and skinned them to use the skins as covers for belts etc. However, the colour faded very quickly and there was always a chance I could get bitten when catching them, so it was a very short lived hobby. Squid and many other species of fish were often caught and cleaned for the cook to prepare a tasty dish, with the smaller red snappers being a favourite.

If the current was not too fierce, some of us did fish in the evenings after work. It was quite interesting to see the variety of fish caught, providing we had not recently been using explosives. It was very usual after getting a good bite to start pulling the catch the long way to the surface and suddenly the rod or line would nearly be pulled out of our hands, and on surfacing all that would be attached to the line was a head. The barracuda could bite off the bodies of substantially sized fish with a single movement. I recall that remora was a funny sort of fish, as on surfacing, it could be taken off the hook and it would stick to a smooth vertical surface as if it was glued. On several occasions sizeable varieties of ray would come up after explosives. When cooked, the wings differed little from the skate we eat from European waters. Another strange phenomena that occurred with the first explosives, were the blocks of rubber, measuring about a meter square, that had been trapped inside the wreck for so many years, and suddenly released. They would nearly pop out of the water as they surfaced. When the first 20 or so bales appeared, we put out the launch to collect them, but they proved very slippery and heavy to recover. It soon became evident that we had no space to stow them, in spite of the fact that they would have been of some value.

Once the main deck of the wreck had been removed, we commenced with the tween deck in the same manner, but put down slightly heavier charges as the extra depth coupled with being in the confines of the wreck, dampened the shockwaves transmitted through the water. The usual distance to pull clear of the wreck to detonate explosives (while still on moorings) was about 600 -700 feet.

After most of the tween deck was removed we commenced with cutting along the sea bed, about level with the tank top, or bottom of the holds. This was followed by vertical cuts so that the shell plate (ship's side) would fall outwards onto the seabed, thus creating a very wide and clear chasm for the remainder of the overburden to be removed and then expose the tin. This method also had the added effect of letting the current run unimpeded through the gap, which in turn would also clear a lot of debris and help improve underwater visibility. We would also take advantage of strong currents to assist with moving large sections of steel plate that had a similar effect to a sail.

Bill O'Neil and I were enjoying an early morning cup of coffee about 0600 on deck one very nice morning. Suddenly the sea around the ship became quite disturbed and rubber started popping up by the thousands. What had happened was that the wreck's side had fallen out by the force of the current, causing all rubber remaining trapped in the after end of the wreck to be released at the same time. Even though we had removed most of the main and tween deck, the side wings fell out with the ship's side. Ronnie Bell later estimated about 1,000 tons of rubber to be on the surface. Luckily we were not in the English Channel, otherwise we would have been guilty of causing a danger to shipping.

The following year a similar event took place on the other wreck, releasing about half that amount, and we actually saw some of the rubber as far away as the Paracel Islands several weeks later.

I found it of interest about 15 years later a wreck I was working on in the Mediterranean also had Malaysian rubber and tin, but in that instance the rubber remained within the wreck, because the water depth was 12,140 feet as opposed to a mere 170 feet in the South China Sea. The tremendous water pressure at half a pound a foot had squeezed every bit of air out of the rubber, leaving it with no buoyancy at all. If any of the rubber did come up in the grab from this depth it did expand a bit when it neared the surface and would float.

On **Hakone Maru** in the Taiwanese Straits a few years later, fishermen had become aware of rubber appearing on the surface, and would stand off near the ship. But when an explosives charge was detonated all hell let loose as they tried to grab hold of as many bales of rubber as they could carry. It was common to see crew members jump into the water and have a bale of rubber under each arm and wait to be picked up by the particular boat they worked on. Many of these boats were quite well kept Hong Kong boats, with green hulls. However they lost all ideas of sensible seamanship on seeing rubber and would run over our mooring wires and often part them or get hooked up by the rudder. At one time I counted 50 boats which stopped us from working. Eventually we would wait until dark before detonating, but generally it made little difference. If those fisherman could only have the patience to wait 15 minutes the strong current would take the rubber well clear of our ship and moorings, but this was not to be.

It was a fairly normal occurrence to see a refugee boat warily watching us late in the evening, and on the following morning at dawn to see it approaching us slowly, usually out of the sun making it very difficult for us to get exact details of size, until it was fairly close. By drawing on the experience of the first encounter with these hapless people, we had one of our big work boats readied at all times with containers of fresh water, canned food, charts, even compasses and fresh fish if we had been using explosives. We did not permit any of these boats to get within hailing distance, but would give them every assistance possible. On one occasion a fairly large boat was more persistent than the average type we encountered. Luckily, when an explosive charge was detonated in the wreck they resumed the course to their choice of destination.

We heard on the World Radio Service that a boat had tied up to an oil production platform or drilling rig about 30 miles from us, and they scuttled their boat. The rig or platform had to stop operations for quite a long time while the situation was addressed. We firmly believed it was a boat that we had intercepted the previous day.

We sailed for Singapore on 20th October to take on freshwater, provisions and fuel; also to let Bill O'Neil return to the U.K. The armature in the main grabbing winch had burned out and needed replacing, or be rewound. We also took advantage of this break to re-rig our derrick slewing system and transfer another winch to the stern.

We left Singapore for the location on 27th October and encountered very rough weather after clearing the Singapore Straits. The passage took us twice as long as usual, thanks to the North East Monsoon, and on arrival at site we moored to just one of our buoys (we had left them at the location) by a head wire as the swell was far too big to consider mooring up.

We managed to moor *Lifeline* over *Taigyo Maru* again on 4th November (my birthday) and continued overburden removal and tin recoveries. Two days later we had to slip moorings for bad weather and continued in this sort of mode for a couple of weeks. Wreck work one day followed by a day or so either hove-to or hanging on to a single mooring. This continued until 18th November when we were told to recover our moorings and proceed to Borneo for orders and discharge.

We had recovered 95tons of tin worth £950,000 so the dear old *Lifeline* had given a good account of herself.

As *Lifeline* was a bit long in the tooth, she had never been fitted with air conditioning. Our cabins opened direct onto the deck. The cabins and mess room below decks were like a furnace. An attempt had been made in Southampton to install some kind of air conditioning but it had failed miserably before the ship even entered the Mediterranean.

Individual units were fitted in Singapore, but they left quite a lot to be desired. For instance, in my cabin the unit was directly above my head, and every time the ship lurched or rolled more than 10 degrees, I was rewarded with a good dollop of icy water, and not being designed for a ship, it rattled like a tin of marbles most of the time.

We arrived in Brunei on 23rd November after a really uncomfortable trip. Captain Roy Martin, who was Risdon Beazley's manager at that time, came out to attend to the details of the recovered cargo, and to get a first hand account of our experiences. This was with a view to a further expedition the following season, and the possibility of another company vessel coming to help recover the cargos that we had discovered.

The Brunei Harbour Master approached Ronnie Bell and I about the possibility of salvaging his launch that had sunk not very far away. We assumed it would be a small fibreglass boat with an out-board motor, so we agreed to see what we could do to help. I took 3 divers in one of our work boats to the location for a survey to evaluate what the easiest method would be. The sunken launch was much bigger than we had expected. It was in fact a twin screw cabin cruiser. Unfortunately we could not get *Lifeline* close enough to have a direct lift, even though the water depth was sufficient. The area where the launch was sunk was congested with all manner of small craft, many of them submerged.

We took every inflatable buoy we could find on **Lifeline** and pulled the buoys inside all the available spaces, to displace as much water as possible, then with one of our 42mm polypropylene mooring lines we circled the craft as no existing bollard or cleat would have been strong enough to take a serious pull, and shackled the rope to itself. The other end we ran up the beach about 600 feet away and attached it to a tractor.

With a bit of arm waving and various changes of direction, the Harbour Master's Launch was pulled to the water's edge. We then had tree trunks laid underneath and resumed pulling until the aluminium and stainless steel boat was high and dry. I guessed the weight must have been in the region of 20 tons.

The Harbour Master was most impressed and grateful, wanting to know how much money he owed us. I said we wanted nothing, as it had all been a bit of fun. The Harbour Master then asked how many crew on **Lifeline**. I replied with the number (about 20 men if I remember correctly). He said he was co-owner of a very large Chinese Restaurant and would like to treat us all to a meal. We actually shut the ship down for a few hours so that everyone could take advantage of this kind offer, plus it would be a great opportunity for all of us to relax at the same time after the work we had done.

I doubt if I have ever had such a fantastic meal. Every crew member was assigned a personal waitress, who did everything except eat the food for us. One diver let the show down momentarily as he asked me what the green slivers of vegetables were on a plate. Jokingly I said "Brussels Sprouts" with that he gestured to his waitress to give him a spoonful of his favourite vegetable, which of course in reality were green chilli peppers. He nearly exploded, and it was not until he had polished off several bottles of Tiger Beer in quick succession, that he was able to resume his meal. I would say that banquet brought a closely knit crew even closer together, thanks to the Brunei Harbour Master.

It was fruitless to attempt further cargo recovery until the North East Monsoon abated, plus there was extra engineering work required to enable **Lifeline** to work more effectively. Not to mention the fact that a good break was due to the crew. We had a very rough run to Hong Kong, averaging about 6 knots due to the head seas and wind, so we were all very pleased to pass Green Island on 5th December.

We had hoped to have the remaining balance of explosives, which was about 2 tons, stored in an explosives barge until we returned the following season. This was not possible, due to red tape and the dubious quality of our explosives, which had become very sweaty. We had no alternative except to put to sea again and go a considerable distance until we found 100 fathoms of water to dump the explosives. To dump the explosives we had to remove it from the wrapping and cut it into small pieces so that it would dissipate in a very short time. Most people get severe headaches with handling this type of explosives, especially when it becomes sweaty. I personally developed a migraine within moments of unlocking the magazine door, and by the time we had completed jettisoning the submarine blasting gelatine, practically every one who was involved was very ill, and it took about 24 hours to return to normal. We took **Lifeline** into the Typhoon anchorage in Hong Kong, leaving her in the very capable hands of the second engineer Geoff Colclough, who had opted to remain with the vessel and oversee the mechanical work that was to be carried out.

Prior to "paying off" I had one of our Singaporeans barter with a scrappie and sell all the non ferrous that had been removed from machinery and various bits and pieces from the wrecks. This came to about £20-£30 each for every person on the ship, regardless of position, and for the lower paid like the messboy, it was a nice little sum to do a bit of shopping with before going home. This practice was continued throughout the South China Sea recoveries. Most of the crew returned to England on 13th December 1978, and the remainder of us a day later.

A few days after returning home one of the Alexander Towing Company's tugs capsized in Southampton water. She was called "**Cherrygarth**". I joined the **Seaford** with a couple of the divers who had just returned home.

We managed to pull her about 100 meters to clear the fairway for shipping to operate normally. We then parbuckled the tug upright and was able to get submersible pumps into her at low water and commence pumping as the tide flooded. **Cherrygarth** was afloat nicely at high water, and was then passed back to her owners, practically undamaged. The **Cherrygarth** had made a very nice finish to quite an eventful and successful year for us, and the company.

My leave was cut short by the disaster at the Whiddy Island terminal in Bantry Bay, when the Tanker **Betelgeuse** caught fire about 6th of January, causing the death of several people. My brief was to dive as soon as possible on the vessel to assess the situation as soon as the fire went out. The water was quite deep. The stern was sitting on the seabed with only the funnel showing above the surface. She had broken her back, but was still attached by the main deck with the fore-end being afloat. I can still remember that the weather was quite foul, and there was a lot of movement and tremendous noise as the tortured steel was moving with the slight swell.

Smit Tak had practically taken over our company, and the intention was to show that, as they had surveyed the vessel (my dive) they were well placed to perform the mammoth operation of cutting the tanker into sections for sinking in deep water, which indeed they did. It was quite interesting in the local hotel, because so many representatives from various salvage companies had gathered to show their interest in the forthcoming salvage operation.

Needless to say, many faces were quite familiar, and to see the various salvage masters and divers talking in subdued tones was amusing, to say the least.

Smit Tak was awarded the contract, and mobilised most of their sheerlegs and salvage vessels to commence operations. I was asked if I could remain, but as I had still quite a bit of leave remaining, plus there was planning to be done for the next trip to the South China Sea, I returned home to Southampton. This later proved to be one of the biggest salvage jobs of its kind ever conducted.

After spending some time in February at our Southampton office, I left for Hong Kong early in March, ahead of the remainder of the crew. The alterations that had been carried out to the stern mooring winch, forward mooring capstans, and derrick slewing arrangement, had been done very well, and there were just a few adjustments needed. Sailing date was fixed for the 20th March 1979.

After we had left the shipyard and gone to anchor for storing ship etc., I was sitting on deck early in the evening and noticed some disturbance in the water near the ship. I thought at first it was a sea creature, but it turned out to be a dog, and it was attempting to claw its way out of the water on to the anchor chain.

We launched a work boat and took a large net on a pole that we used for catching surface fish at night. I managed to net the bedraggled dog, which was totally hostile and not at all grateful. It was similar to a large sort of spaniel. The poor dog turned out to be totally wild, and where he had come from was a mystery. He soon became accustomed to being tied up, and I kept him under the decompression chamber on the boat deck. Initially I had a work glove on a broom handle that I used to stroke him with. He could tear the glove to pieces in seconds. Very gradually he started to trust me, and I would spend long periods sitting close to him, perhaps reading a book or talking to him.

After a few weeks I released him from the leash, and his place was outside my cabin on deck, where he would sit for hours gazing at the door, and then get excited when I appeared. Eventually he would leap up into my arms.

He tolerated other crew members, but would not befriend anyone, and bared his teeth if approached. He had a special dislike for Asian people, and would go mad if a Chinese Junk came close, or a whalla whalla boat. Even the Singaporean divers he eyed with disdain. The next time we went to Hong Kong I am sure he knew somehow I was leaving the ship, as he had whined and whimpered for a couple of days previously. Geoff, the 2nd engineer, had offered to look after Chink whilst I was on a short leave.

I returned from leave to find Chink really pleased to see me after about 5 -6 weeks absence. Geoff said he had no trouble with Chink, except when local boats approached **Lifeline**, but he was never able to befriend him, and for the first couple of weeks he never left his place outside my door. He proved to be the best watch dog imaginable.

Before sailing I went ashore one evening with some of the crew and returned about midnight. I was really angry to find that Chink had attacked an officer. The guy in question had known Chink ever since I had rescued him, and after a few drinks with some others who did not go ashore either, he had decided to make a fuss of Chink, as he said he could not understand why the dog did not trust him. Chink had badly bitten this guy's hand, and put deep scratches in his arm.

I had no alternative except destroy Chink later that night. I find it difficult, even all these years later, to recall that poor animal who trusted me, and I guess all I achieved was to give him a few happy months.

After loading explosives in Hong Kong, we set off for the location of the two wrecks. My instructions from Southampton were to do as much cutting and preparation work on both wrecks as possible, so that the latest addition to the Risdon Beazley fleet **Ashford** could start recovering tin as soon as she arrived in the South China Sea. After a very pleasant 6 day passage to the location, we arrived on 26th March. We laid our moorings the following day and resumed cutting and recovering tin from the **Taigyo Maru**'s No 4 hold.

The refugee situation had not altered. We generally attended to one or two boats a week. During the spell in Hong Kong the **Lifeline** had been painted grey in the hope she could resemble a naval vessel from the distance (albeit a very strange one). We even flew the Vietnamese flag to try and give us breathing space for the bigger and faster refugee boats.

About this time we noticed what appeared to be a fairly large Japanese or Korean fishing vessel. The fishing vessel was not actively fishing, and on closer scrutiny we could see an "A" frame over the stern, several zodiac type boats and lots of binoculars trained on us. It was a very uneasy feeling. Gradually, after several days, the ship came closer and we tried contact with V.H.F. and Aldis lamp, but got no reply. Whenever we brought tin to the surface I had to lower the grab inside the ship's hatch to unload, so that they could not actually see what we were bringing up.

Eventually I did manage to talk to a crewmember who spoke in very broken English. We spoke via the V.H.F. and I asked him what they wanted. Firstly I was told that we were working illegally on Japanese war losses, and then there was a request to board us to discuss the matter. I agreed for two persons only to come on board, as they wanted to bring six or seven. When they did come onboard, I noticed the two guys looked as nervous as we felt. They asked what we were doing. I replied that we were surveying shipwrecks. They said they wanted to send several divers to look for human remains, to which I replied that it was not possible, besides there were no remains to be seen. They asked to see our contract. Luckily they seemed not to be able to read English, as I think it was probably little more than a letter of intent. They left very dissatisfied, and saw nothing of what we were doing. Several hours later they were obviously trying to pinpoint our position, and ran across one of our mooring wires, which was really annoying, as we had to completely stop work. After that final episode they disappeared and we never saw them again.

With about 50 tons of tin onboard we had to proceed to Borneo to rendezvous with the **Ashford** in order to pass on information about the wrecks, also take on fuel, water and provisions and, the most important reason, was that one of the divers had an ear infection that needed medical attention.

We arrived in Muara on the 11 April, discharged cargo, bunkered and provisioned the **Lifeline.** **Ashford** arrived in Muara on 16th April. Ronnie Bell, and I went on board to meet the captain who was new to Risdon Beazley to swap notes and pass information about the situation of both wrecks.

There were only a few of the crew who had been with the company for some time, one of these was Don Jones, who was Risdon Beazley's leading chamber diver for many years. Simon Hartog was also on board as a diver. Simon had worked with us for several years dispersing war time wrecks in Dunkerque, Le Havre, and the English Channel. This made quite a good combination, as Don could use the atmospheric observation chamber whereas Simon and the 3 or 4 other divers could perform any soft suit diving. Hopefully they would not need to use explosives to any extent, as the majority of cutting had already been done.

I tried to explain to the Master our strategy with regard to the Vietnamese Refugees and was more or less told not to bother, as he had also been at sea for many years, therefore could deal with the situation should it arise. Two weeks later we had a R.T. call from **Ashford** saying that a large refugee boat had come alongside and required some medical attention. The refugees piled on board **Ashford** (about 30 I think) and their boat sank shortly afterwards. Needless to say this caused enormous problems, as **Ashford** tried landing them in both Singapore and Hong Kong but was denied permission and spent many weeks steaming, rather than recovering the remaining cargo.

While in Muara four of the crew asked permission to take one of the workboats to a pretty little island that could be seen from our berth for a picnic and swim. They took some refreshments promising to return about 1800 hrs. On looking with the binoculars, I could see the boat was high and dry. We had no tidal predictions, so had no idea when they would be afloat again. Three of us went over with the other boat with a radio and food. The stranded guys elected to remain until the boat floated, but would remain in contact. The boat had not floated by the following morning, and appeared even higher up the beach, so we had no alternative but to take **Lifeline** close ashore and pull the boat off with our heavy winches. The guys had suffered a spooky and sleepless night. They could sense people moving undercover of the foliage, plus the crickets and other creatures kept up an endless chirping.

One of the men had dropped off to sleep with his back against the launch, which they found was swarming with soldier ants. He knew he had been bitten but didn't really feel much until later in the day back on **Lifeline**. The acid from the ants injected into the poor guy's back started to weep, and he was covered in lumps of about fingernail size. He was unable to sleep for about two weeks, and caused us a lot of concern. The only relief we could give him was to keep daubing his back with bicarbonate of soda. His job was a watch keeping engine room rating, and after his watch he would come to the wheelhouse and take the helm for a couple of hours at a time. He said the concentration helped keep his mind of the discomfort and pain. Very gradually the lumps subsided and he suffered no after effects.

We resumed working on **Engen Maru** and were finding considerably more tin than was thought to have been on board. One afternoon I decided to take a dive. This I did frequently, but without any routine, as it kept everyone on the ball, and more to the point, gave me a first hand account of progress. As conditions were so good, I decided to take a quick look at the forward hatches and to avoid lengthy decompression, kept as high as possible above the wreck. The midships superstructure had racked over to the Starboard side, and as I passed over it, I noticed a body amongst the wreckage. I took very little notice, as it was not long since we had worked several wrecks sunk in European waters, where many people had been lost. It was a couple of minutes before I realised that the remains could not possibly be a crew member belonging to the ship, as it was clothed and not fully decomposed. All I could think of upon reflection, was that it was possibly the remains of a Vietnamese refugee, as many of their boats did founder.

A couple of days after returning to the **Engen Maru**, we assisted a very large Vietnamese refugee boat that had at least two hundred people on board. I felt that these people were slightly different, as they used different tactics, and did not try to get close to **Lifeline**, and were really grateful for the fuel, water and provisions we gave them. Several months later they acknowledged as being helped by what they thought were Australians.

We now had recovered well in excess of tin thought to be loaded onto **Engen Maru**, so every ingot was now a bonus. I decided to take a closer look in the No1 hold and photograph sea snakes or fish if the visibility was good enough. One of our divers had taken a quick look about a week previously, and said there was no overburden or cargo visible.

I lay on my stomach to get a good shot of some barracuda that was attacking another fish, and I could sense a slightly uneven surface, and on fanning away the covering of silt with my hand I realised there was at least one layer of tin (later proved to be two). The tin was as it had been stowed in Singapore or Penang, and had not moved when the ship was torpedoed, so it was completely flat. 100 tons was eventually recovered from this hold.

The armature for the main grabbing winch had burned out again, and to make a jury rig would have made grabbing painfully slow and difficult, therefore we slipped our moorings and headed for Hong Kong. We had over 130 tons of tin onboard, so the company was more than happy to get it sold while the price was at an all time high. We arrived in Hong Kong on 14th May after a nice trip. The faulty armature was rewound and the tin discharged. A Typhoon had passed through the area we had been working in, so our departure had been quite timely. After heavy testing of the newly rewound armature, we weighed anchor and proceeded to the explosives anchorage, to take back the explosives that had been temporarily stored while we were in the normal ship's anchorage. We left within a couple of hours for our location.

The trip had been very slow due to South Westerly winds and a slight head swell. It took very little wind and sea on the nose to slow poor old **Lifeline** to about 4-5 knots. The reason for easily losing headway being that the configuration or construction of her stem, which was designed for lifting heavy weights and very large anchors, was flat rather that the normal ship shaped stem, and would only cut through the water like an ordinary ship in near flat calm conditions. Several years earlier the **Help**, which was a sister to **Lifeline**, had been working in Canadian waters. For the long passage, a false bow had been bolted over the flat stem, which actually increased her speed by one knot in average head seas.

On 29th May we arrived back on site, and discovered that two moorings were missing. We located both moorings with grapnels within 3 or 4 hours, thanks to the excellent navigational skills of Ronnie Bell. One buoy had broken adrift, caused by a broken shackle. The other still had the buoy attached, but was squashed beyond repair. We were unsure what could have happened to this mooring. It may well have been run down by a passing vessel (not uncommon) or sprung a leak during the recent Typhoon. Cutting and grabbing was soon resumed, and looking back through my records, I see we had recovered 26 tons of tin in 3 days. We often found traces of other substances, like various ores, that we would have no idea of identifying. I recall once getting a message to keep a look out for zirconium. I asked what does it look like? I never did get an answer, I wonder why.

On those particular wrecks, tin ore, tin concentrates and other various concentrates were contained in rubber sacks, which was quite ingenious, as the rubber was also obviously part of the consignment. It was thought not worth the time and expense to have these various packages analysed and tested for purity, because over the years sand and silt contamination would have made assessing difficult.

Our main winch let us down again on 12th June, but with over 100 tons of tin in our hold we didn't feel too badly about it. Because there was so much tin exposed we made use of the other heavy lifting winch to lift some rather large sections of the wreck's shell plate from the seabed (about 15 tons), and cover the cargo in case unwelcome visitors like the Japanese returned to the location during our absence. Their ship seemed not to have grabs, and there was no way divers could recover except manually, and certainly they would not be able to lift the plate without cutting it first.

We lifted all our moorings and had a rare rendezvous with **Ashford**. The refugees could be seen watching us from her foredeck. At least **Ashford**, being a fairly large ship, had space enough for them.

A fair trip to Hong Kong was enjoyed by all onboard, and we arrived on 20th June. The cargo was discharged and **Lifeline** was anchored in the Typhoon anchorage so the winch could be repaired again, and everyone could take a mid-season break (unheard of in the past years of Risdon Beazley).

I returned to Hong Kong about the middle of August, followed not long after by the divers, officers and crew. The new equipment that had been fitted to the ship was tested. This included a new H.P. diving compressor. The existing one had been having difficulty in keeping up with demand. Prior to taking on some explosives, our divers spent the best part of three days cleaning the growth from the ship's bottom, to help with our speed. The antifouling paint had about worn off, and the growth of barnacles, weed and a small shell like crustacean had been quite prolific.

We finally left Hong Hong waters at 1400 on 29th August 1979, and had a fair, but busy trip to the location. There was a lot of work to be done, such as running on and splicing new mooring and riser wires, new grab wires were carefully run on the grab winches and all diving equipment tested. Because there was so much to do, the divers were not able to help out with watch keeping duties this trip.

We laid our normal pattern of 6 moorings round the forward end of **Engen Maru** on 7th September, moored over the wreck, and removed the two pieces of shell plate that was covering the cargo. By 2000 hrs we had recovered 3.5 tons of tin, not a bad day's work by any standards.

On the 11th our good fortune was marred by a diving accident, that could easily have been a fatality, had it not been for the professionalism of our diving team. I had sent two divers down in the normal manner. One being on surface demand, complete with telephone communications, and his buddy using S.C.U.B.A (h.p. air cylinders on his back). The task was to make a quick survey and move some loose ingots that were out of reach of the grab, in places like under bilge brackets or corners of bulkheads. The surface demand diver requested emergency recovery procedure, and to stand by to resuscitate the second diver on surfacing while preparing to go into the decompression chamber.

As the cage surfaced, the standby diver jumped into the water in case the unconscious diver was not properly inside the shark cage. The shark cage was always used as a lift to get the divers to the wreck and back, rather than swim down a rope attached to the wreck (shot rope). In doing so, the standby diver badly gashed his knee on the side of the cage, which required a few stitches. The diver was semi-conscious on surfacing. Thanks to the experience of the surface demand diver and his Royal Naval training, he had pushed the demand valve into his buddy's mouth, and was able to get some air into his lungs within seconds of it happening.

While I was assisting with the decompression tables that the divers required, the crew was busily letting **Lifeline** go from the moorings so that we could proceed to Singapore. At that stage we had no idea what had happened on the wreck, or if therapeutic treatment or a diving doctor would be required. Not to mention the fact that by this time we had not had a chance to have a good look at the injured knee of the standby diver.

It remains a mystery as to what really happened. It may have been a slight case of narcosis (better known in the old days as raptures of the deep), which is basically inert gas like nitrogen that becomes narcotic under pressure and can render a diver incapable of logical behaviour. I eventually locked in to the chamber with both divers to clarify the situation. The diver who had got into trouble had not the slightest idea of what had happened, his first recollection was us bundling him into the decompression chamber.

The surface demand diver, who had undoubtedly saved his buddy's life, stated that moments after reaching the safe distance above the wreck with the cage (about 2 meters) they both left the cage to commence work. The lead diver noticed that his pal had stopped for some reason, and on looking at him, realised that his mouthpiece was out of his mouth. He was obviously in severe trouble, and was not attempting to retrieve his mouthpiece. The lead or surface demand diver thrust the mouthpiece back into the unconscious diver's mouth, and dragged him the short distance back to the cage for a faster than usual recovery to the surface.

I have deliberately not named these divers, as I would not wish to embarrass them. I do know that the diver who had the near miss, is now in a senior position in the oil industry. As it turned out the standby diver who had injured his knee required medical attention, but the other diver was perfectly o.k. within a couple of hours. We did however continue to Singapore, just in case there happened to be delayed shock or after effects. From that time on, all S.C.U.B.A. divers on any job I was involved with, had to wear a strap, so that the mouthpiece could not fall out or be easily removed.

We off loaded 64 tons of tin ingots in Jurong (Singapore) and proceeded back to sea on 20th September, arriving at the location early on Saturday 22nd, and was moored up by midday. We had recovered 91 ingots, which equalled about 4 tons, before stopping work for the day.

The weather was starting to deteriorate as the North East Monsoon intensified, but we did manage to make fair recoveries. On a fairly calm day someone noticed a very large dark shape not far from the **Lifeline**. At first we thought it may have been a semi-submerged tree, but as there was about 1 knot of current, it had to be something else. After an hour or so, the creature came to within a couple of meters of the ship. It turned out to be a very large female whale shark, that had a baby with her. We estimated the length to be at least 40 feet, with a very large cavernous mouth, feeding we guessed on small creatures like plankton that was in the water. We resumed work, which did not seem to bother the creature at all, and after a couple of hours or so she disappeared. I recalled watching one of Jacques Cousteau's interesting programmes and he said that up until that time he had never seen a whale shark because they are so rare and little was known about them. We cut the chain of the **Engen Maru**'s anchors, and recovered the anchors that were still quite serviceable (weighing about 5 tons each).

We left the **Engen Maru** as the tin had mostly been recovered, except for isolated ingots which proved too time consuming to have divers collect. We recovered our moorings on 9th October and re-laid four moorings round **Taigyo Maru**. We then went to Singapore to discharge 86 tons of tin and replenish the ship with water, provisions and fuel. The weather by now was quite bad and it was the 22nd before we resumed wreck work, spending many days either moored to a mooring or 'hove to'.

We made another run to Singapore because of bad weather and landed 11 tons of tin. We returned for the last time to **Taigyo Maru** on 8th November. We had more time off the wreck for bad weather than actual work, and by 17th November it had become hopeless to try and do more. Besides, there were not a lot of ingots remaining to be seen, but without doubt, enough to cover the costs of another trip, if the price was to remain the same. We recovered all our moorings and rolled our way back to Singapore to discharge the last 14.5 tons of tin, demobilise the ship and return to England.

Fergus Hinds and Mike Hatcher returned to the wrecks about a year later and recovered enough loose ingots by divers to make it a worthwhile venture, as their overheads were considerably less than Risdon Beazley.

Several years later I was working from Vietnam on similar shipwrecks, and the boss of V.I.S.A.L.(the state salvage company) told me that there were two more wrecks untouched not very far from the Vietnamese Coast. They believed these to be in their waters therefore belonging to them. He was quite upset when I told him that the two wrecks in question had been salvaged several years earlier. I did not feel badly about this, as V.I.S.A.L. had done very well from other Japanese tin carriers, and will continue to recover a little bit more each season.

As it happened, this was to be the last ever cargo recovery made by Risdon Beazley, and probably one of the most profitable. Sadly the Dutch company, Smit International, had taken over our company, and as far as I am aware, none of the revenue from the South China Sea recoveries was used to finance future recoveries from shipwrecks, or improve or maintain any of the ships left in the rapidly diminishing fleet[1].

Now, some 25 years later, I am positive that very few (if any) cargo recovery projects have proved as profitable, and probably none involving the bulk removal of valuable heavy metal ingots. I believe there are three main reasons for this; one being the real value of the metals had changed little. Tin, admittedly an exception, is much lower than in 1980. The second reason is the lack of experienced men from senior management, researchers, to professional wreck divers (with merchant ship construction knowledge) and riggers. Thirdly, fuel/labour and all other costs make this kind of venture very precarious. New companies wishing to take on this type of work usually say they will achieve treble the feasible daily recoverable amount.

Practically all of the companies that I have dealt with since the Beazley years overlook the fact that the wreck has to be opened up first. The decks, and often the sides, have to be removed. Then several thousand tons of overburden (unwanted cargo) need to be moved before getting a glimpse of the heavy cargo that is usually stowed in the bottom of the ship. I have dealt with a few companies who have projected to recover a specific cargo from a wreck, usually one that has not even located or surveyed, at a faster rate than the ship would have been discharged while berthed in Port.

---

[1] The proceeds were paid to the parent company, having been routed via the Dutch Antilles, the sum almost equalled that year's profit declared by the parent company, which had just become a public company. The *Ashford* was sold by Dave Smiley of SISEA for a sum close to the sum that RB had paid for her and the *Lifeline* was sold for scrap on instructions from Rotterdam. The rest of the fleet was dispersed among other Group companies (SISEA bought *Seaford, Telford & RB35*). The Yard and the equipment were auctioned and, except for the few that joined SISEA, the staff were laid off.   **RVM**

Chapter Eleven   The Final Decade 1969 to 1979

Early in 1970 things moved forward, the **Great Britain** contract was taken on following Bill O'Neil's report. Risdon Beazley were to salve the ship and Ulrich Harms were to transport the vessel back to Bristol.   At much the same time Risdon Beazley Ulrich Harms (RBUH)[1] started trading and in April the redoubtable Martha Gäbel arrived to get us organised. Martha became a family friend[2].

One of my first jobs was to oversee the crating of the equipment to go to Port Stanley for the salvage of the **Great Britain**.   I called the local builders merchant to open an account and started to spell the name of the company, fortunately not the Ulrich Harms bit as well, when the person I was talking to said "no need lad, Risdon Beazley has had an account here since 1936". The **Great Britain** was salvaged and transported 'at cost' and inside the budget.   Neither Risdon Beazley Ltd, Ulrich Harms GmbH, nor Mr 'Union' Jack Hayward who funded the work, get a mention on the **Great Britain** website.

At first RBUH leased the yard and bare-boat chartered the ships: both were bought from RAB during the next three years, with the cash from earnings.   Hans-Erich Borucki, the General Manager of Ulrich Harms GmbH, was keenly interested in recovery and did everything he could to encourage RBUH.   He was concerned that we could not get our vessels up to 'the yard' and told me to look for an alternative site for the company, where we could bring our own vessels alongside.   There was nothing in the Southampton area, but I found a suitable place at Poole, where Hamworthy Engineering were moving to a bigger site. This site, Yard Quay as it is now called, was ideal but there was no enthusiasm from the management of RBUH who felt that we should stay where we had always been.   Poole Harbour Commissioners were equally opposed, but in their case because they wanted the site for themselves.   We did not move, but in the years to come we found it harder and harder to find places to discharge the **Droxford** and to lay our ships up over the winter.

Erich Borucki left Ulrich Harms in August 1971 to set up Interbergung GmbH owned by Smit Tak of Rotterdam, Martha Gäbel, and others joined him.   Much to everyone's annoyance I kept in touch with my friends in the new organisation.

Little more than a year later I was making a routine visit to the Harms office in Hamburg when I got a message from Ulrich Harms that, rather than fly back to London, I was to join him on a flight to Amsterdam.   When we both arrived at Hamburg airport there was Erich Borucki - strange things were happening, another takeover?   I flew on to London and reported to my boss Allan Crothall, he said "nonsense old man, if anything like that was happening I would be the first to know" (he was after all the only other shareholder in RBUH).

With all that was going on it would seem that we had no time for salvage, but we were as busy as ever.

The pattern was one of almost continuous employment for the recovery and wreck removal vessels, plus crane work using the Harms fleet. Their cranes worked in all parts of the UK salvaging, among others, **Lairdsfield, Seacon, Dutch Master Sand Skua** and **Loch Seaforth,** jobs that were contracted by RBUH, as were a number of transport jobs.   **Droxford** found and salvaged cargoes from the **Empire Soldier, Metric, Urbino, Harrovian** and **Hollington**, plus several 'gleaning' jobs. Ulrich

---

[1] RBUH had been incorporated on 13th January 1969.
[2] She wrote a summary of the Beckedorf / Harms companies, a copy of which I have on file..

Harms were able to secure the contract for the **Droxford** to recover a cargo of metal from the German coaster **Metric,** which had been loaded with 400 tons of copper and 50 tons of gunmetal, when she sank in the Irish Sea. **Droxford** recovered 371 tons of copper and 38 tons of gunmetal from the wreck, which was lying on her beam ends. They found that structural steel in contact with the copper was so holed that it resembled Gruyère cheese.

The **Hollington,** just South of the Faroe Islands, was the next cargo recovery operation and involved the **Droxford** working at the then record depth of almost 900' and at the highest Latitude that they ever worked. In all they recovered over 700 tons of tin from this wreck. During this operation the **Droxford** visited Lerwick to allow the Shetlanders amongst the crew to show the ship to their families.

The **Harrovian** had been repeatedly sought without success. Captain Brackenbury's summary of the wrecks that had already been found showed that one of the sailing ships that had been located might be one of two sunk on the same day as the **Harrovian**[1]. This proved to be correct and to the SSW was the **Harrovian**, almost 30 miles from her reported sinking position. **Droxford** recovered over 700 tons of copper from this wreck.

The wreck removal fleet was employed in the English Channel and in France, Lyle has covered the biggest job, near the Varne Bank .

In 1971 RBUH took over the transport pontoon **Mulus IV**, which was under construction at HDW Kiel. I went over to see the vessel finished and registered, after that she joined the Harms fleet. By October 1973 we knew that Smit Tak's takeover of Ulrich Harms and therefore of RBUH had been completed. In that month Allan Crothall received a visit from Paul van den Berg (PvdB) and Z S W 'Willem' Moerkerk. Several of us were taken to a hotel and introduced to our new masters. After the meeting was over we went on to another hotel for a meal and a few drinks.

Allan Crothall told me to go in the car with our visitors and tell them about the **Empire Manor** operation, at that time most of the others knew little about that job; PvdB was particularly interested. I think that Erich Borucki had explained the type of work that we did and he saw it as a useful broadening of the group's activities. By the end of November most of the vessels had returned for winter refit and a valuer arrived from Rotterdam. I was surprised to learn that half of the price that Smit Tak had paid for the Harms group was for RBUH. The large Harms fleet was modern, but there was quite a bit of debt; the RBUH fleet was mostly old and tired, but was owned outright. The valuer had been given the total figure for the valuation and as I took him from ship to ship he became more and more depressed.

Droxford was particularly showing her age. She went to Sheerness for her winter refit and Bram van Dintel came back with a lump of rust scale that had been cut out of the base of her funnel. He came into ACC's office, put the scale on his desk, and said "there you are Mr Crothall, that's some of the most sophisticated rust in the world". This followed a press release that ACC had given saying something to the effect that **Droxford** was the most sophisticated salvage ship in the world.

Bram was unhappy about the takeover and let it be known; when he was introduced to the Rotterdam top brass and they started talking to him in Dutch he said "See here, this is an English company and we talk English here". Another group who were

---

[1] 'Brack' then set to work on the North West Approaches in the hope of flushing out another perennial – the **Oldfield Grange.** In this case the exercise did not seem to succeed, but examination of these records suggests that he may have pin pointed this wreck.

equally unhappy were the few survivors from Overseas Towage and Salvage, which Smit had closed down a few years before. One of their number, Captain Alfred Sims warned me that it was only a matter of time before RB went the same way. I was impressed with PvdB, and disbelieved Alf, but he was right. I still feel that, had PvdB not died, the result might have been different. Alf took the sensible course and moved to Neptun.

On the 17th April 1973 Risdon Beazley Marine took over the assets and activities of RBUH[1]. An EGM was held at Clausentum Yard on the 30th April 1973 when it was decided that Risdon Beazley Ltd should be put into voluntary liquidation: a General Meeting was held at Littlebourne on the 14th May ' at 11 o'clock in the forenoon' to complete the liquidation. So, 48 years after it was formed, one of the most successful marine salvage companies ever, ceased to exist.

Under Paul van den Berg it seemed that the new company's future was assured, though Smit Tak did call in management consultants to recommend a new structure for the group under which RBM's future salvage activities were confined to the UK and Eire, with the exception of cargo recovery. But van den Berg was stricken with lung cancer and died in December 1977. Well before that Dr Donath had been given responsibility for the company, but it seemed to be a side line for him.

By 1977 it was judged to be time for **Droxford** to make another attempt on the **Glenartney.** Fergus Hinds, who was by then the Cargo Recovery Manager, made painstaking preparations for the project and another thorough search was made using a different type of sonar[2]. The side scan sonar team worked by night whilst the ASDIC was used to sweep an extended area by day. At 0715 on the morning of the 29th March, the 11th night of the search, Hind's team found a wreck. Because the **Droxford's** deck was cluttered with survey gear it was not possible to examine the contact so the whole search area was completed, and the equipment landed, before the dive could begin. Don Jones, Beazley's senior diver and a veteran of hundreds of such dives, identified the **Glenartney.**

The casualty lay at the mouth of an undersea trench in just over 1,000 feet of water. It is most unlikely that she would have been found by the ASDIC that was standard equipment on the recovery vessels. The wreck was hidden in a submarine canyon and could only be seen from one angle. In a two-year operation, that was something of an epic, the **Droxford** recovered 750 tons of tin worth a staggering £4 million.

In 1977 we were given approval to buy and convert a supply vessel to relieve the **Droxford** of the location work. Much of the remaining work was to the West of the British Isles so we decided to equip the vessel as a station tug as well. As it was the Technical Department in Rotterdam would not approve my choice of vessel and the towage department were against the vessel being a station tug! The vessel I had picked was later bought by Smit Lloyd! We finally settled on the vessel that became the **Seaford**, the conversion took longer than we had hoped as the vessel had an engine room fire whilst in the shipyard. As it was the vessel came too late and spent too much of it's time towing the cranes.

1954 Risdon Beazley Ltd. had approached the British Government to discuss terms

[1] There is confusion surrounding these dates. My memory of the Empire Manor story is borne out by the Treasury's file where they state that the contract was given to RBUH and the cheque was to be paid to RBM. ACC gives the date of the formation of RBM as 17th April 1973 – and he should know; though he made a mistake when talking about the fleet when RBUH was formed - the two pontoons were not part of the RB fleet, they were bought later. It has not been possible to check the dates and it would appear RBUH was renamed Risdon Beazley Marine, rather than RBM being a new company. In March 1973 when we were at the Sand Skua arbitration we were still trading as RBUH though we knew that the company had been taken over.
[2] Fergus Hinds has provided his logbook of the operation and his notes.

for the recovery of the gold that was stowed in the bomb room of **HMS Edinburgh**. RB got little encouragement because the **Edinburgh**, being a warship, had been declared to be a war grave. In the seventies the British and Russian governments agreed that the British should seek salvors to recover the cargo. Much to the surprise of the management at RBM a little known consortium that had been formed for the purpose obtained the contract and recovered the cargo. At the time RBM were given the excuse that their method of recovery would not treat the casualty and the drowned naval seamen with due reverence.

Three years later it was disclosed in court that an official of the Salvage Association who was to handle the bids and who had recommended the consortium, felt it his duty to "break Risdon Beazley's monopoly". He admitted in court that he had sent copies of the RB submissions to the successful contractor; both he and the contractor were acquitted. As it was it was doubtful if RB's technique would have succeeded in this case and the men who might have undertaken such a mammoth task were no longer with the company[1].

The **Droxford** was only twenty-two years old when Smit decided that she should be scrapped, as there was "no future in cargo recovery". No other recovery vessel has exceeded the achievements of this fine steamer, or her master for the last 13 years - Captain William A. Ross.

By the time of the **Oregis** operation we owned and operated the **Magnus II**, later renamed the **Telford** and then, when the **RB Brunel** joined the fleet, the **RB Telford**; plus the **Pullus 1** [2] a 47 meter barge that became the **RB47**. Our experience with the **Telford** showed that there were opportunities for a larger crane and in 1975 we bought the **Magnus XI** from Harms and had it rebuilt at HDW as the **RB Brunel**. This new unit joined the fleet in March 1976. I had written a business plan predicting two years work for a bigger crane, as it was what we got was just that - two years successful work. After that we sold the crane to SISEA.

At the same time Fergus Hinds was busy with reports on the future of cargo recovery. Fergus had been pointing out that we needed to be thinking of a completely new recovery vessel to take us into deepwater. As it was the lead that we had was wasted over the next four years; though Fergus was still gamely writing these reports as late as February 1980.

By this time the **Lifeline** was in the Far East[3]. We had been across to Hamburg to buy the **Taurus**; I negotiated Erich Borucki down to 60% of what we were told to pay for the vessel, only on return to Southampton to be told that the price was back up to the 'asking' price. After a refit at Avonmouth the new unit, **Ashford**, also went East.

---

[1] The Times 20. 3.84, - Press Journal 21.3.84 and Daily Express 29.7.85
[2] Latin for Pony, to differentiate it from the bigger Mulus (the Mule of course) barges
[3] See Lyle's chapter on the South China Sea

RB Brunel, Seaford and Queen Mother   *Risdon Beazley photographs*

Topmasts 16.17,18 and 20　　　　　　　　　　**Risdon Beazley photographs**

Lifeline & Ashford   Risdon Beazley photographs

Lairdsfield and Dutch Master

Lairdsfiled & Dutch Master   *Risdon Beazley & Ulrich Harms*

On 6th February 1970 the British cargo ship **Lairdsfield** capsized shortly after dropping the Tees pilot.   The vessel was on a voyage to Cork with a cargo of steel products. The upturned bow of the casualty was sighted about half an hour later, but there was no sign of the ten man crew of the vessel.

We obtained the contract to lift the casualty and **Magnus III** was sent to the site, when it was lifted on the 24th February only three bodies were found.   The vessel was declared to be a Constructive Total Loss and was towed away for scrapping.   Both the crew of the crane and the RB salvage team and divers felt the loss of these fellow merchant seaman strongly.   The **Topmast 20**, under the command of Captain Alf Sims, recovered all but one piece of the steel cargo.   A folk song was written about the loss.

Seacon

Seacon at Dover Harbour entrance   *Harms brochure*

Seacon was a single hatch coaster of 137 gross tons, built in 1968. She was run down just two years later by a Belgian ferry whilst approaching the Eastern Entrance at Dover, the entrance was immediately closed. An RB team from the **Topmast 18** and the **Queen Mother** located the wreck, in 50 feet of water, within 48 hours. It was the worst possible location as far as the divers were concerned; the currents were treacherous, the water was pitch black and the best slack waters were predicted to last only three minutes! This meant that the diving team spent almost all their time working in conditions that they would not normally have dived in.

Bill (Peggy) O'Neil, the salvage officer, sent the **Queen Mother** to Portland to tow back two 'camels'; but these were of no use because of the strong currents so the **Topmast 18** was pinned down to the wreck with 82mm strops that the divers had, with great difficulty, fed under the hull. At 0400 on the morning of the lift Lyle Craigie-Halkett was having a cup of coffee before his dive when another of the divers, Charlie Hibbert, warned him to be careful as he believed that the wreck had moved during the night. Lyle groped his way down through the black water to find that the lifting strop was slack, it would normally be 'snatching' because of the movement above: Lyle found the reason, the casualty had indeed moved, through 90°; Charlie was correct, as he had been before!.

Topmast 18 'pinned down' on the wreck and, with a lift of about 100 tons, lifted her clear of the seabed. But the **Topmast 18**'s propellers were well out of the water and she had to ask for the two Dover tugs to tow them to shallower and quieter water. During the few fair weather days that they had, they prepared the wreck for lifting. They found that the steel hatch covers were missing; so Lyle went with one of the **Topmast 18**'s salvage launches to locate them and strop them for lifting. He found them in the initial sinking position and, whilst stropping them, was disconcerted to hear a ship's engines; the engines came nearer and nearer until the vessel, a Belgian ferry (again), passed right over him, he clung on for dear life in the black water. Lyle recalls that "the hatch lids were reverberating with shock waves, plus the noise was horrendous", The duty officer on the **Topmast 18** had failed to alert the port control in order that all traffic could be stopped "not a very good career move". The much shaken crew in the launch were fully expecting not to see Lyle again.

Ten days later the **Magnus V** and the **Argus V** arrived and, using the gear rigged by the Beazley divers, parbuckled (uprighted) the **Seacon** and carried her, clear of the water, into Dover harbour, where the RB team cleaned her out ready for tow. The only damage that she had sustained was a two meter cut from the main deck to justbelow the sheer strake and the usual damage to the radar mast etc. A few months later the **Seacon** was trading again as the **Sea Trent.**

Transport of quayside cranes from London to Cardiff, South Wales   ***Harms brochure***

The Harms transport fleet was managed from Rotterdam by three people who were the whole staff of Harms Nederland B V.   Their speciality was transporting dredgers and similar equipment.   Until Harms pioneered this method of floating 'cargo' onto pontoons the rate of loss of dredgers was high.   Owners and underwriters realised that this was the way of the future and reduced their premiums accordingly.   The first to be hurt were Smit, for this work was their bread and butter.   Three of the pontoons were owned by Harms and the fourth by Beazley.   The development of this technique opened up all sorts of new possibilities, the most newsworthy of which was the salvage of the **Great Britain** and her safe transport back to Bristol.

In the above instance we were intending to lift the cranes on to the **Mulus** with a **Magnus** crane, but the client, a South Wales Port operator, felt that this method was too expensive.   Their engineer decided that we could drive the cranes on and off and he designed the equipment to do so.   The two girders that were the link spans are on the port quarter of the barge.

Lumey

There were also the little jobs, such as the salvage of the schuyt *Lumey* which was hard aground on St Aldhelms Head in Dorset in 1970. The Owner/Master fell asleep whilst on watch. He was not a happy Dutchman, he felt that somehow his misfortune was caused by English wreckers, who were now about to rob him!

Lumey at St Aldhelm's Head, Dorset **photograph Charles Cooper**

Talking to him later we found what had happened: 30th April is Queen's Day in the Netherlands and his crew were due overtime pay for working on that day: rather than pay the money the Master had remained on watch with the autopilot on. He was bound for Portland to load stone, after having discharged his previous cargo in Shoreham. The ship had been steadily set in and just failed to clear the Head. He was fortunate in one thing, his ship had grounded on the neap tides when the range was only 0.5 meters so it was in little danger. A week later he would have ended further up the cliff and at real risk of being a permanent fixture.

We agreed a contract on the job and sent the **Queen Mother,** which was working on the **Highland Brigade** off the Isle of Wight. The Master was L V Tomlinson, an experienced tugmaster, and Charles Cooper and Ted Hosking, two top divers who were on the verge of becoming Salvage Officers. The **Queen Mother** received the call at 0940 on the 30th and was in Poole by 15.45 to load pumps and equipment. She arrived at the casualty at 19.45. Roy Martin had driven from Poole and, after a quick inspection, it was agreed that work would begin in the morning at first light. Charles Cooper and Roy Martin remained on the casualty. After listening to the late night shipping bulletin, which forecast winds of force 6 for the morning, they returned to the **Queen Mother**. The crew turned to and ran a wire to the casualty. Three attempts were made to refloat the vessel but the wire kept snagging on the large rocks which lie at the foot of the cliff. On the third attempt the **Queen Mother** clipped one of the rocks, but a diving survey ascertained that the propeller damage was minor.

After laying a mooring buoy to hold the casualty off Queen Mother again went to Poole. On arrival at 13.25 she loaded a new polypropylene tow rope and was back on site by 15.45. The weather forecast continued to be poor and Charles Cooper and Ted Hosking loaded as much of the polypropylene as they could in the launch to connect to the casualty. By this time the tide was running strongly and they just managed to grab the casualty's anchor chain as they went by and shackled the tow line to it. By 18.45 they had the casualty afloat and at 20.30 both vessels anchored in Poole Bay to allow an inspection. On Saturday the 2nd they were given permission to enter the Harbour and picked up the anchor at 09.00. The afternoon was spent alongside Poole Quay pumping out water and at 19.00 the vessel was slipped at Bolson's Yard and on Sunday morning the vessel was surveyed.

Sand Skua

Sand Skua and Magnus X   Western Solent   Charles Cooper

On 30th May 1972 the wreck clearance vessels were in port at Dover over the Spring Tides when they were called by the Office and asked to send a team down to Southampton where the sand suction dredger **Sand Skua** had partially sunk whilst dredging on the Solent Bank.   A team of four, including Lyle Craigie-Halkett, Charles Cooper and Ted Hosking, loaded their gear into a taxi and were delivered to Town Quay Southampton where they boarded the **Willbetty** which had already loaded two four inch Rapier Pumps.   By the time they were en route to the casualty the wind was blowing WSW force seven.   They arrived at 20.10 and relieved Capt Alfred Sims, who had been holding the fort.   They discovered that the **Sand Skua**, whilst loading ballast, had flooded the forward buoyancy space/pump room and sunk by the head. They sounded round and checked for leaks before bedding down in the excellent accommodation, which was at a rather crazy angle, especially at high water.   A 400 ton **Magnus** crane had been requested from Hamburg; but after calculations were made this was changed to a 1000 ton crane, **Magnus X,** was substituted and the 400 tonner was recalled.

On the 31st they made a more thorough inspection of the hull and the fo'c'sle.   The Harms tugs **Argus 5** and **Argus 8** arrived on site, as did the **Queen Mother**.   They laid the mooring that the **Queen Mother** had brought to stop the vessel slewing with the tide and connected one of the **Argus** tugs to hold the vessel when the current was at its worst.   In the pump room they discovered several unexploded artillery shells and the Bomb Disposal Team were called..   On Saturday 3rd June the salvage crane **Magnus X** arrived in tow of a chartered tug and **Argus 5** went to Cowes to take over the tow.   Harm's Salvage Officer Ove Jäckstein was in charge, with a diving team from Risdon Beazley.   Work began at first light on Sunday 4th June when the lifting strops were hauled underneath the casualty using the messenger wires that had been positioned by the RBUH team.   By 16.30 that afternoon lifting was underway with a series of breaks when the load exceeded the capacity of the crane and the vessel needed to be pumped.   By 23.30 the vessel was on the surface and being pumped out.   The Harbour Board officials arrived in the early hours and the vessel was cleared for tow by 10.15.   The Bomb Disposal Team left with six 6"shells at 11.10 and the casualty was towed to Northam with the **Magnus X** following.   The re-delivery note was signed in the Yacht Tavern at 20.00 that evening.   After many months RBUH were awarded £182.000, by which time the company had been taken over by Smit Tak.

Loch Seaforth

Magnus III and the Loch Seaforth   **Photograph Charles Cooper**

On the 22nd March 1973 the coastal passenger steamer **Loch Seaforth** ran aground on Gunna Rock during a gale.   The crew and the few passengers abandoned ship and made it safely to Tiree.   The **Loch Seaforth** was re-floated 5 hours later and towed to Tiree with her engine room still flooded.   She sank alongside the steamer pier.

On Saturday 24th March Charles Cooper was called at home at 6.30 and was asked to charter an aircraft to fly to Tiree via Glasgow where he was to pick up the Salvage Association's Surveyor.   He phoned Blackpool Airport and was told to call back in half an hour because a suitable aircraft was at the time launching parachutists. When he called back a rate was agreed and they took off at 11.00.   On arrival on site they met Caledonian MacBrayne's Superintendent and examined the casualty.   On Monday morning he left Tiree with the other members of the team to look at one of the Company's vessels, the **Loch Carron,** which was aground further north.

On the 30th April Roy Martin and Charles Cooper flew to Glasgow where the contract to lift the **Loch Seaforth** was signed.   Charles Cooper again visited the site to check on the condition of the casualty and make the necessary preparations for the arrival of the crane **Magnus III.**   On the 7th he was called away again, this time to visit another casualty, the **St. Ronald** at Kirkwall.   This casualty was aground on gently sloping rocks but close to a near vertical drop.   Cooper telexed the office with a full report and the job was passed to the Smit Tak vessel **Biber** that was in Peterhead.

He then flew back to Tiree where the **Magnus 3** arrived on Saturday 12th, by which time a gale was blowing from the SW.   As they were in the Western Isles work was not permitted on Sunday.   Lifting started on Monday morning and by late afternoon the casualty was clear of the bottom and was beached in Gott Bay.   On Tuesday 15th she was patched and pumped and filled with empty oil drums, a management team from Caledonian Macbrayne was on site and they helped with the oil drums.   The redelivery note was signed on Tiree Piping Club notepaper.

On Monday 21st the vessel was floating without assistance and on Wednesday 23rd it was decided that she was a CTL[1] and she was sold for scrap. The casualty left for Troon at 18.15 that day in tow of the **Argus 7** whilst the **Argus 8** and **Magnus III** left at 19.00.   After delivering the **Loch Seaforth** to the breakers the next day, **Argus 7** sailed to rendezvous with the **Magnus 3** and the **Argus 8.**

---

[1]Constructive total loss, where the anticipated repair cost is likely to exceed the value of the repaired vessel

Hvassafell

Hvassafell aground at Iceland, with Lifeline
in the background   Photo Charles Cooper

In the Spring of 1973 the Icelandic cargo vessel **Hvassafell** grounded on an island off the North Coast of Iceland, only a few miles from the Arctic Circle.. The Coastal class salvage vessel **Lifeline** had just come off a charter and was equipped and sent to Iceland. This was the first time that the vessel had ever left the UK and, with her squared off bow, she had a difficult passage. On several occasions she had to seek shelter which caused the casualty's owner to remark that "Your ship has very good anchors".

Charles Cooper flew from Glasgow to Reykjavik and then on to Husavik to join the **Lifeline** and they set about rigging the ground tackles and wires to the casualty. Charles had chosen comparatively light gear, because of the necessity of hauling the wire across through shallow water with a rocky seabed. Hauling began and the casualty was swung, in steps through 80°. The tackles were being overhauled to make the final pull when the carpenter's stopper disintegrated, seriously injuring the two hands on deck and catapulting Charles Cooper into the icy sea. He tried to swim towards the salvage ship, but realised that neither of his legs would function, nor would one of his arms. As soon as they could the **Lifeline's** launch was put in the water making for their salvage officer and expecting the worst, but Charles was a very fit man and a fighter; he later said that, whilst he was a Brit, his limbs were full of Icelandic blood and Swedish steel.

The only good fortune that they had on that day was that a nurse from Akureyri Hospital was watching the salvage attempt with her boyfriend. She swung into action and arranged for all three to be hospitalized. It was several months before they were fit to travel to the UK, the P&I Club arranged for an air ambulance to bring them home, accompanied by two nurses from the hospital. All concerned were extremely grateful to the staff at the hospital, all the more so because this accident happened at the time of the 'cod war' between Iceland and the UK.

RB did not have a relief salvage officer available, so Jaap Pols went from Rotterdam and completed the job; sadly Jaap himself later died as a result of another accident at work.

Oregis 10th March 1974

Oregis, with RB Telford & Pullus 1 lightening the vessel

Oregis at Low Water
Photos RBM brochure

On the 10th March 1974 the **Oregis**, which had just been converted from an ore carrier to an offshore installation vessel, left for sea trials off the Tyne. Shortly after slipping her tugs the ship suffered engine failure and, despite the efforts of the tug **Northsider**, ended up on the Black Midden rocks off North Shields, with the **Northsider** aground near her. The Northsider was refloated on the next tide but the **Oregis** was hard aground. The ocean going tug **Statesman 1** attempted to tow the vessel off but abandoned the attempt once a young crewman from the tug lost his life.

The **Oregis** was operated by Houlder Brothers from their offices in London. We offered for the job and I went to London to explain what we intended to do. When I arrived I was shown into the board room, where several of the directors were meeting; the meeting was being chaired by Mr John Houlder, who had been flying over the casualty at the time of the grounding. I explained that, as far as we knew, the vessel needed to be lightened, lifted and then towed back into the channel – and we had the gear to do the job. We were given the contract and I travelled up to the Tyne to see things first hand. I was able to walk right round the casualty, followed by a small group of doleful Geordies, saying 'why aye, nuthin' comes off the Black Middens'.

We mobilised three 400 ton cranes, ours from the Tees, one from Rotterdam and one from Hamburg, together with tugs and salvage craft. I began to believe the Geordie tales of woe when the **Magnus X**'s jib collapsed during the salvage attempt, but as always the team stuck to their task and refloated the ship.

Some months later when she went back into service we were surprised to see that the temporary stiffening that we had put on in way of the moonpool was still there.

RB Brunel about to lift HMS Reward

On the 11th August 1976 **HMS Reward** was returning to Rosyth after acceptance trials following a refit. When she was between the two Firth of Forth bridges the **Reward** was in collision with the West German container vessel **Plainsman** and the **Reward** sank within 15 minutes, all 40 crew were rescued by the **Plainsman**. **Reward** was one of a series of war built **Bustler** class rescue tugs and the refit had included modifications to enable the vessel to serve as a stop gap Fishery and Oil Rig Protection vessel. When the collision occurred **RB Brunel** was in Narvik installing a new ore loading terminal. After visiting Nigg Bay for oil related work the **Brunel** arrived at the site of the sinking and, after loading two specially made strops, that British Ropes had made at five days notice, the crane started work.

Salvage Officer Charles Cooper was already on site and after a few days the 1,200 ton casualty had been lifted and carried to the North side of the Forth where an inspection was carried out. The Admiralty decided that the damage from the collision was so severe that the vessel should be scrapped. On completion the **Brune**l sailed for the River Tees to upright and load out an oil jacket.

RB Brunel at the Tees both pictures from RBM brochure

Gold Coin

The Greek owned motorship **Gold Coin** was a 300-foot cargo vessel built in 1952 by Gebr.Pot, Bolnes   She sailed from Europoort December 3rd 1972 bound for Dakar with 2,000 tons of bulk maize. The weather was very bad with gale force winds and heavy seas.

The following day she sent out a distress signal that was picked up by North Foreland Radio Station; nothing further was heard. The next day a Belgian Ferry reported an upturned life raft and life buoys five miles off Dover Western Entrance. Dover Lifeboat was launched and from a position North East of the South Goodwin Light Vessel picked up five bodies wearing life jackets marked with the ship's name **Gold Coin**. Twelve other persons were ascertained to be missing from the ship but their remains were never found.

A month later a British bulk carrier reported striking a submerged object off Hastings this turned out to be the **Gold Coin** laying on her Starboard side with no apparent damage. Risdon Beazley was awarded the Trinity House contract to disperse the wreck to allow safe passage over the top: from memory I believe that the depth required was roughly 70 feet, or 10 feet above the seabed.

Topmast 18 was used for the operation, which took about 2 weeks to cut with explosives and disperse. It was a relatively easy job as the main engine was just low enough for us not to have to lift it; if there was a problem it was the maize cargo that remained trapped on board, as once disturbed there was no underwater visibility during the entire job.

This operation was typical of the wreck removal work that was 'bread and butter' work for the **Topmast** vessels, both in the English Channel and French ports.   The wreckage was always cut a couple of feet deeper than Trinity House required, as it was a matter of pride that we did not fail the clearance sweep.

On at least one occasion this practice worked to our disadvantage. Smaller companies were always at our heels and one undercut our price to do further work on a wreck that we had originally cut down.   They went out, did a diving survey and notified the authorities that the wreck had been reduced to the new depth. The Trinity House vessel arrived and issued a clearance certificate, so the contractor was paid without having to do the work.   While this was annoying for the company, the certificate was correct as the wreck was down to the required depth.

El Tambo

Early in 1980, although the company was nearing the end, Risdon Beazley must be credited with being the first, and to date, the only British company to completely remove a sunken vessel by cutting it into 400 ton pieces with massive high tensile steel chain.

This method had been developed by our associate German Company, Ulrich Harms, mainly for use in waterways where the current was too strong for divers to work. Smit also quickly adopted this method to remove wrecks which were impossible to salvage by conventional means. In spite of the experience that Harms had, and to a lesser extent Smit, we received absolutely no advice from either company, even though by this time we had worked closely together on numerous jobs.

We had been working for many years with similar equipment, albeit perhaps on a smaller scale and that experience stood us in good stead, we soon applied our own style of safe working practises and got on with the job.   It was to be a good training ground, because shortly after this Smit International employed a couple of us to operate the salvage sheerlegs in South East Asia, where we removed many wrecks using the chain cutting method.

The wreck in question was the Panamanian registered **El Tambo**. Her owners at the time of sinking were recorded as being Cugado Shipping Co. S.A.   Her present role was as a cattle carrier, for which she had been converted from a general cargo vessel. **El Tambo** was built in 1961 by Werft Nobiskrug Rendsburg Germany, as the **Maria Russ**, for the West German company, Ernst Russ.   In 1972 she became the **Corinthian,** and much later sold on again and converted to carry cattle when she was renamed **El Tambo**.

El Tambo sailed from the Republic of Ireland for Libya, with just over 900 head of cattle and on 8th February 1977 she was off the South Bishops Light, West Wales, when a serious fire broke out in her engine room. Her crew of 21 was safely taken off the burning vessel by life boats launched from the British Ferry **Avalon**.   At that time the conditions were stated as being unpleasant with fog, and a heavy swell running. Initially, ships stood by in case assistance was required.

A supply vessel called **Arctic Seahorse** managed to get a tow line made fast to the burning ship and was able to keep her head into the wind and swell to help confine the fire to the stern section. After being on board for several hours some crew from the **Arctic Seahorse** and a fire fighting team from **H.M.S. Herald** managed to extinguish the fire.   The tow was then directed towards Fishguard. Off Strumble Head the **Arctic Seahorse** relinquished the tow to the R.M.A.S. Salvage Vessel **Garganey,** and with **H.M.S. Herald** standing by, she towed **El Tambo** into Fishguard Harbour and secured her to an Admiralty mooring.

The vessel was later boarded by a RSPCA Inspector to evaluate the condition of her live cargo. Luckily, in spite of what must have been a terrifying ordeal for the unfortunate animals, only one was found to have died. By this time the cattle had been standing for 8 or 9 days, with no space to lie down but, at least they had sufficient feed. Four days later the cattle were successfully transferred to two Dutch vessels, presumably to continue their voyage to Libya.

One or two watchmen were placed on the **El Tambo** by her owners to look after the vessel while a decision was made regarding the ship's future.   On March 27th, with the ship still attached to the Admiralty mooring, she sank during a gale. This surprised many people who had been following the fortunes of the ship. Only one watchman was reported as being on the ship at the time, and he was rescued from the water by the local R.N.L.I. Lifeboat, and subsequently hospitalised at Haverfordwest, suffering from cold and shock.

I was later told quite an amusing story regarding this event.

A local boat owner had been celebrating a family birthday, and it had developed in to a very lengthy session. When the alarm went out that the **El Tambo** was sinking, the boat owner rushed to give assistance, and on approaching the wreck, he noticed someone (the watch keeper) apparently walking on the water, and instantly blamed the preceding celebrations. He was about to return to the quay when his companion noticed, that in fact the survivor from El Tambo was perched somehow on top of banded cattle feed that had not become waterlogged.

The **El Tambo** was now a navigational hazard, and owing to the confines of the port of Fishguard, the wreck would have to be removed. She was sitting very near upright, with the masts and funnel protruding above the surface at all states of the tide.

For some reason the salvage contract was awarded to a local diving company, rather than to one of the more established salvage companies. In actual fact, the small company that took on the job did a very good job of sealing all the hatches and other openings.

Sadly they failed. When the time came to test their handy work all seemed in order and compressed air was forced into the ship to displace the sea water. I was told that, as the operation was taking much longer than anticipated, they went ashore for some supplies leaving the compressors remained running. Presumably the suction created over the entire length of the vessel was far greater than anticipated. Suddenly some observers on the shore noticed the entire wreck rise really quickly amid foam and bubbles and rear up, then turn over on her starboard side and sink once more.

Obviously the air internally had expanded rapidly as the ship broke the suction on the seabed, but in doing so, blew out the ship's side plates as the air could not escape This caused her to go down in a much worse condition than she had been previously. She was abandoned officially by her owners shortly after.

Very close to three years after she had entered Fishguard, a comprehensive diving survey was conducted by Risdon Beazley's salvage divers, and following their report a contract was negotiated to completely remove the wreck in 4 or 5 sections. Our 400 ton lifting capacity self propelled Sheer Legs **R.B. Telford** in tow of Risdon Beazley's tug/supply vessel **Seaford,** arrived in Fishguard Harbour on March 10th 1980. Whilst the sheerlegs was preparing all the chains, slings, shackles and other equipment, also topping the sheerlegs from the transport position, further surveys were conducted on the wreck. At low water the **El Tambo's** port side was awash, so the **Seaford** was able to moor against the ship's bottom.

We decided to remove all "top hamper" first, such as King posts and superstructure and rove messenger wires completely around the bridge section in preparation for the cutting chain. The work was quite weather dependant, as any surge from the swell outside the breakwater would roll over our location and make it impossible for divers to work, except on the sheltered side (the wreck's bottom), but generally, if the swell was difficult we would pull clear of the wreck until it abated.

With all preparation in place, we moored the **R.B. Telford** to the landward or bottom side of the wreck. We rove our messenger wire, followed by a 52 mm wire, and then normal 3 inch chain, which parted after we put about 50 tons tension on it. So we reverted to the special high tensile steel anchor chain that had been delivered for hull cutting.

Once we had finished the reeving of messenger wires, the large chain was pulled through and our first cutting attempt was carried out. We quickly got the feel of the best way to cut with chains, and that was by exerting only enough pull to keep the chain moving. **R.B. Telford** had two main hoisting tackles; the pulling tackle had about 50 tons, while the other tackle would be slowly lowering, with about 30 tons weight so that it created a see-saw movement. There was quite a lot of vibration transmitted through the sheer legs, and we also used a diver's bone conducting transmitter and were able to hear the chain ripping through the light steel. It took about 3 hours for the actual cut. The after housing followed and then the King posts, which proved to be no problem at all.

Popeye

Early in May, we had orders to leave Fishguard for the Isle of Bute in Scotland, to salvage a capsized backhoe dredger called **Popeye**. The dredger had capsized in poor weather whilst under tow in the Irish Sea. **Popeye** had not sunk, but was floating comfortably upside down. Fortunately, there were no crew on board during the tow. The tug slowly towed the capsized dredger to the sheltered waters of Kames Bay in the Isle of Bute.

The job lasted about a week. All openings plugged and relief vents fitted, we then rove heavy wires 92mm and parbuckled or rolled the **Popeye** onto even keel. The most amazing thing was that, after uprighting the dredger, we found there had been no ingress of water inside the hull, and it was still perfectly dry. The only slight damage was confined to machinery above the deck.

There followed several cargo lifting jobs for the **R.B. Telford**, and some diving surveys on other wrecks, such as the Liberty vessel **James Egan Layne**, not far from Plymouth and a recent wreck that had foundered off Spurn Head called the **Revi**.

It was to be Saturday 31st May before we resumed work on the **El Tambo** in Fishguard. The bridge section of El Tambo which we had cut previously, was lifted in one piece and weighed about 70 tons. At high water we placed it on the shore near the breakwater. From the distance the structure looked as if it was some kind of large office block or factory building.

The after castle followed shortly afterwards, and was actually a bit heavier. The real task of cutting the hull now began in earnest, and not without considerable problems. The locations of the cuts had been predetermined by our company Naval Architect, and it was crucial to cut as near as possible to the nominated places. This would be very near to a transverse bulkhead so that the hull form would be as rigid as possible. The fact that **El Tambo** was laying on her side made it much easier for cutting; had she been upright the chains would have had difficulty in gaining an opening on the flat bottom. She had sunk into the seabed about 3 meters.

Sections of the Samson posts were welded to the high side of the wreck so that at all times we could see how we were lined up for the cutting, at all states of the tide and also to use as mooring points. We positioned **Seaford** on the bottom side of the wreck and **R.B. Telford** on the deck side. Both were equipped with clamshell grabs to dig enormous basins either side of the cutting locations. It was slow going as the seabed tended to back fill very quickly, especially if there was a period of bad weather and swell.

Once we had removed about 300 tons of seabed it was reasonably safe for the divers to grope around in the black water. The next phase was to tunnel under the wreck, which is a very dangerous task for divers as the seabed can back fill and trap them; so for this very reason we had two divers at a time working - or rather one working, and the other making sure the exit was clear at all times.

Against the hull we used large air lifts that vacuumed loose silt as the divers worked with smaller hand held air lifts, and jetting hoses combined with compressed air. In this manner, the seabed material was liquidised into slurry, and therefore easier to remove. We quickly found that the team attempting to tunnel from the deck side was having very little success, and the conditions were too dangerous because of loose debris falling on top of them as it became dislodged. Also the seabed on that side had much more tendency to back fill rapidly.

When the first tunnel under the wreck was as far as we had calculated, we tried to locate the tunnel from the deck side but that only became possible when we injected air through the diver's lance and bubbles would appear on the surface. A polypropylene cord with very small floats attached was blown through. Eventually these floated to the surface to act as the initial messenger.

The next stage was to pass messenger wires under the wreck through the newly dug tunnel which filled in within hours but remained soft enough for pulling wires. The first wire was about 18mm and fed out from the stern of the *Seaford* then pulled on the deck of the *R.B. Telford*. When the first wire reached the *R.B. Telford* the size was increased until we had a 72 mm wire passed under *El Tambo*.

The following procedure was rather tricky. It was important to try and get lifting messenger wires underneath at the same time as the cutting chains. The 72mm final messenger wire was attached to the cutting chain by a type of "Union or Triangular Plate" with one hole cut for the 72mm messenger at the tapered end and on the other end 3 holes cut for attaching the chain in the centre and the two outside holes for further 42mm messenger wires. As the chain was being pulled from one side to the other, the two 42 mm wires were also slackened off, but kept well away from the chain. Eventually these two wires would become the messengers or forerunners for the lifting slings that would be pulled under after the cut was completed. We dug three tunnels and all the wires draped and attached to the high side of the wreck for easy retrieval.

R.B. Telford was positioned on the bottom side of the wreck for commencement of cutting. Very quickly we found the perfect tension to ensure that the chains were doing their job. We heaved about 250 tons on one hook and kept about 100 tons on the lowering hook. When the lowering hook reached the water's surface, the procedure was reversed. Our first attempt took about 8 hours which, considering that *El Tambo* was in good condition, was quite acceptable, if divers were to use conventional underwater cutting equipment, it would take at least a month for one cut because of double bottoms, tween decks and internal debris to cut through, all in zero visibility. When the bight or loop of the chain appeared after one final lurch we knew that we would achieve what we had set out to do.

Two areas gave us problems. One was hatch coamings. These would become balled up with the cutting chain and form a kind of steel bar, about 1 meter in diameter and was very difficult to cut. The ship's propeller shaft was exactly the same. We just put a very small amount of explosives on the couplings which severed the bolts, and the cutting chain just pulled the shaft clear or slipped over it. For this we had permission from the Harbour Authority to use 5lbs of explosives; the shock wave was hardly noticeable from the shore, but enough to fracture the material giving us problems.

Lifting the sections cut in 400 ton pieces was not difficult, as we only kept them clear of the sea bed as *Seaford* assisted us towards the shore. Once beneath the seawall we would then have to lighten the sections as much as possible, by cutting them into smaller pieces with oxyacetylene torches at low water. This was a particularly difficult and dangerous job, because on conversion to carry cattle, the ship's sides had been coated with cement to the depth of the frames, adding many tons to the weight of each section. This fact had gone unnoticed until we started work on the wreck. It is very difficult to cut steel that has cement on the other side, as the cutting gas blows back onto the burner, complete with molten metal and cement dust. This cement also accounted for the extra weight we encountered that had not previously been calculated.

Fortunately we were all adept burners, and got the job done, but not without numerous burns to any skin that happened to be exposed.

I was passed a message one day saying a fellow would like to meet me in a particular pub in old Fishguard on Saturday evening at a specified time. Being curious, and having a liking for different pubs, I went along to see him. It was obvious that I was a stranger, as everything went quiet when I stepped inside. A middle aged chap introduced himself, and we sat down in a corner. After a lot of small talk about **El Tambo**, I was getting fed up, so asked what did he really want. The answer was "Would I like to buy a ship's bronze propeller?"

The truth slowly came out that this guy along with some diver friends had removed the propeller from **El Tambo** by using explosives at night. With lifting bags they had managed to tow it several miles to its present location, where it had nearly disappeared in the muddy seabed, but had a chain attached to it, and was being used as a mooring anchor.

I declined the offer; it would look very suspicious if we tried selling a bronze propeller the same weight as **El Tambo's**. It is possible that the propeller is still there to this day. It seemed very strange that the Harbour Authority never sensed something had happened, because at least 20lbs of explosives must have been used to blow the propeller off the shaft, which would send off quite a crack in the shallow water. We had noticed the propeller had gone and as there had been at least one previous salvage attempt, surmised it had been taken to help defray costs.

Another strange unexplained occurrence was that on lifting the heavy engine room section on shore we noticed that all the crank case doors on the main engine and auxiliaries had been smashed inwards with a very heavy object. This must have been done before she turned on her side, as there was no access for divers after she had sunk. I did report this but little to no interest was shown.

We had one very near disaster on the operation. We were busily cutting up the beached sections to enable us to deposit as far ashore as possible, and suddenly noticed that the **R.B. Telford** was taking a slight list. It was immediately apparent that we were sitting on a piece of wreckage and the tide was falling rapidly. The **Seaford** was alongside the docks taking on fresh water. I called George Crawford, her exceptional captain, and told him we were in real danger of getting impaled. He cast of immediately and within ten minutes had pulled us clear. The piece we had sat on was starting to show, luckily it had a flat surface, and the slight damage was limited to one of **R.B. Telford's** bottom plates. However, we learned a valuable lesson, as the tide had to fall another 10 feet and the consequences could have been disastrous. Our own Schottel propulsion units would not budge us at all.

The **R.B. Telford** was called away to Singapore to start a new life in the Far East, and I joined the Dutch Sheerlegs, **Taklift 1**, to lift the last 3 or 4 pieces from the beach, onto the shore. The lessons learned on **El Tambo** were put to good use for future wreck cutting in Indonesian and Singaporean waters.

Epilogue

On January 8th 1979 the French tanker **Betelgeuse** exploded whilst discharging in Ireland. Smit decided that the removal of the wreck should be undertaken by the parent company as Risdon Beazley Marine 'lacked sufficient experience'!

Mr Risdon Beazley CBE died at his Twyford home on the 31st January 1979.

By the end of May, when Roy Martin left to take over at SISEA, things were already looking grim. Risdon Beazley had been profitable for nine out of the ten years of the 70s, with cargo recovery as usual being the star performer and, even in that final year, it was this that accounted for almost all of the group's profit! But Fergus Hinds' proposals for the company's future in cargo recovery were not accepted and none of the earnings were ploughed back into Risdon Beazley Marine.

By July 1979, when the capsized **Tarpenbek** had to be removed from the Eastern Solent, the company had only the **Telford.** It was necessary to bring a crane from Rotterdam to assist in raising the wreck.

The final blow came in 1980 when RBM's proposal for the salvage of the gold from **HMS Edinburgh** was rejected and the **Droxford** was sold for scrapping in October of that year. SISEA sold the **Ashford** at a price close to that paid to Harms and, after 36 years service, the **Lifeline** was scrapped in Singapore at Tak's insistence.

There had been yet another reorganisation in the first half of 1980. The new team in Rotterdam seemed to have no interest in their Southampton subsidiary and they began to lay off staff from September. It was a very bad year for Risdon Beazley Marine and for the Smit Group as a whole. As Fergus Hinds wrote in his notebook "Demise inevitable by the year's end".

Roy Martin took over the **Telford, Seaford** and **RB35** – the **Seaford** towed the other two to Singapore, where they joined the SISEA fleet and a number of RB people.

Risdon Beazley Marine closed in 1981, a sad end for an organisation that had quietly, but diligently, served the UK in war and peace and generated employment for thousands of staff at sea and ashore. The masters, salvage officers and crews displayed courage and superb seamanship, successfully completing every task. Ashore labour relations were good and the work force turned out high quality work.

The recovery vessels travelled the world; recovering 55,000 tons of non-ferrous metal, working down to over 300 metres. The bulk of the work was done under contracts with the UK government that generated substantial amounts for the UK exchequer.

Risdon Beazley, and the company he formed and ran so successfully, lives on in the memories of men and women across the World. All concerned were a credit to Britain and to their home port of Southampton[1].

---

[1] Clausentum Quay is now covered with flats and the yard by industrial units, nothing marks the site. Nor can any record of the man or his company be found elsewhere in Southampton. A yellow diving chamber stands in the front entrance to Southampton Maritime Museum. This chamber was donated by Risdon Beazley. Several years ago it was pointed out that, despite what is written on the label, it is not a Seibe Gorman diving bell. It is an observation chamber manufactured in Italy for Risdon Beazley by Roberto Galeazzi. Labels with the correct description were given to the museum; these have never been used because 'budgetary restrictions would not allow it'. It has had a slot cut in it for donations and has recently been named 'Fred the Diver'.

Allan Crothall gave the company's artefacts collection to the City, were stored in an industrial unit and could be 'inspected on request' – but how can you ask to see something when you don't know it is there? They may have since been sold! It seems that Southampton's interest in maritime matters is limited to the **Titanic;** very strange for a major port with a long maritime history.

Appendix 1

Requisitioned vessels under R B management, as at May 1945 (in addition to the 29 Admiralty vessels)

Name	Built	GRT	Owner	Manager	Dimensions	Engines	Remarks	
Ahershus	1914	832	Fred Olsen	R A Beazley 44			Salv v/l Iceland 1941/44, May 44 for Normandy	
Alita	1920	109	Risdon Beazley	R A Beazley	100x16x7	Oil Twin screw	Barge	BU Limerick 60
B.H.C. No.9	1909	290						
Carmenita	1920	109	Risdon Beazley	R A Beazley	100x16x7	Oil Twin screw	Barge	BU Norresundby 74
Dapper	1915	419	Dover Harbour Board		125x30x13	Steam C 2 Cy		BU Dover 51
Doria	1919	150	William Watkins	J R Watkins	96x21x11	Steam T 3 Cy		BU 1957
Dorita	1920	109	Risdon Beazley	R A Beazley	100x16x7	Oil Twin screw	Barge	Hulked Gibraltar 51
Dormouse	1924	41						
East	1913	246	Risdon Beazley	R A Beazley	106x28x10	None?		
Empire Demon	1943	268	MOWT	C Rowbotham	108x26x13	Steam T 3 Cy	'Near Warrior' class tug, to MoT45, BU Dublin 66	
Foremost 18	1911	583	Ex James Dredging	Not shown	174x32x13	Steam T 3 Cy	PLA salvage, hopper for James	BU Groningen 58
Freija	1917	326	Ex van den Tak	Not shown	119x31x10	None?	LR 1940, Tak deleted as owner.	
Gallions Reach	1936	797	Ex Tilbury construction	Not shown	179x34x15	Steam T3Cy	LR 1941, Tilbury deleted as owner	Sank Tees 1971
Innishowen	1913	142	Risdon Beazley	R A Beazley	89x19x9	Oil 6 Cy		Mined Denmark 1950!
Lady Southborough	1923	704	Ex Tilbury construction	Not shown	171x34x13	Steam T 3 Cy	LR 1941, Tilbury deleted as owner	BU 1950
Longtow	1919	358	Risdon Beazley	R A Beazley	138x24x13	Steam T 3 Cy	To Overseas Towage 1945	BU Grays 1951
Maggie Lough	1908	129	Lady of the Isles SS	None	92x22x10	Steam C 2 Cy	Wood	BU Penryn 1947
Miss Elaine	1933	364	Risdon Beazley	R A Beazley	152x25x12	Oil 6 Cy	Trawler	Missing 1952
Nessus	1912	328	MOWT	R A Beazley	119x30x14	TS steam 6Cy	Tug built Nantes ex Fr Navy	
Ogarita								
Palmston	1907	430	Risdon Beazley	R A Beazley	160x31x9	Steam C 2 Cy	Cargo	BU Randers 1962
Polita	1920	109	Risdon Beazley	R A Beazley	100x16x7	Oil Twin screw	Barge	Hulked Gibraltar 52
Ramier	1917	441	MOWT	R A Beazley	136x27x12	Steam T 3 Cy	Ex French Navy	
Recovery of Leith	1906	408	Risdon Beazley	R A Beazley	138x27x14	Steam T3Cy		BU France 1960
Reliable No.1.	1930	148	Risdon Beazley	R A Beazley	95x20x7	Oil 6 Cy	Ex William Kipping	
Richard II	1912	181					ex Richard ex HS49 Dutch built	
Roselyne	1918	138	C T Dixon		94x22x9	Oil 4 Cy	IronAuxK	
Thoma II	1909	87					Harwich	
Topmast No. 1	1902	106	Risdon Beazley	R A Beazley	85x18x10	C4Cy TS	Ex HMS Nettle	
Trela								
Trottebec								
Venture III			(Venture II 1925 510 Built Leith, US flag, deleted 1955?)					
Watercock	1923	200	Gamecock Steam Tow	LHG Walford	97x25x12	Steam T 3 Cy	ex Masterman	
Wayfarer								

Sources Lloyds Register via www.plimsollshipdata and fates from www.miramarshipindex, both excellent sources.
Original list from Mr Bert Maidens Assistant Marine Superintendent

The five 109GRT barges and the *Innishowen* were from the fleet of John Summers and Sons, Shotten.

Appendix 2

ADMIRALTY OWNED FLEET under Risdon Beazley management- (29 vessels)[1].

American Lease Lend Salvage Vessels   Part of a class of eight fully equipped salvage wooden vessels 183' x 37' x 14.75' Diesel Electric 1,200 BHP 12knots. Displacement 800 tons, Crew 35. Rest of the class were retained by the USN and were at the Utah and Omaha beaches on D-Day.

American Salvor	(USN BARS 5)	1943	Barbour Boatworks, New Berne, North Carolina
			(Returned to USN 1946)
Boston Salvor	(USN BARS 6)	1943	" "
			(Reduced to wreck, Antwerp, flying bomb attack 1944)
Lincoln Salvor	(USN BARS 9)	1943	Bellingham Ironworks, Seattle
			(Returned to USN 9/46)
Southampton Salvor	(USN BARS 10)	1943	" "
			(Returned to USN 10/46)

King Salvor Class Part of a class of twelve deep-sea salvage vessels; balance under the White Ensign. A thirteenth unit was completed as the Diving Vessel HMS Reclaim. The RB managed vessels were sent to the Mediterranean, plus Colombo. At the end of 1945 they were transferred to the Royal Navy for service in the newly liberated Far East where salvage was to be a Naval activity. 200' x 37' x 15'. Steam 1,500IHP

Name	Delivered	Builder	
Ocean Salvor	1943-9	Simons (Renfrew)	
Prince Salvor	1943-9	Whites (Hebburn)	
Salvage Duke	1944-12	Simons (Renfrew)	
Salventure	1942-11	Simons (Renfrew)	
Salviking	1942-12	Simons (Renfrew)	Lost 14.2.44, torpedoed
Sea Salvor	1944-2	Whites (Hebburn)	

Coastal Salvage Vessels

Dispenser	1943	Smiths Dock	Malta, Naples, Genoa and Marseilles.
Help	1943	Smiths Dock	*Chartered by RB, became Krab -Wijsmuller*
Kinbrace	1945	Alexander Hall	
Kinloss	1945	Alexander Hall	
Kingarth	1944	Alexander Hall	*RHN 1946-9*
Lifeline	1944	Smiths Dock	*Sold to RB, scrapped in Singapore 1981*
Swin	1944	Alexander Hall	

Plus Lifting craft Numbers: 1, 3, 12, 15, 17, 21, 22, 23, 24, 25, 26, 27, and 28.

---

[1] Information from Jane's Fighting Ships 1944/5, Warships of World War Two - Ian Allan 1962 and Admiralty Coastal Salvage Ships by David Sowden

Appendix3

VESSELS OPERATED BY OTHER MANAGERS

Liverpool & Glasgow Salvage Association, Manager G R Critchley, salvage officer Captain Kay

Ranger	L&G's own salvage vessel built 1880.
Salveda	Only example of class - tug/salvage vessel
Salvage Chieftain	A ship of this name is listed as being in an HX convoy.
L.C.14 and L.C. 20	Dumb lifting craft
Forde	From 1943

LGSA minutes also show that they took over the Dispenser before the end of the war, the RB list shows her as still being under RB control at that time.

Metal Industries, Commodore Thomas McKensie RNVR (Sp)

Succour	Coastal Salvage Class
Uplifter	Coastal Salvage Class
Abigail	
Bertha	
Metinda	Metal Industries vessel pre-war?
Le Luttier	

Rounds

Foremost 17	Self propelled hopper, sister to Foremost 18 (RB)
L.C.16 and 19	Dumb lifting craft

PLA (Port of London Authority)

?? Own fleet?

Leith Towage & Salvage Ltd.

Bullger	Total loss 1941?, replaced by Rampant? ex Empire Sentinel. See page 440 The
Empire Ships	

Dover Harbour Board

Lady Brassey	(Requisitioned - returned 1946)

Appendix 4

FAIRMILE DESIGN VESSELS BUILT

Risdon Beazley built, 22 Fairmiles, they were the lead yard in the south and fourth nation-wide. Risdon Beazley's average building times were: - "B" type, 9 boats, 21 weeks (24.8), "C" type, 1 boat, 27 weeks (29) and "D" type, 12 boats, 33 weeks (43.3) - top yard. (In the brackets are national averages). Other vessels in footnote[1]

Boat	Rated	Completed	Fate

B Type

Boat	Rated	Completed	Fate
204	ML	27.02.41	To Burma RNVR 1.11.45, for disposal 1946
208	ML	12.03.41	RNN 12.3.41, for disposal 10.45
265	ML	30.05.41	Lost by fire, Freetown 1.7.44
338	ML	28.09.41	Became ML2338, sold 17.12.56
347	ML	17.10.41	Sold 1.47 = yacht *"Venturer"*. Still in operation as an inter island ferry in Greece under the name Eastern Princess 2005
467	ML	06.12.41	For disposal 10.45
468	ML	29.01.42	For disposal 9.45
498	ML	15.04.42	*"Sea Eagle"* 1955, Derry SCC 11.57, sold 9.63
499	ML	00.05.42	Sold 4.3.46

C type

Boat	Rated	Completed	Fate
327	MGB	22.08.41	For disposal 10.45

D type

Boat	Rated	Completed	Fate
646	MTB	19.11.42	For disposal 8.45
649	MGB	07.01.43	For disposal 9.45. Mediterranean
676	MTB	13.05.43	To RAF 6.45 = LRRC024
680	MTB	00.04.43	To RAF 6.45 = LRRC028
705	MTB	07.08.43	Mined 23.03.45 in the Adriatic
706	MTB	00.10.43	For disposal 9.45 to 7.46 Mediterranean
738	MTB	15.12.43	To SCC Ipswich, sold 25.04.58
744	MTB	00.03.43	RCN 3.44 - 5.44, to RAF 1945 = LRRC040
772	MTB	12.07.44	To SCC Chelsea 1.46, sold 29.04.55
789	MTB	17.10.44	Lost 14.02.45 by fire and explosion, Ostend
5013	MTB	00.03.45	MTB3053 49, MASB3053 53, SCC 57, sold 69
5019	MTB	13.04.45	To RAF 4.45 = LRRC011

---

[1] HSL (Harbour service launches) 441130, 441131, 441136, 441137, 441142, 441143, 441152, 441153, 441160, 441161. And smaller boats of which *Cerf III* may be the only survivor. This boat was built by Risdon Beazley in 1945, as boat no. 45772, a 36ft HL(P) Harbour Launch (Philip Simons – Lloyd's Register–Fairplay)

Appendix 5

RECOVERIES OF NON-FERROUS METAL BY RISDON BEAZLEY COS. 1947/80

Worked	Vessel's name	Flag	Feet	Area	Tons	Metal recovered
1947 - 1950	Alaska	Fr	216	English Channel	2,097	Copper
1965 - 66	Alex Macomb	US	240	George's Bank USA	1,735	Copper, aluminium
1971, 1975	Anglian	Br	400	S.W. Approaches	350	Brass, zinc
1970	Apapa	Br	200	Irish Sea		Silver coins
1970, 75	Athenia	Br	447	North of Ireland	109	Brass
1959	Aztec	US	104m	Celtic Sea	33	Copper, cadmium
1955 -56	Ballarat	Br	230	English Channel	702	Copper, lead
1952	Binnendijk	Du	100	English Channel	184	Copper etc.
1964	Boniface	Br	168	North of Ireland	342	Copper
1952	Bradglen	Br	24m	Thames Estuary	123	Zinc
1949 - 51, 74	British Prince	Br	132	North Sea	968	Copper
1955	Cairnmona	Br	180	North Sea	1,065	Copper, zinc
1954, 57	Calchas	Br	230	South of Ireland	269	Nickel
1958	California	Br	350	S.W. Approaches	287	Nickel, brass
1950, 51	Cambank	Br	115	Irish Sea	174	Copper
1952	Candia	Br	170	English Channel	648	Lead
1952	Carlo	Br	200	South of Ireland	455	Lead
1948	City of Birmingham	Br	50	North Sea	2,045	Copper, steel etc
1950	City of Brisbane	Br	50	North Sea	1,802	Lead
1958	City of Corinth	Br	300	Western Approaches	91	Tin, copper
1976	Clan Davidson	Br	560	Western Approaches	350	Copper, lead
1968	Collamer	US	480	Off Nova Scotia	719	Aluminium
1959	Counsellor	Br	21m	Irish Sea	678	Steel
1957	Cubana	Br	190	English Channel	33	Tin etc.
1952	Cumberland	Br	318	Eastern Australia	1,858	Copper, lead
1954	Efstathios	Gr	483	Bay of Biscay	1,299	Copper, brass
1951, 52	Empire Kingfisher	Br	145	Off Nova Scotia	512	Copper, bismuth
1973	Empire Manor	Br	330	South of Newfoundland	75	Gold, zinc
1969	Empire Soldier	Br	600	East of Newfoundland	644	Copper
1978 - 80	Engen Maru	Ja		South China Sea	750	Tin
1977 - 78	Glenartney	Br	1,020	Mediterranean	900	Tin
1971	Gorizia	Ur	190	English Channel	105	Brass
1961	Guido	Br	240	North Sea	217	Tin, lead etc.
1953, 56	Hannington Court	Br	250	Off South Africa	916	Copper
1973 - 74	Harrovian	Br	480	S.W. Approaches	716	Copper
1956	Heddernheim	Ge	180	North of Denmark	964	Copper matte
1964	Helga Smith	Gr	480	E. of Newfoundland	1,285	Copper, nickel Ali
1970, 72	Highland Brigade	Br	84	English Channel	28	Tin
1955	Hispania	Sw	30m	West Scotland	9	Tin
1970-72	Hollington	Br	894	Faeroes	680	Tin
1974	Indian City	Br	107m	Celtic Sea	84	Zinc
1956 - 57	Julia Luckenbach	US	200	Off South Africa	960	Copper matte
1953	Juno	No	240	English Channel	674	Copper
1955 - 56	Kaarparen	Sw	210	East Coast Canada	353	Nickel matte, Ali.
1950 - 51	Karmt	No	90	North Sea	743	Tin
1971	Kioto	Br	420	South of Ireland	436	Copper
1953 - 54	Klipfontein	Du	160	Mozambique	1,166	Copper
1969	Kolkhosnik	Ru	135	Off Nova Scotia	1,062	Nickel, molybdenite
1955	Kong Sigurd	No	660	Oslo Fiord	156	Copper
1955	Ladywood	Br	294	S.W. Approaches	2,390	Copper matte
1958	Lewis Luckenbach	US	340	S.W. Approaches	145	Copper, zinc
1949, 51	Mahseer	Br	50	North Sea	279	Copper

1958	Manipur	Br	200	West coast of Scotland	610	Copper, zinc
1973, 75	Medina	Br	160	English Channel	28	Tin
1970	Metric	Ge	258	Irish Sea	365	Copper etc.
1975 - 76	Modavia	Br	180	English Channel	700	Copper, zinc etc.
1955 - 56, 67	Mount Pindus	Gr	720	Gulf of St. Lawrence	764	Copper
1958, 67	Mount Taygetus	Gr	720	Gulf of St. Lawrence	884	Copper
1949 - 50	Norhauk	No	50	North Sea	1,121	Copper, zinc etc.
1947 - 49	North Eastern Victory	US	50	Goodwin Sands	1,288	Lead
1953	Niagara	Br	438	New Zealand	½	Gold
1953	Ocean Venture	Br	156	East coast USA	1,350	Lead
1950 - 51	Oronsa	Br	288	Irish Sea	494	Tin concentrate
1956	Parthenia	Br	180	West coast Scotland	35	Nickel
1959 - 60	Philadelphian	Br	340	S.W. Approaches	570	Copper
1953	Port Nicholson	Br	90	North Sea	165	Lead
1980	Sansei Maru	Ja		Korea St.	120	Copper
1949 - 50	Savona	Br	50	North Sea	623	Lead
1958	Seang Choon	Br	190	South of Ireland	601	Lead
1961	Skyro	Br	55m	W. Spain	662	Lead
1955 -56	Spectator	Br	55m	S. Ireland	40	Copper
1955	Strathdene	Br	240	East coast USA	1,230	Copper, brass, zinc
1979 - 81	Taigyo Maru	Ja		South China Sea	825	Tin
1956, 1975	Ternfjell	No	57m	Eng. Channel	7	Tin
1972	Urbino	Br	446	S.W. Approaches	221	Brass
1955 - 56	Vedamore	Br	420	South of Ireland	1,676	Copper
1956, 75	Vinovia	Br	200	English Channel	694	Copper, brass etc
1968	Warrior	US	180	North of Trinidad	536	Copper, brass etc.
1952	Winkfield	Br	34m	North Sea	91	Lead

Source various RB summaries and records

COMPANIES

Risdon Beazley Marine Trading Company Ltd Southampton 1926 - ?

Risdon Beazley Ltd., Southampton ~ 1939? - 1973

R A Beazley, Manager - wartime manager for Admiralty vessels.

Lloyd's Albert Yard and Motor Boat Packet Co. Southampton

Lloyd's Albert Yard & Motor Packet Services Ltd (R.A.Beazley, Manager) Cork? 1950

Irish Salvors. 1964 (may be another name the preceding company?)

Risdon Beazley Ulrich Harms 1970 - 1974?

Risdon Beazley Marine Ltd. 1974, still in existence, but not trading.

Appendix 6

Treasury's Summary of Payments. Financial Years 1953/4, 1954/5, 1955/6 & 1956/7
Source - Treasury file at the National Archives

Risdon Beazley Ltd.

Vessel		Date of Payment	Amount for Contract	Date of Payment	% of Proceeds of metal sales		
Cumberland		10.1.52	£ 1,000.00				
				22.7.53		£ 20,000.00	
				1.11.53		£ 6,386.87	
				23.11.53		£ 2.00	
Port Kembla		19.2.52	£ 1,000.00				
Seang Cheong	)				*		
Boniface	)				*		
Carlo	)			23.1.53		£ 4,986.55	
Candia	)			3.12.52		£ 8,063.88	
Oldfield Grange	)						
Calchas	)			18.1.57		£ 19,472.34	
Feltria	)						
Kioto	)	16.7.52	£13,997.50	24.1.53		£ 4,777.89	
City of Corinth	)				*		
Folia	)						
Vedamore	)			24.1.53		£ 9,362.18	
	)			31.12.54		£ 13,457.59	
	)			25.11.55		£ 10,879.85	
	)			18.1.57		£ 15,492.55	
Vinovia	)				*		
Philadelphian	)				*		
Pilar de Larrinaga	)						
Ballarat				25.1.57		£ 8,192.20	
Niagara						£ 30,732.45	
Nydal		13.7.53	£ 1,000.00				
California		10.9.53	£ 1,000.00		*		
Damao		24.8.55	£ 1,000.00				
Bostonian	)						
Miniota	)						
Volnay	)	19.10.56	£ 1,500.00				
Fluent	)						
Braunton	)						
Efstathos		13.7.53	£ 1,000.00	11.1.55		£ 14,491.86	
Total			£21,497.50			£ 166,298.21	£ 187,795.71

Less £25,000 paid towards cost of new vessel (Droxford?)		£ 25,000.00
Risdon Beazley Ltd. **Net contribution**		£ 162,795.71
Gray & Thompson Salvage Co. £ 3,000.00	£ 7,950.24	£ 10,950.24
		£ 173,745.95

* = Recoveries and payments made in later years

Fleet List, includes Sale & Purchase and vessels acquired and disposed of before 1939[1]   [a]

Abigail	Built 1908, bought 1947, sold 1947 - *Esperanza*, B/U 1965
Afon Alaw	Built 1975 for work at Amlwch Anglesey, transferred 1983?
Afon Braint	Built 1975 for work at Amlwch Anglesey, transferred 1983?
Aid	Ex Ministry of Transport, lost Nov 1940 in attack by German destroyers
Alita	109 grt. From John Summers ~ 1939
Ashford	Ex *Empire Sandy* chartered 1948 -1952 Larch class built in 1943 by Clelands 1200ihp
.	Became three masted schooner in Canada in 1985
Ashford	Bought from Harms as *Taurus* 1978, sold to Thai Cement 1982 by SISEA
Ashford 24	1943 TID 24. 1952-1953. Sold to United Towing Company. *Bowman*
Ashford 47	1943 TID 47 1947-1953. Sold to United Towing Company. *Fenman*
Ashford 90	1944 TID 90 1952-1953, Sold to United Towing Company *Yeoman*
Attendant	Acquired from Malet Salvage Syndicate 1950 by Lloyds Albert Yard Motor Packet Services, Cork Built for Elder Dempster Steel T S Sold 195??
Averse	Built France? 1936 Admiralty water tanker, traded
Bargate	?? Southampton sludge v/l, owned by Henry Beazley?
Barmouth	1938, *Topmast 19*, bought 1964 sold Jos de Smidt Antwerp (for B/U?) 1966
Beaumont	Built 1907 1920 -??
Bertha	*Topmast No6*, bought 1946, sold 1948
Bijo	Built 1901 1924-1930
Bittern(e?)	No information
Brunel	Bought from Ulrich Harms *Magnus XI,* substantially modified. Named *RB Brunel* transferred to Smit International SEA *Smit Cyclone*
Bulldog	Built 1884 1934-1934
Carmenita	109 grt. From John Summers, 1939?
Couchy	*LC24*
Dispenser	*LC12*
Dorita	109 grt. From John Summers 1939?
Droxford	Built 1958 by John Lewis Aberdeen, scrapped at Troon? 1981
East	Pre war fleet
Empire Aid	1947-1952 Larch Class tug, became *Marina* OTS, B/U Basrah
Empire Dean	No information, not in Empire Ships. Could be *Empire Demon*?
Empire Flora	See *Topmast 14*
Empire Rest	Castle class Corvette, became convoy rescue ship. In fleet 1951/ 2, broken up 6.6.1952 Briton Ferry
Empire Maydream	C type dry cargo coaster, 1947 to Mollers HK *Wing Hing*
Empire Mayring	C type dry cargo coaster, 1947 to Mollers HK *Sing Hing*

---
[1] From a list provided by Mr David Asprey

Empire Mayrover	C type dry cargo coaster, 1947 to Mollers HK *Wa Hing*
Florence	No Information bought 1949?
Foremost 17	Bought 1946.ex PLA. Managed by T Rounds during the war. B/U Passage West 1958
Foremost 18	" " Managed by Risdon Beazley " " B/U Groningen 1958
Help	Steam Coastal class salvage ship, became Wijsmuller's Krab
Innishowen	Bought 1946, clearance Le Harve
J W Brankley	Built 1914 1920-1930
Laboe	*Topmast No10* 1948-1951 *Albatros, Rolf Gerling – Letzer, Lugano* 1980
Lady Bevis	Off requisition 1946, B/U 1947
Lady Southborough	Bought 1946, bottom damaged 1947 B/U?
LCT NSC(1) 112	Bought 1947
LCT NSC(1) 113	Bought 1947
Lifeline	Steam Coastal Class salvage ship, chartered 1047-1959, bought 1959,converted to motor 1961, scrapped Singapore 1981. Longest serving RB ship 37 years.
Lightwell	[ex OHM] generator vessel harbour service, in fleet 1948
Lumme	*Topmast No9* 1948-1949 *River Orwell* then *Ocean Puller*
Maria Catarina	1947/8 No other information
Marlton	Built 1914 1920-1930
Metinda	Topmast No 7, bought 1946 ex Metal Industries. Sold? 1949
Miss Elaine	Bought before 1940, requisitioned, sold 1946
Monarch of Bermuda	No information, this vessel burnt out and was rebuilt as *New Australia*.
Mulus 4	Built 1972 Transferred to Smit Tak as *RB Giant 15*
Ogarita	109grt. From John Summers, 1939?
Ole Wegger	Whale Factory ship, scuttled by Germans in the River Seine, bought/sold 1946
Pagniston	No information
Palmston	Pre war fleet Cargo Ship
Polita	109 grt. From John Summers, 1939?
Poole dredger No2	Pre war fleet
Pullus 1	See RB47
Queen Mother	1955 1968-1978 ex Bristol Channel pilot cutter, acquired ****, sold to Mid-Mar
Recovery of Leith	Pre war fleet salvage lighter self propelled
Reliable No1	1930 water boat, in fleet 1940 and still in 1946
RB 35	1976 1976 – 1980 transferred to Smit International South East Asia 1980
RB47	Built ****, transferred to Eerland became ******
RB Giant 15	see *Mulus 4*
RB Telford	Bought from Harms as *Magnus II*, 1975, transferred to SISEA 1980. sold to India ****, brought back to Singapore by Kasel Salvage
Salventure	Admiralty King Salvor, no information on involvement
Sea Salvor	Admiralty King Salvor, no information on involvement

Sir Walter Raleigh	Bought Jan 1947, sold to Overseas Towage & Salvage April 1947
St Clears	Built 1919 purchased from the Admiralty 1948-?
St Giles	Sold 1947, in Plymouth same year
Stockton	Ex Tees floating crane, B/U Briton Ferry 1972?
Stanwood	1948 No other information
Succour	Admiralty Coastal Class, no information on involvement
Swin	Admiralty Coastal Class, no information on involvement
Topmast No 1	ex HMS Nettle 105/101/35tons built 1902 J Samuel White Cowes. Sold to Cork where it worked for many years
Topmast No3	No information
Topmast No4	Built 1907 1939-1941
Topmast No 6	see *Bertha* Metal Industries
Topmast No7	1890 see *Metinda*
Topmast No 9	1943 ex *Lumme*
Topmast No10	1943 ex *Laboe*
Topmast No.14	1945 ex Empire Flora 1948-1949 *Flora* 292 116 28 36 1945 Coastwise tug. MOWT sold to Venice 1949
Topmast 15	Ex Empire Tigress, tanker, in fleet 1949-53. had been involved in PLUTO.
Topmast 16	ex Mark 111 Landing Craft *Segundo*, in fleet 1955 - 1975
Topmast 17	ex Free French inshore minesweeper acquired from Forth Conservancy *Conserver*
Topmast 18	Mk 111 Landing craft *Rampino,* sold to Mid-Mar 1964-1976 had been coaster
Topmast 19	ex *HMS Barmouth* which see
Topmast 20	ex Mark 111 Landing craft, rebuilt 1966, sold to Mid-Mar 1976
Topmast 21	*Severn Knave* 1967-1976 Built to push sections of Severn Bridge, sold to Holyhead Towing Ltd. (John Meade) renamed *Llanwern Island,*
Trela	Pre war fleet
Trottebec	No information
Twyford	*HMS Warden* (Bustler class tug). Chartered 1947-1951.
Twyford	Steam salvage vessel built 1952 by John Lewis of Aberdeen Transferred to Ulrich Harms GmbH ****. broken up at Cuxhaven 1980
Vigilant	HM Customs cutter? Bought from MOT
Viscol	Admiralty tanker blt 1916, 1163 grt, traded 1947/8, sold, B/U Brindisi
Ylevil ex Lively!	Built 1908 1939-1939

In all 16 salvage launches listed, usually two per ship, built in own yard until 1964. Four LCMs. Various crane barges and ten steel barges mentioned. Lighter C160. Pike 10 (presumably a barge built for transporting clay from Ridge to Poole (Dorset). PB8 and PB9 (may also have been Pike's barges?)

BHC 9 Blyth Harbour Commissioners, BHC 10 war loss

Appendix 8

Books & files that refer to the Beazley companies (several hundred files have been examined) .

National Archives (formerly Public Record Office) Kew

PRO Reference	Title/scope and content	Dates
ADM 1/11095.	ADMIRALTY (5). Admiralty control of salvage agreement *Visits by Doust's teams with Messrs Risden Beasley (sic) Ltd.*	1940-1941
ADM 1/11097	Formation of the Admiralty Salvage Section	
ADM/17183	Salvage operations Mediterranean, Naples	
ADM1/17274	Salvage operations. Normandy and Northern Europe	Sept-Dec
BT 356/3447.	River Itchen, construction of river wall by Risdon Beazley Ltd.	1966
MT 82/86	Maintenance by Riston (sic) Beazley *Mooring contract*	1959
MT 82/87	Maintenance by Riston (sic) Beazley Ltd *Mooring contract*	1952-1962
T 231/1215.	Risdon Beazley Ltd. (Mr Pickford). *Research/contracts, gold and silver*	1953-1956.
T 161/1203	Finance Banking: Opening of public banking accounts Admiralty, with Messrs Risdon Beazley Ltd, Southampton in connection with 'salvage' work.	1942 June 12- 1946 Nov 29
T 199/726	Risdon Beazley Ltd: tracing of records concerning purchase Sweden by Ministry of Supply of BISCO of a large quantity of valuable cargo, which was not insured (1942)	1959-1960 from
T 199/727	Risdon Beazley Ltd: metal cargoes shipped on Ministry of Munitions account, which were lost through enemy action	1951-1960
BT 381/various	Crew Agreements & Official Logs for the wartime salvage ships – by Official Number.	

The files that refer to RB's recovery of the gold from the *Niagara* and to the early attempt on the *Empire Manor* were 'lost while on loan to a government department', the name of the department is not recorded!

Wealth from the Sea	Allan Crothall 1993	ISBN 0 9522747 0 1
Riches from Wrecks	Fergus Hinds	
The Empire Ships	W H Mitchell and L A Sawyer	ISBN 1-85044-275-4
D-Day Ships	John Winser World Ship Society	
Admiralty Coastal Salvage Vessels	David Sowdon World Ship Society	ISBN 0-9543310-4-4
Operation Victor Search	Douglas A Koster Terence Dalton	ISBN 0-900963-95-6
Admiralty Salvage in Peace and War	Tony Booth Pen & Sword	ISBN 978-1-84415-565-1

Websites:

http://www.convoyweb.org.uk - Mike Holdaway's invaluable website, now contains Arnold Hague & Don Kindell's research.

http://warsailors.com – Siri Lawson's site, started as a tribute to her father, now a vast store of information

www.plimsollshipdata.org - scans of all 1939-1945 Lloyds Registers, can be searched for individual ships.

www.miramarshipindex.org.nz – individual ships, both merchnat and naval, including fates.

Also the Naval Museum at the University of Alberta, Calgary; archives contain John K Burgess' research.

Plus various manuscripts, memoirs and diaries that are acknowledged elsewhere